James Ridley

The Tales of the Genii

Or, the delightful lessons of Horam, the son of Asmar. Faithfully translated from the Persian manuscript and compared with the French and Spanish editions published at Paris and Madrid by Sir Charles Morell

James Ridley

The Tales of the Genii
Or, the delightful lessons of Horam, the son of Asmar. Faithfully translated from the Persian manuscript and compared with the French and Spanish editions published at Paris and Madrid by Sir Charles Morell

ISBN/EAN: 9783337068615

Printed in Europe, USA, Canada, Australia, Japan

Cover: Foto ©ninafisch / pixelio.de

More available books at **www.hansebooks.com**

THE
TALES of the GENII:
OR, THE
DELIGHTFUL LESSONS
OF
H O R A M,
THE SON OF ASMAR.

Faithfully TRANSLATED from the
PERSIAN MANUSCRIPT;

AND

Compared with the French and Spanish EDITIONS
published at PARIS and MADRID.

By Sir CHARLES MORELL,
Formerly Ambassador from the British Settlements
in India to the GREAT MOGUL.

VOL. II.

THE FOURTH EDITION

LONDON:
Printed for G. WILKIE, St. Paul's Church-Yard.
MDCCLXXXI.

TALES

OF THE

GENII.

THE CONTINUATION OF THE TALE OF THE INCHANTERS; OR MISNAR THE SULTAN OF THE EAST.

THE Sultan, though much averse to such pageantry, was yet persuaded by his vizier to sleep in his new pavilion, and the glorious appearance which it made, brought thousands to view the magnificent abode of their Sultan.

The account of this splendid tent soon reached Ahubal's army, and every one extolled the glorious pavilion, so that Ahubal's tent seemed as nothing in comparison of the Sultan's.

Ahaback and Defra, who were in the Prince's pavilion, hearing the account, refolved to go invifibly and examine it.

They left the prince, and putting each a ring on their fingers, paffed the centinels and watches of both armies.

But if the fight of the pavilion filled them with malice and envy, the hiftories of their brethren's death increafed that malice, and urged them to revenge.

They returned haftily to Ahubal's pavilion, and related to him what they had feen.

Ahubal's heart rankled at their account, and his vifage fell, to hear how much his brother had outdone him in magnificence.

Give me a tent more fplendid than the Sultan's, faid he to the inchanters, or difband your armies, and leave me to my fate!

My Prince, anfwered Ahaback, let not fuch a trifle difcompofe you: It is true, we could in a moment erect a pavilion more magnificent than the Sultan's, but it will be moft glorious to difpoffefs him of that which he has built, and to fet my Prince upon the throne of his father; for which purpofe, let the trumpets found on the morrow; the truce is at an end, or if it were not, we mean not to keep our faith with an ufurper; and ere the Sultan be prepared, let us fall upon him; who knows but we may fleep tomorrow night in this pavilion, which now caufes our uneafinefs?

The counfel of Ahaback pleafed both Defra and Ahubal, and they gave orders for the troops

troops to march in the morning, and attack the army of the Sultan.

The forces of Mifnar were sleeping in their tents, when the alarm was spread that the enemy were upon them.

The viziar Horam arose in haste, and put himself at the head of the army; but, instead of leading them to their enemies, he fled off to the right with the choicest of the troops, and took possession of a pass in the mountains behind the pavilion; from whence he sent a messenger to the Sultan, that he had secured him a retreat, in case the armies of Ahubal should conquer.

The Sultan being at the extremity of his army, knew not of the confused attack, till it was too late to redeem his lost opportunity. He collected his scattered troops together, and led them toward the enemy, at the same time sending a message to Horam to leave the mountains and support him.

The captains and officers that followed Mifnar, behaved with great resolution and intrepidity, and the Sultan exposed himself frequently to the darts and missile weapons of his enemies; till overpowered by numbers, and his own troops on all sides giving way, through the confusion which prevailed, he was forced to make to the mountains, where his viziar still continued, though he had received the Sultan's commands.

The troops of Ahubal pursued the Sultan's scattered forces to the mountains, where the viziar's troops opened to receive their friends, and then opposed the rebels, who were faint with the fatigues of the day.

After a great slaughter, the rebels were forced to give over, and returned to the encampment of the Sultan, from whence they loaded themselves with the spoils of their enemies.

Ahaback and Desra were greatly elated at their success, and Ahubal, in one day, found himself master of India; his brother defeated; and his gaudy pavilion wrested from him.

Ahubal beheld with surprise the magnificence of the pavilion, and seeing the invidious workmanship on the outside, where the deaths of his former friends were displayed:

Ahaback and Desra, said the Prince, it is but just that you should revenge yourselves on my proud brother. For my part, I can never inhabit a pavilion which was meant to triumph over my friends; but you may justly take up your abode here, that the nations may at once learn, when they see you in this pavilion, the former misfortunes of your brethren, and your present and well-earned success. Wherefore to-night, my friends, take up your residence here, as this place is most worthy to hold you, and to-morrow I will order my workmen to remove the pavilion next my own.

The inchanters were pleased at the speech of Ahubal, and the banquet was prepared for the conquerors, in the gay pavilion of the unfortunate Sultan, while he remained among the mountains, wanting even the necessaries of life for himself and his army.

But

But the Sultan's misfortunes did not make him forget the cause of them. He called a council of his captains, and commanded the viziar Horam to be brought before them. The viziar was condemned by every voice, and Misnar, with tears in his eyes, pronounced the sentence of death against him.

To-morrow, said the Sultan, must the ill-fated Horam be numbered with the dead.

Horam heard the sentence without emotion: My life, said he, is in the hand of my Lord, and he is welcome to the blood of his slave.

The viziar was then ordered into the custody of an hundred men, and a captain was appointed to guard him until the morning.

The unfortunate Sultan then retired to rest, in an obscure tent, or rather not to rest, but to an irksome contemplation.

My kingdom, said he, is passed from me, and worse than my kingdom, my friend, my dearly beloved Horam, has proved a traitor to his master! Were we not as the cedars of the forest, and grew together as the trees that are planted beside the rivers of Arvar! Our souls were as twin sisters, and our minds we e like the stars Leman and Upnor, which twinkle not singly in the dead of night! The heart of Misnar was in the bosom of his friend; it lay upon his bosom as the infant lieth in its mother's arms; it smiled, and was secure on the bosom of Horam——.

As the Sultan was filled with these meditations, his guards gave him notice, that the captain who was set over the viziar, had brought

brought Horam to communicate an affair of moment to him.

Is there deceit in Horam, said the Sultan, that he cometh like a thief in the night? If Horam is false, farewell my life! let him that destroyed my kingdom, complete his ingratitude by finishing my fate!

The captain then entered the tent of his Sultan, with Horam in chains.

Life of my life, and master of my thoughts, said the viziar, ere I die, I am constrained to shew thee, among these mountains, far greater riches than are in thy palace at Delly, or in the tents of thine enemies; riches that will restore thy affairs, and turn thy tears into showers of joy.

Are you not satisfied, said Misnar, O ill-fated Horam! that you come to deceive me with new illusions? Where is my kingdom! where my royalty! where my army? by thy fatal counsels destroyed, overwhelmed, confounded! Now then lead the way, and let me see these curious treasures which are to recompense the loss of all my hopes.

The captain then led Horam out of the tent, and the Sultan followed.

The viziar being in chains, moved but slowly, and the captain of the guard dismissing his men, drew his sabre, and held it naked it over the head of the viziar.

The darkness of the night prevented the Sultan from seeing whither he was carried by his viziar.

They passed over various rocks, and were obliged to wade through some small brooks

or

or rivulets, which fell from the tops of the mountains, till at length they arrived at a spacious cavern, which was formed by two pendent rocks.

Here the viziar entered, and lifting up his chains, knocked against a small door, which was at the extremity of the cavern.

In a moment the door opened, and four slaves came forward with flambeaux in their hands.

The slaves seeing their master and the Sultan, fell prostrate, and Horam enquired, whether all was safe.

Yes, my Lord, answered the slaves; we have not been disturbed since my Lord first brought us to this gloomy cavern.

Where is Camul, said the viziar?

He watches, replied the slaves, with the ax in his hand.

What hour of the night is it? said Horam to his slaves?

The third watch of the night is passed, answered his slaves.

Then enter, my Sultan, said Horam, and see thine enemies perish from before thee.

What enemies, and what mysterious place is this? said the Sultan. Who is Camul, and what ax doth he bear in his hand? Lead me, Horam, not into danger, and remember, that the sabre of my captain hangeth over thy head.

The Sultan then entered in at the little door, and followed the viziar and his guard, and the four slaves with flambeaux in their hands.

In this manner the Sultan passed through a long passage, hewn out of the solid rock, till he beheld at a distance a man seated on a stone, with an ax in his hand, and nine lamps burning before him.

As they drew near, the man fell prostrate before them, and the viziar also falling prostrate, desired Misnar to take the ax out of the hand of Camul his slave.

What wonderful ax is this, said the Sultan, that is thus preserved in the bowels of the earth?

The Sultan took the ax, and Camul the slave removing the stone on which he sat, there appeared a strong rope underneath, one end of which passed through the rocks, and the other was fastened to an enormous ring of iron.

Strike, royal master, said Horam, and sever that rope from the ring of iron.

The Sultan did as Horam desired, and struck the rope with his ax, and divided it from the ring.

The rope being released, flew with great swiftness through the hole in the rock, and Misnar waited some time to see what might be the consequence of cutting it asunder; but nothing appearing, he said to the viziar, Where are the riches, Horam, which I left my bed to view? is this like the rest of your promises, and am I brought here to be again deceived?

Royal master, answered Horam, let me die the death of a rebel; I have nothing more to discover; pardon my follies; and avenge thine own losses by the sword of justice.

What,

What, said the Sultan enraged, hast thou brought me through the dangerous passes of the mountains by night, only to cut a rope asunder? And was I called forth to see only a passage made in the rocks, and the slaves of Horam as ill employed as their master lately has been? Lead me, villain, continued he, back to my tent, and expect with the rising sun the fate you have so amply merited.

Thus saying, the Sultan returned, and the captain of the guard led Horam back in chains to his place of confinement.

In the morning the army of the Sultan which had escaped to the mountains, were all drawn out, the cymbals sounded, and a gibbet forty feet high was erected in their front, to which the captain of the guard led the unfortunate viziar Horam.

At the sound of the cymbals the Sultan came from his tent, and gave orders that Horam should be led to his fate.

The viziar, unmoved at his doom, surrendered himself to the officer, who was to execute the sentence of the Sultan, and the ignominious rope was put about his neck; when a messenger, attended by several centinels, came running into the camp.

The messenger hastened to the Sultan, and thus delivered his message:

Ahaback and Desra, the wicked inchanters who have upheld thy rebellious brother, are dead; the army of Ahubal is in the utmost consternation; and the friends of the Sultan wish to see thee hunting thine enemies, as the lion hunts the wild asses in the forests.

This messenger was succeeded by several of the Sultan's spies, who confirmed the account.

Misnar then put himself at the head of his troops, ordered Horam back to his former confinement, and hastened to fall upon the troops of the rebels.

Early the same morning the Prince Ahubal was awakened by his guards, who with a countenance of woe declared to him the death of his friends Ahaback and Desra.

Are my friends dead? said Ahubal trembling. By what misfortune am I bereaved of them? What new device has Misnar practised against them? Are not these wise and sage magicians, then, a match for a boy's prudence? Alas, what can I effect against him, when these fall away before his victorious arm!

Prince, answered his guards, we have too late discovered the wiles of our enemies. Over the magnificent pavilion of the Sultan, which Horam built for his master, the artful viziar had concealed a ponderous stone, which covered the whole pavilion. This, by some secret means, he contrived in the night to release from its confinement, while Ahaback and Desra were sleeping on the sofas beneath it; and ere day began to arise, their guards were surprised by the fall, and ran to release their masters from the stone: But, alas! their bodies were crushed to atoms, and still remain buried under the pavilion, as fifty of the strongest of thy troops were unable to remove the stone from the ground.

At

At these words the countenance and the heart of Ahubal sunk, and ere he could recover, word was brought him, that the Sultan's troops were in the midst of his army, and that none dared stand against them, unless he approached to encourage them.

Ahubal was so overwhelmed with fear and grief, that, instead of leading his troops, he prepared himself for flight, and Misnar pursuing his good fortune, was in a few hours in possession, not only of his own tents, but also of those of the enemy.

Having gained a complete victory, and sent part of his troops after those that were fled, the Sultan commanded his viziar to be brought before him, and in the sight of his army, asked him, what merit he could challenge in the success of that day?

Glory of mine eyes, and light of my paths, said Horam, the contrivance of thy slave had been useless, if a less than my Sultan had afterward led his troops to the battle. Therefore thine only be the glory and the honour of the day; but my Lord must know, that some time since we were informed, that the inchanters Ahaback and Desra were preparing to uphold thy rebellious brother, and well I knew that prudence, and not force, must prevail against them.

I therefore besought my Lord, to grant me the chief command for twenty days, and neglected to take such advantages over Ahubal's troops, as the captains of thy armies advised.

This

This I did, knowing that any victory would be vain and fruitless, if the inchanters were not involved in the ruin; and that while they were safe, a second army would spring up as soon as the first was destroyed.

For these reasons, I endeavoured to strengthen my Sultan's army, that when the reinforcements of Ahaback and Defra should arrive, their number might not prevail against us.

In the mean time, the sumptuous pavilion which was built for Ahubal, inspired me with a device, which I hoped would put the inchanters in my power.

Studious that no one might interrupt or betray my designs, I inclosed a place near the mountains surrounded with trees, where I began to build a pavilion, which I gave out was erected in honour of my Lord the Sultan. Within this pavilion I concealed a massy stone, which was sawn out of the solid rock, and which, by the help of several engines, was hung upon four pillars of gold, and covered the whole pavilion.

The rope which upheld this massy stone, passed through one of the golden pillars into the earth beneath, and by a secret channel cut in the rock was carried onward through the side of the mountain, and was fastened to a ring of iron in a cave, hollowed out of the rock on the opposite side.

By the time the inchanters were arrived in the camp of Ahubal, the pavilion was finished; and although I had secret advice, that my Sultan's troops were to be attacked on the morrow,

morrow, yet I chose to conceal that knowledge, and so to dispose of the army, that the chief part might fly with me behind the mountains which hung over the pavilion, and that the rest, having no conductor, might be put to flight with as little slaughter as possible.

This I did, expecting that Ahaback and Desra, puffed up with their success, would take possession of my Sultan's pavilion.

Rise, faithful Horam! said the Sultan Misnar; your plot is sufficiently unravelled; but why did you hide your intentions from your Lord?

Lord of my life, answered the viziar, because I was resolved, in case my plot did not succeed, to bear the burden myself, that my Sultan's honour might not be lessened in the eyes of his troops.

This noble confession of the viziar's pleased the whole army, and they waited with the utmost impatience to hear his pardon pronounced.

The Sultan then embraced his viziar, and the shouts of his army were, Long live Misnar the Lord of our hearts, and Horam the first, and the most faithful of his slaves!

The army of Ahubal still continued to fly after their Prince, whose fear did not suffer him to direct those who came up with him. And now, in a few days, the army had been totally dispersed, had not the giant Kifri, enraged at the death of his brethren, and travelling in his fury, appeared before the eyes of of the terrified Prince and his troops, in a narrow pass among the rocks.

The presence of Kifri was not less terrifying than the noise of the pursuers, and Ahubal, at the sight of the monster, fell with his face to the ground.

Who art thou, said Kifri, with the voice of thunder; that fliest like the roebuck, and trembleſt like the heart-ſtricken antelope? Who art thou, that flieſt as the virgin from the noiſe of the battle, and that increaſeſt the ſhrieks of the fallen, being wounded by thy fears?

Prince of earth, ſaid Ahubal, I am the friend of Ulin, of Happuck, of Ollomand, of Tafnar, of Ahaback and Defra. I am he, who, through the power of the inchanters, have contended for the throne of India.

Curſed then are they that league with thee, anſwered the giant Kifri, thou ſon of fear, thou wretch, unworthy of ſuch godlike ſupport! Was it for thee, baſe coward, that Ollomand poured forth his unnumbered ſtores, that the plains of India were dyed with the blood of Defra, the miſtreſs of our race? Be witneſs for me, earth! this reptile is unworthy of our aſſiſtance, and to fight for him is to league with Mahomet, to offer up the blood of freedom on the falſe altars of faith. O ye ſpirits of the brave, my ſoul is on fire, to ſee ſo many of our friends lie ſtretched on the plains! their blood, curſed and ill-fated coward, overwhelm thy head!

As Kifri ſpake thus, his broad eye-balls glowed like the red orb of day, when covered ed with dark fleeting clouds, and from his nostrils issued forth the tempest and the flame.

In an instant he seized on the fear-shaken Ahubal, as the vulture shuts within her bloody talons the body of the affrighted trembling hare; and lifting him high in the air, he dashed the wretched Prince against the ragged face of the mountains. The blood of Ahubal ran down from the mountain's side, like the rain which is poured forth out of the stormy cloud, and his mangled limbs, crushed by the fall, hung quivering on the pointed rocks.

The death of Ahubal lessened not the fury of Kifri, but all that followed the unhappy Prince experienced his rage; till glutted with blood, and tired of his revenge, the monstrous giant sunk to rest, and stretched out his limbs upon the tops of the mountains.

But the sleep of Kifri was cumberous as his body, and the dreams of the giant were as the thoughts of the enemies of God. In the visions of the night came Ulin before him; and the ghost of the murdered Happuck was in the eye of his fancy.

Enemy of our race, said they, where is he who was to redeem our glory, and to revenge our blood? Where is Ahubal, of whom the dark saying went forth, that none but our race could overpower him? The dark saying is now interpreted by thy shameful deed, and the powers of inchantment are at an end!

The

The giant, disturbed at his visions, started up: the moon rode high above the mountains, and the trees of the forest looked broad with the shades of night: He cast his black eyes to the south, and saw the storm rolling forth its clouds: The tempest gathered around him, and poured its fury against him. His long disordered locks streamed out like the shattered canvas of the shipwrecked vessel.

The lofty pines rolled down the rocky precipices, and the fragments of the mountains tumbled in wide confusion at his feet.

The eye-balls of Kifri, inflamed with anger and despair, appeared like two meteors in the storm; he viewed the war of elements with contempt, and mocked Alla and Mahomet aloud, and said:

Is this the God of Nature's work? Is he angry with the bauble he has made? Has he given his parsimonious drops of rain to these forests, and toiled for years to raise their head to heaven, that he may scatter them in sport, and destroy them with his thunderbolts? Let him then view a new ruin beyond his power to compass, for Kifri will no longer live his slave upon earth, but will join his fate to the fate of Ollomand, his brother *!

* The original speech of Kifri's is much longer; but his blasphemies, though in character, are yet too offensive for christian ears. The Editor would not have inserted any part of this speech, did not the immediate death of the giant, and the manner of it, lead to an excellent moral; for as infidels and atheists are in real life always railing at Providence, so their wicked thoughts generally end like Kifri's, in a violent attempt on their own lives.

So saying, the giant bent his body toward an huge rock whereon he had slept, and straining his tough sinews, tore up the mighty fragment from the ground.

The earth felt the shock, and its dark entrails trembled; but Kifri, undismayed, threw the wild ruin to the clouds.

The labouring mountain returned quickly on the rebellious head of the giant, crushed him beneath its ponderous substance, and finished, by its descent, the life and the presumption of Kifri. The cities of India were shaken at its fall, and the ocean ran back from the shores of Asia; fear and dismay were on the inhabitants of the east, till Alla sent his sun on their borders, and enlightened the realms which his favourites inherit.

The news of Kifri's death was brought to the Sultan by one of the followers of Ahubal, who, at the first approach of the giant, had ran from his presence, and hid himself in a cave in the rocks.

Horam, said the Sultan, our enemies are no more, seven are destroyed, and one weak woman only remains; but since Kifri, the terror of Asia, has fallen a sacrifice to the cause of Ahubal, and since the rebel is himself destroyed, what has Misnar more to fear? However, let our army be yet increased, let trusty nabobs be sent into every province, and nothing omitted which may preserve the peace of my empire; 'tis the part of prudence to watch most, where there is the least appearance of danger.

The

The viziar Horam obeyed his master's command, and Misnar having regulated his army, returned in triumph to Delly, his capital.

The Sultan having restored peace to his kingdoms, began to administer impartial justice to his subjects; and although the faith of Horam had been often tried, yet Misnar chose not to rely altogether on any but himself.

Viziar, said the Sultan, as Horam was standing before him, are my people happy? 'Tis for them I rule, and not for myself; and though I take pleasure in punishing the licentious and rebellious, yet shall I ever study to gain the hearts of my obedient subjects; a father's frown may restrain his children, but his smile can only bless them. Dost not thou remember, Horam, the story of Mahoud, the son of the jeweller? And how am I sure, but even now, private malice may be wreaking as great cruelty upon some innocent person, as the Princess Hemjunah suffered from the inchanter Bennaskar?

My Prince, answered the viziar, the toils and the dangers of the war have never for a moment driven from my mind the memory of that Princess, who, with Mahoud, underwent the most odious transformation, through the power of Ulin.

Nor have I, answered the Sultan, forgot their distress, but the cares of empire have hitherto prevented my search after them: As to the Princess, she is possibly with her father at Cassimir; but Mahoud is doubtless an inhabitant of Delly, where he lived before his transformation: Therefore, O viziar,
give

give immediate orders, that the respective cadis of each division of the city, who have the numbers and the names of every inhabitant within their district, be questioned concerning this jeweller's son; and let him to-morrow be brought before me.

The vizier Horam did as he was commanded, and sent for all the cadis of the city, and examined them concerning Mahoud, but no one could give any account of him.

The next morning Horam attended the Divan, and acquainted the Sultan with his fruitless search.

The Sultan was much dissatisfied at his vizier's report, and after he had answered the petitioners and dismissed them, he sent again for his favourite vizier.

Horam, said the Sultan, my cadis are remiss in their duty, Mahoud is certainly hid in my city; all is not right, Horam; the poor son of the jeweller would be proud to own, that he was formerly the companion of the Sultan of the Indies, though in his distress; he had long ere this been at the foot of my throne, did not somewhat prevent him.

Prince of my life, answered the vizier, if Mahoud is in this city, he is doubtless disguised, and has reasons to conceal himself; and how shall thy officers of justice discover, among many millions, one obscure person, who is studious to conceal himself?

In a well regulated city, answered the Sultan, every one is known, and sound policy has always invented such distinctions, as

may

may prevent the disguise of designing and wicked men. The man who cannot give a just account of himself is an enemy to society, and it is no infringement on the freedom of the honest, to oblige them, by their dress and appearance, to shew forth their manner of life. They only need conceal their actions, who are ashamed of their deeds, and it behoves the magistrate to place such in the sight of all men. Secrecy and retirement are the handmaids of sin; and the Prince who would prevent both private and public wrongs, should study to fix a mark of distinction on all his subjects, for villainy loves the masque of hypocrisy, and evil-minded men affect the appearance of the sanctified. But till my capital is better regulated, I mean to take advantage myself of the confusion of my city, and examine, in disguise, those private outrages which are screened from the public eye of justice. Wherefore, Horam, procure two disguises for yourself and me, and let the emir of Matserak be sent ambassador to the Sultan of Cassimir, to enquire after the welfare of the Princess Hemjunah.

The viziar, in obedience to the Sultan's orders, sent the habits of two Fakirs into the palace; and at evening the Sultan, accompanied by his viziar, went forth in his disguise.

As they passed through the second street from the royal palace, one habited like a Fakir, with his horn in his hand, saluted them, and asked them to partake of the alms he had received.

The

The Sultan readily accepted his offer, left the brother of his order should be offended.

They immediately retired into a remote place, and the strange Fakir pulling out the provision he had received, they began their repast.

Brother, said the Fakir to the disguised Sultan, you are, I perceive, but a novice in your profession; you are neither so free nor so ready as I could wish; you have seen but little of life, and you would be puzzled, were you to encounter such wonders as I experienced but last night in my approach to this city.

What, answered the Sultan hastily, were they? Perhaps; brother, you mistake me, possibly; though not so communicative as yourself, I may nevertheless be as brave and resolute.

Alas, answered the Fakir; I begin to suspect you are no true brother, you know we are communicative among ourselves, but secret to the world about us. What severities have you practised? what scars of self-inflicted austerities have you to shew? By the faith which I profess, I will hold no longer converse with you, unless you give me some convincing proofs of the genuineness of your profession.

Here the viziar perceiving the Sultan to be hard pressed, interrupted the Fakir, and said,

O holy Fakir, but stranger to our tribe, from whence comest thou, that thou knowest not Elezren, the Prince of devotees in the city

city of Delly, to whom the emirs bow, and before whom the populace lay proſtrate as he paſſes; thou art indeed but newly come to Delly, ſince the fame of Elezren hath not been founded in thine ears.

Brother, anſwered the Fakir, the fame of Elezren is not confined to Delly alone, ſince all Aſia receives him as a ſaint; but where are the ſilver marks of wiſdom on his cheeks, and the furrows of affliction which are deep wrought in the aged front of Elezren the favourite of Heaven? No, young hypocrites, age and experience are not to be caught in the ſnares of youth, nor the ſagacious elephant in the toils of the unwiſe. But think not your idle preſumption ſhall go unpuniſhed, or that the holineſs and purity of our caſt ſhall be ſtained by the unhallowed mirth of a boy's folly.

At theſe words the Fakir ſprung from the ground, and running into the ſtreets, he made the air echo with his complaints.

The mob hearing, that two young men had perſonated the appearance of the holy caſt, crowded to the place where the Sultan and his viziar ſat trembling at their own temerity, and were juſt about to tear them to pieces, when the viziar, ſtepping forward to meet them, cried aloud, Slaves, preſume not to approach your Sultan, for know, that Miſnar, the idol of his people, ſits here diſguiſed as a Fakir.

Luckily for the Prince, ſeveral of the foremoſt were well acquainted with his features, or it is probable the mob would have looked upon
the

the viziar's speech, only as a device to prevent their fury. But when the Fakir perceived the foremost of the crowd acknowledged Misnar as their Sultan, and fall down before him, he endeavoured to escape.

My friends, said the Sultan, secure that wretch, and suffer him not to escape; and, Horam, said he, turning to his viziar, let him be confined in a dungeon this night, and to-morrow brought before me in the Divan of justice.

The words of my Lord, answered Horam, are a law which cannot be changed. But let me beseech my Prince to retire from the crowd.

Misnar willingly did as Horam advised, and the people made way for him to the palace, crying out, Long live Misnar, the pride of his slaves!

The Sultan being returned to his palace with his viziar,

Horam, said he, each man has his part in life allotted to him; and the folly of those, who, leaving the right and regular path, strike into the mazes of their own unconnected fancy, is sufficiently seen from our adventure this day: Wherefore I would have every man endeavour to fill his real character, and to shine in that, and not attempt what belongs to another, in which he can gain no credit, and runs a great hazard of disgrace. But as the examination of this Fakir in our public Divan, may rather increase, than cover our shame, I would have him brought before me immediately; and with as little noise

noise as possible. Alas, Horam, since the follies of Princes are so glaring, how cautious should we be in our deportment and behaviour!

The vizier obeying, went forth, and in a short time brought the Fakir bound in chains, before the Sultan.

The Fakir advanced to the presence of the Sultan full of shame and fear, and falling at his footstool cried out,

I call Mahomet to witness, I slew not the man in wrath, but in mine own defence!

What man? said the Sultan, astonished at his words: whom hast thou slain, O wicked Fakir, that thine own fears should turn evidence against thee?

Alas, answered the Fakir, hear me, most injured Lord, for the blood of my brother presseth me sore.

As I journeyed yesterday, and was arrived within a league of the city of Delly, I turned me toward a place walled round, which I supposed was the repository for the dead, and finding the iron gate open, I entered into it, intending to shelter myself for a few minutes against the scorching sun.

As I entered, I perceived at one end a stone sepulchre, whose mouth was opened, and the stone rolled from it. Surprised at the sight, I walked forward toward the vault, and heard within the voices of several persons. At this I was in doubt whether to proceed or retire, supposing that some robbers had taken up their residence there.

In the midst of my confusion, a young man, with a turban hanging over his face, came out, and, seeing me, drew his sabre, and made toward me to kill me. Whereupon I took up a large fragment of the wall which lay at my feet, and, as he came forward, I threw it, and felled him to the ground; then, running up, I snatched the sabre from his hand, and would have destroyed him, but he cried out, saying, Take care what thou doest, rash man; for it is not one, but two lives, that thou takest away, when thou destroyest me.

Amazed and confounded how it was possible for me to destroy two lives, by revenging myself on one wretch, who without offence had meditated my death, I stopped my hand; which the young man seeing, he aimed to pull the sabre out of my hand; whereupon, avoiding his effort, and lifting up the sabre above his head, I at one blow severed it from his body.

Immediately, seeing the blood start from his veins, I ran out of the inclosure, fearing lest any of his company should overtake me, and flew till I reached the city of Delly, where I subsisted that night and this day on the alms of the Faithful, till I met my Sultan and his viziar in the habit of two Fakirs.

And what, said the Sultan, has made thee thine own accuser, since the life you shed was in your own defence?

Pattern of the Just! answered the Fakir, my revenge on the young man made me not sorrowful, as my conscience bears me witness,

I took not his life, till neceffity and mine own prefervation required it; but my mind is reftlefs, becaufe he faid I fhould take two lives away when I deftroyed him; therefore I concluded, that there was fome myftery in his fate, or that he prophefied, in his laft agonies, that his death fhould occafion mine.

If thy tale be true, continued the Sultan, his blood refts on his own head who was the aggreffor: But the ftory is fo very fingular, that I fhall detain thee till my viziar and a party of foldiers be fent to fearch the inclofure you have mentioned.

The viziar then gave orders for the guard to mount their horfes, and the curiofity of the Sultan was fo great, that, although it was night, he refolved to accompany his viziar.

In a fhort time, the guards being drawn up, the Sultan and viziar mounted their courfers, and the Fakir was carried between two of the guards, to point out the fcene of his encounter.

The party being arrived at the iron gate of the inclofure, Horam, with ten of the guards, went in on foot, and marched with the Fakir to the tomb where he had heard the voices, and from whence the young man iffued forth.

As they approached to the tomb, they beheld the body of the young man on the ground, and his head at a diftance, which induced them to give the more credit to the Fakir.

The guards, entering the tomb, found no one within; but at the upper end they faw a
ftone

stone case, supported by two blocks of black marble.

The stone case was covered with a flat marble, which the guards could not remove from its place.

The viziar, being acquainted with these particulars, returned to the Sultan, and related to him what the guards had discovered. But Misnar, recollecting the many devices which the inchanters had prepared to ensnare him, was doubtful what course to take.

On a sudden the moon, which shone exceeding bright, was overcast, and the clouds appeared of a glowing red, like the fiery heat of a burning furnace: Hollow murmurs were heard at a distance, and a stench arose of a putrid and suffocating smell; when in the midst of the fiery clouds a black form appeared, of an hagged and distorted female, furiously riding on a bulky and unwieldy monster with many legs.

In an instant the clouds to the east disappeared, and the heavens, from that quarter, shone like the meridian sun, and discovered a lovely graceful nymph, the brightness of whose features expressed the liveliest marks of meekness, grace, and love.

Hyppacusan, said the amiable fair one, addressing herself to the hag, why wilt thou vainly brandish thy rebellious arms against the Powers of Heaven? If the Sultan, though he be the favourite of Alfa, do wrong, the Mighty One, who delighteth in justice, will make thee the instrument of his vengeance on the offending prince. But know the extent of thy power, vain woman! and presume not to war against the will of Heaven, lest the battle of the faithful Genii be set in array against thee, and thou be joined to the number of those who are already fallen.

Proud vassal of light! answered the inchantress Hyppacusan, I fear not thy threats, nor the bright pageants that surround thee; war, tumult, chaos, darkness, fear, and dismay, are to me more welcome than the idle splendours of thy Master's heavens: For know, spruce gilded spirit! I had rather inhabit the gloomy caverns of death, and brood over the mangled carcasses of the slain, than sit, with slaves like thee, in the soft tasteless bowers of Paradise——

Graceless and abandoned wretch! answered the bright fair one, defile not thy Maker's creations by thy blasphemous tongue; but learn at least to fear that Mighty One thou art not worthy to honour!

Thus saying, she blew from her mouth a vivid flame, like a sharp two-edged sword, which entering into the red clouds which surrounded Hyppacusan, the hag gave an horrible shriek, and, the thick clouds rolling around her, she flew away into the western darkness.

The fair one then descending toward the Sultan, the brightness disappeared; and Misnar, the viziar, and his guards, fell prostrate before her.

Arise,

Arise, Misnar, said she, Heaven's peculiar favourite, and fear not to enter the tomb, where the inchantments of Hyppacusan are now at an end.

The Sultan was about to answer, but the fair one led the way to the tomb, and commanded the Sultan to enter with her, and uncover the stone case which stood at the upper end.

As the lid was removing, a sigh issued from the case, and an exquisite beauty arose as from a deep sleep.

Adorable fair one! said the Sultan kneeling, inform me whom it is my happy fate to release from this wretched confinement.

Alas! answered the beauteous maid, art thou the vile Bennaskar, or the still more vile Mahoud? O let me sleep till death, and never more behold the wretchedness of life!

What! said the Sultan, starting from his knees, do I behold the unfortunate Princess of Cassimir?

Illustrious Hemjunah! said the viziar Horam, as the Princess stared wildly about her, Misnar, the Sultan of India, is before thee.

Yes, interrupted the fair spirit, doubt not, Hemjunah, the truth of the viziar Horam; for behold Macoma, thy guardian Genius, assures thee of the reality of what you behold.

Helper of the afflicted! answered the Princess of Cassimir, doubt vanishes when you are present; but wonder not at my incredulity, since my whole life has been as a false illusion before mine eyes. O Alla! wherefore

fore haft thou made the weakeft the moft fubject to deceit?

To call in queftion the wifdom of Alla, anfwered the Genius Macoma, is to act like the child of folly, arrayed in the garments of reafon: Go then, thou mirror of juftice and underftanding, and fpan with thy mighty arms the numberlefs heavens of the Faithful; weigh in thy juft balance the wifdom of thy Maker, and the fitnefs of his creation; and, joined with the evil race from whom I have preferved thee, rail at that goodnefs thou canft not comprehend——

Spare me, juft Genius, anfwered the Princefs of Caffimir, fpare the weaknefs of my difordered head. I confefs the folly of my thoughts; but weak is the offspring of weaknefs.

True, replied the Genius; but, although you are weak, ought you therefore to be prefumptuous? Knoweft thou not that the Sultan Mifnar fuffered with you becaufe he defpaired; and now would Hyppacufan return thee to thy former flumbers, did not Alla, who has beheld thy former fufferings, in pity forgive the vain thoughts of mortality.

Bleffed is his goodnefs, anfwered the Princefs, and bleffed are his fervants, who delight in fuccouring and inftructing the weak and diftreffed.

To be forry for our errors, faid the Genius, is to bring down the pardon of Heaven; and Hemjunah, though fo long overpowered by the malicious, is neverthelefs among the lovelieft of her fex. But I fhall not anticipate

cipate the fair one's relation of her own distresses; since they best can describe the misfortunes of life, who have been used to feel them.

Sultan of India, continued Macoma, turning to Misnar, I leave the Princess of Cassimir to your care, in full assurance that the delicacy of her sentiments will not be offended by your royal and noble treatment of her. But let an ambassador be immediately dispatched from your court, to inform her aged and pious father of the safety of his daughter.

The dictates of Macoma, answered the Sultan, bowing before her, are the dictates of virtue and humanity, and her will shall be religiously obeyed.

At these words the Genius vanished, and the Sultan bid part of his guards return to Delly, to the chief of his eunuchs, and order him to prepare a palanquin, and proper attendants, to convey the Princess of Cassimir to the royal palace.

While these preparations were making, the Sultan and his viziar endeavoured to sooth and entertain the Princess of Cassimir; and, though Horam was desirous of hearing her adventures, yet the Sultan would not suffer him to request Hemjunah's relation, till she was carried to the palace, and refreshed after her strange fatigues.

The chief of the eunuchs arrived in a short time, and the Princess was conveyed, ere morning, to the palace of Misnar, where the female apartments were prepared for her reception,

ception, and a number of the first ladies of Delly appointed to attend her.

The Sultan, in the mean time, having ordered the Fakir to be released and sent out of the city, entered the Divan with his viziar; and, having dispatched the complainants, retired to rest.

In the evening of the same day, the Princess, being recovered from her fatigue, sent the chief of the eunuchs to the Sultan, and desired leave to throw herself at his feet, in gratitude for her escape.

The Sultan received the message with joy, and ordering Horam his viziar to be called, they both went into the apartments of the females, where the Princess of Caffimir was seated on a throne of ivory, and surrounded by the slaves of the seraglio.

The Princess descended from her throne at the approach of the Sultan, and fell at his feet; but Misnar taking her by the hand, Rise, adorable Princess! said he; and injure not your honour, by thus abasing yourself before your slave.

Fame, answered the Princess, which generally increases the virtues of the great, can represent but part of the merit of the Sultan of India; they, who have not seen him, can form no true judgment of his perfection.

Could flattery, answered the Sultan, be ever pleasing to me, it must be from the mouth of the Princess of Caffimir; but I mean to turn your thoughts from me to a more worthy subject, where you may safely lavish your praises, without fearing to exaggerate. The lovely Hemjunah

Hemjunah has promised to relate her wonderful adventures, and Horam, the faithful friend of my bosom, and our former fellow-sufferer, is come to partake with me in the charming relation.

Prince, said Hemjunah, I shall not conceal what you are so desirous of knowing.

The Sultan then waved his hand, and the slaves withdrew.

THE HISTORY OF THE PRINCESS of CASSIMIR.

TALE THE EIGHTH.

IT is often, said the Princess of Cassimir, the fate of the greatest, to have their private interests sacrificed to the public good. Glory and honour in your sex, O Prince, are motives which make this sacrifice the less lamented; but, in ours, we have no way of becoming useful to the public, but by joining hands where hearts are rarely consulted. Such was to have been my fate. Ere I had attained my thirteenth year, my father proposed to marry me to the Prince of Georgia. It was in vain that, when my mother disclosed the fatal news to me, I urged my youth, and my entire ignorance of the Prince, or his qualities.

My child, said Chederazade, to make ourselves happy, we must be useful to the world. The Prince of Georgia has done your father great service in the wars, and you are destined to reward his toils; all the subjects of Cassimir will look upon your choice as a compliment

compliment to them; and they will rejoice to see their benefactor blessed with the hand of their Princess.

But, Madam, answered I, does the happiness of my father's subjects require such a sacrifice in me? Must I live in a country to whose language and manners I am a stranger; must I be for ever banished, and must the realms of Cassimir look upon me as a monster, whose absence alone can effect their comfort and glory? O where will be the soft intercourse of hearts, or the mutual pleasures of love, in a match with such a stranger!

The idle dreams of love, said my mother Chederazade, were invented by the evil Genii, to increase the number of the children of disobedience. Sound reason and policy acknowledge no such intruder. Convenience should first beget alliance; and mutual affection must be the fruit of mutual intercourse. The flame of love is subdued by caprice, by satiety, by disgust, and reflection; and the strongest band, either of private or public societies, must be interest and utility. These, Hemjunah, are sufficient reasons to engage your compliance with your father's desire, and these will influence you, if prudence and wisdom are the motives of your choice; and, if you want prudence, it is fit those who are able to instruct you, should also guide and direct your actions.

At these words, Chederazade left me bathed in tears, and trembling at my fate.

My

My nurse Eloubrou was witness to the hard command my mother had imposed upon me, and endeavoured to comfort me in my affliction; but her words were but as the wind on the surface of the rock; and, to add to my griefs, in a few minutes after, the chief of the eunuchs entered the seraglio, and bid me prepare to receive the Sultan my father.

The Sultan of Cassimir entering my apartment, I fell at his feet.

Hemjunah, said he, the Prince of Georgia is my friend, and I intend to give my daughter to his arms.

Shocked at these successive declarations of my fate, which I had no reason to suspect the day before, I fainted away, and, when I recovered, found myself on a sofa, with Eloubrou lying at my feet.

My lovely Princess, said Eloubrou, how little am I able to see you thus! and yet I fear the news I have to impart to you may reduce you to your former condition.

Alas, said I, nurse! what new evil has befallen me, what worse can happen than my marriage with a stranger?

Princess, replied Eloubrou my nurse, the Prince is to see you this night; nay, the ceremonies are preparing, the changes of vestment, the dessert, and the choral bands.

Ah, said I, nurse, cruel Eloubrou! what hast thou said? Am I to be sacrificed this night to my father's policy? am I to be given as a fee to the plunderer of cities and the ra-

visher

visher of virgins ?, for such are they whose profession is arms!

No, most adorable Princess! said a young female slave who attended on Eloubrou, trust but to me, and the Prince of Georgia shall in vain seek the honour of your alliance.

The faithful Eloubrou shrieked at the words of the female slave, and endeavoured to clap her hands, and to bring the chief of the eunuchs to her assistance; but the female slave waved her left hand, and Eloubrou, and the rest of the slaves, stood motionless before her.

Most adorable Princess! said she, I am the friend of the distressed, and I love to prevent the severe and ill-natured authority of parents; give me your hand, and I will deliver you from that monster the Prince of Georgia.

What! answered I, shall I trust to a stranger, whom I know not, and fly from my father's court? No——

Well then, said she, I hear the cymbals playing before the Prince, and the trumpets, and the kettle-drums; farewel, sweet mistress of the fierce and unconquerable Prince of Georgia!

As she spake, the warlike music sounded in my ears; and not doubting but that the Prince and my father were coming, I held out my hand to the female slave, and said, Save me, O save me from my father's frown!

The slave eagerly snatched my hand, and blowing forth a small vapour from her mouth, it filled the room, and we arose in a cloud.

The

The manner of my flight from my father's palace I know not, as I immediately fainted; and, as soon as I recovered, I found myself in a magnificent apartment, and a youth standing before me.

Charming and adorable Hemjunah! said he, falling at my feet, may I hope that the service I have performed, in delivering you from the Prince of Georgia, will merit your attention?

Alas! said I, what service hast thou performed? Who art thou, bold man, that durst stand before the Princess of Cassimir? Eloubrou, said I, faithful Eloubrou! where art thou? where is Pickfag, the chief of my eunuchs? where are my slaves, where are the guards of my seraglio?

Princess, answered the young man, fatigue not yourself with calling after them, since they are in the kingdom of Cassimir, and you are in the house of Bennaskar, the merchant of Delly: But, not to keep you in suspense, O Princess! know, that I have for several years traded from Cassimir to Delly; and although I never saw you till lately, yet the fame of your opening beauties was so great, that it fired the hearts of all the young men in your father's kingdom. Every time I arrived at Cassimir, the subject of all conversation was the adorable Princess Hemjunah, and it was in vain any other beauty was mentioned.

Fired by these encomiums, I resolved to see you, or die. For this purpose, I attempted at different times the faith of the guards, the

eunuchs,

eunuchs, and even of Eloubrou your nurſe; but in vain; your faithful ſervants were deaf to my intreaties. Finding human policy fruitleſs, I ſought after thoſe who have power in inchantment; but I began to doubt even the reality of theſe, as I could no where hear of any one who profeſſed magic.

As I was one day returning from my warehouſe, I heard one call me by my name; and, looking behind, I perceived a female dreſſed in a dark-coloured mantle, with a veil upon her face: Bennaſkar, ſaid ſhe, follow me.

As we are always apt to hope every unexpected adventure will lead us to the wiſhed-for point; ſo I had no doubt but the female behind me was appriſed of my deſires, and willing to forward them. I therefore gathered up my garments, and followed her through ſeveral ſtreets.

At length the female ſtopped at the door of a large houſe; and, when I expected the door would have been opened unto her, ſhe ſunk into the earth, and diſappeared from my ſight.

I waited at the door of the houſe till night, every moment expecting to ſee it open, or that the female would appear again.

But my hope was vain; and, after ſeveral hours expectation, I was obliged to return to my lodging, full of vexation and diſappointment.

The next morning I aroſe, and went into the ſtreet, and ſaw the ſame female beckoning

ing to me; I hesitated not a moment to follow her.

She is certainly, said I to myself, possessed of supernatural powers; and, as she has taken notice of me, I will shew myself obedient to her commands.

She led me again, by the same way, to the house before which I had spent the greater part of the preceding day; and, as soon as we arrived there, sunk again into the ground.

Though I was heartily vexed at this second illusion, yet I resolved to stay on the spot, till night and the city guard made my stay impossible.

But night came without satisfying my curiosity; I returned again to my lodgings, and knew no more than at first the meaning of the female's appearance.

The third day I proceeded as usual to my warehouses; and, as I was about to unlock them, saw the female again in the market-place, beckoning to me as before.

As I had now entered into her service, so I resolved to continue in it, and therefore went behind her to the house, which I remembered well, having contemplated its front two days successively.

The female stopped, as before, at the entrance of the house, and sunk a third time into the earth.

But I will not tire your patience, adorable Princess! with a minute relation of my fatigues. For eleven days successively was I

thus

thus deceived; and, on the twelfth, as I was standing in my usual place, several slaves issued out with chaboucs, saying that I was a thief, and had for some time been seen lurking about, and examining the house.

Though I assured them I was a merchant, I did not find the chabouc come the slower on my back; wherefore, supposing it vain to resist, I ran as fast as I could from them; and, as fear and pain are excellent remedies against sloth, so I found I had soon left the slaves behind me.

Having entered my lodging, I began to lament my fate, and the cruelty of her who had so often deceived me. But, in the midst of my lamentations, I felt the room shake; and in an instant saw the female rise through the floor, and stand before me.

Bennaskar, said she, I am Ulin, the friend of the distressed, and the helper of all those who will put their trust and confidence in my inchantments; I have long watched your motions, and know your thoughts; and, willing to try your faith in the magic arts, I have thus often deceived you. Alla requires a reasonable worship from his votaries; but we, who love to contradict him in all things, expect in our dependents a blind and obsequious obedience.

Princess, or Genius, or whatever thou art, answered I, give but Hemjunah to my arms, and my life shall be spent as you direct.

If I find you faithful, answered Ulin, you shall, ere to-morrow's sun, depart hence, and have the Princess in your possession.

Ulin

Ulin then declared to me what she expected, in return for her goodness to me; and I swore to act in obedience to her commands.

Go, happy bridegroom! said Ulin, and prepare thy palace at Delly; my slaves shall carry thee thither, and I, in the mean time, will personate one of the slaves of the palace of Cassimir; and doubt not but, ere the promised time, I will convey the Princess to thy palace.

She then muttered with her lips, and a tall black slave arose through the floor.

Carry my friend, said Ulin, to Delly, and heap in his treasury a large portion of my niceties.

The black slave took me in his arms, and in an instant I found myself in the saloon of this palace; and this day my mistress Ulin has fulfilled her promise, and brought the lovely Hemjunah to my arms.

Merchant, answered I, talk not so boldly; it would better become you to apprise the Sultan of India of my arrival, that I may be carried to the Sultan's my father's.

Nay, pretty Princess, answered Bennaskar, be not so imperious; but recollect that you are at my disposal.

Wretch! said I, Mahomet will never suffer thee to destroy the innocence of one who never offended thee.

Alas, answered Bennaskar, Mahomet would be well set to work to prevent all the evils of this world: No, no, my Princess, we are secure here, and I fear no interruption while Ulin is my friend.

And

"And what promise didst thou make her, returned I, what hast thou given up, to make such a wretch of me as you seem to wish?

"That, said Bennaskar, you will shortly see; nay, you shall see it this instant, if you will but vouchsafe, adorable Hemjunah, to ascend the bridal chamber.

"Infamous wretch! said I, bursting into tears, how durst thou make use of such expressions?

"Nay, continued the wretch, I must be plain with you, Madam; either attend me with cheerfulness, or expect to be compelled.

"O, said I, with an aching and distracted heart, where is my dear mother Chederazade! where is my royal father, the Sultan of Cassimir! where the millions of subjects that doat on their Lord! that his daughter must be ravished by a vile merchant, and there is none to help her!

"The wicked Bennaskar paid no regard to my tears, but, taking me in his arms, carried me by force out of the room where first we met.

"I filled the house with my cries and lamentations, but in vain; Bennaskar still continued to carry me through several apartments, and was deaf to my tears, my cries, and my prayers.

"Seeing my honour thus at the disposal of an hardened wretch, the creature of a vile magician, a sudden thought came into my head, which, I hoped, would at least put off for a
short

short time the villanous intentions of the dishonourable merchant.

O Bennaskar, said I, why do you thus hurry me, like a criminal, and a slave, through your apartments? Surely you will not dishonour the royal blood of my family; let me loose from your arms, and send for the cadi, that, since it is my fate to be the consort of Bennaskar, I may at least have a writing of marriage.

No, no, Princess, answered the fierce, cruel wretch, our sex seldom desire the trouble of marriage contracts to prolong the days of impatience, when we have the fair in possession without them; to-morrow we shall have leisure to talk of those matters, but the present moments are too precious to waste in needless forms.

As the villain said this, he arrived with me in a vaulted chamber, where releasing me from his arms, he secured the entrance.

And now, Princess, continued the wretch, I am bound to perform my promise to Ulin, before I take possession of your charms.

Though I was dumb with terror and vexation, yet I hoped for a short release from the words of the vile merchant; nor was I deceived; Bennaskar took the lamp from the centre of the chamber, and sprinkled a little powder on the flame, and repeated these, or the like words.

Silly guardian of Hemjunah's virtue, hasten hither, and behold the triumphs of Ulin thy foe!

At thefe words the apartment shook, and the countenance of Bennafkar fell; but a voice iffuing out of the wall, cried, Bennafkar, feize thy prey, and fear not the harmlefs prefence of my foe Macoma.

The vile merchant then feized me in his arms, and was about to lead me to his detefted bed, when, in a gentle cloud, a venerable and majeftic perfonage defcended into the apartment.

Unhappy Princefs of Caffimir! faid fhe, how has thy imprudence weakened my power, and deftroyed thine own fafety! If thou hadft not yielded to the falfe female flave, the forcerefs Ulin had not triumphed over thee and me; but now fhe has given thee unto the power and poffeffion of Bennafkar, and I am not permitted to refcue thee from the clutches of this detefted merchant.

Then, faid Bennafkar (who before was awed by the prefence of the Genius Macoma), Hemjunah is my own, and my faithful Ulin has not deceived me. Come, continued the abandoned villain; come, Princefs, let us divert your guardian Genius with our connubial rites.

At thefe words, exerting all his ftrength, the villain threw me beneath him; but his triumph was but fhort, for the Genius advancing, immediately touched him with her wand, and faid,

Wretched flave of iniquity, think not Heaven will fuffer thee to complete the curfed purpofe of thy black heart. Though I am not permitted to refcue the Princefs, yet have

I power

I power over thee, base tool of sin! Therefore, whenever you look upon the Princess, you shall deprive her of sensation, and yourself be deprived of desire.

Then, cried Bennaskar, rising and turning from me, I will at present disappoint thy power, till I receive my commands from the mouth of Ulin, the mistress of my fate.

Ah, cried the inchantress Ulin, who that moment entered the vaulted chamber from the closet (which, my Prince, you have heard described by Mahoud), What hast thou done, thou enemy of our race! Accursed and fatal neglect, that I had not first secured Bennaskar from thy power! But since the inexorable word is gone forth, I will add to thy sentence.

Here, continued she, stamping with her foot, and an ugly dwarf arose through a trap door in the chamber, Nego, be it thy business to attend my servant Bennaskar, and whenever thou seest that female deprived of sensation, do you bury her in the earth beneath this chamber: And, Bennaskar, continued the inchantress, do you take this vial, and whenever you want to converse with this stubborn female, let one of your slaves, whom you can trust, pour part of the liquor into her mouth, and she shall recover; only retire yourself into the closet, that you be not seen of her, at least till she consent to your will, for then the inchantments of Macoma shall no longer prevail against you.

The

The inchantments, said Macoma, O wretched Ulin! are not yet complete; there is yet a moment left, and both our power over Hemjunah and Bennaskar will be at an end.

Therefore thus shall it be, although Bennaskar is possessed of the Princess, yet shall these apartments be, hidden from the sight of all men, except on that day when thy evil race prevails. On the full of the moon only shall Bennaskar be able to explore these rooms; and fear not, amiable Hemjunah! said the Genius, addressing herself to me, for neither force nor inchantment shall work your ruin without your own consent; and although Mahomet, displeased at your late imprudence, for a time permit this inchantment, yet at length, if you continue faithful and virtuous, he will assuredly deliver you.

At these words Bennaskar turned toward me, with anger and disappointment in his eyes, and immediately I was seized with a deep sleep, and what passed afterwards I know not.

I found myself awakened by the descent of some liquor in my mouth, and saw a black slave standing before me. At the same time the voice of Bennaskar issued forth from the closet:

Ill-fated Princess Hemjunah, thy tyrant Genius hath now hidden thee a month from my sight, while thy friends Ulin and Bennaskar seek to restore thee to light and to life; say but therefore thou wilt yield to my will,

will, and the inchantments of Macoma will be destroyed.

Wretched Bennaskar! answered I, I knew not that my sleep had continued a month; but if it be so long since I saw the Genius Macoma in this chamber, I thank Mahomet that he hath so long hidden me from the persecutions of Bennaskar.

Haughty Princess! answered the vile Bennaskar from the closet, my slave shall inspire you with humbler words. Whereupon he ordered the black slave to give me fifty lashes with the chabouk.

But it is needless, O Prince, to repeat the various designs of that wretch; for three months was I thus confined; and Bennaskar having exercised, through the hands of his slave, the cruelties of his heart, used at length (when he found me persist in my resolution) to come forth, and, by his presence, deprive me of sensation.

The adventures of the third month you have heard from the mouth of Mahoud; I shall therefore only continue my adventures from the time that he left me with the book in my hand.

Bennaskar seeing his friend Mahoud had left him, went out, and soon returned again with him, and taking him into the closet, in a moment came forth, and touching me, he said, Come, fair Princess! the inchantments of Macoma are now at an end, and thou art given up entirely to the possession of Bennaskar.

I shrieked

I shrieked at his words, hoping the Cadi would hear me, but in vain; Bennaſkar roſe with me through the vaulted roof, and I found myſelf with him in a wide-extended plain.

Wretch! ſaid the Genius Macoma, who that moment appeared, haſt thou dared to diſobey my commands, and remove the Princeſs from the vaulted chamber, where even thy miſtreſs yielded to my power? But I thank thee; what the imprudent Mahoud could not accompliſh againſt thee, thou haſt effected thyſelf.

As ſhe ſpake, the form of Bennaſkar periſhed from the face of the plain, and his body crumbled to atoms, and mixed with the duſt of the earth; but from his aſhes the inchantreſs Ulin aroſe, and with an enraged viſage turned toward me, and ſaid,

Thou art ſtill the victim of my power; and ſince Bennaſkar is no more, go, ſweet Princeſs, and join thy delicate form to the form of thy preſerver Mahoud, whom I deſigned for the flames; but my will being oppoſed, he is reſcued from thence, and now defiles the air of Tarapajan with his peſtiferous breath.

Such, Sultan of India, were the conſequences of my imprudence; and thus are our ſex, by the ſmalleſt deviations, often led through perpetual ſcenes of miſery and diſtreſs.

Lovely Princeſs of Caſſimir, ſaid the Sultan Miſnar, I have felt more anxiety during this ſhort interval in which you have related your adventures, than in all the campaigns I have made.

made. But suffer us, O Princess, to add a further trouble to you by a second request; for I am as anxious to hear by what misfortune you were inclosed in the tomb of death, as I was to know in what manner you were subjected to the villanous cruelties of the wretch Bennaskar.

The Tale, O Prince, said the fair Hemjunah, is wonderful; but, alas! new indiscretions drew upon me the severities I have experienced.

As soon as, by our restoration to our pristine forms, we were apprised of your victory over the inchantress Ulin, I found myself in the seraglio of my father's palace.

In the apartment from which I was taken by the wicked inchantress, I beheld my nurse Eloubrou. She was prostrate on the ground, and the palace was filled with her cries.

Faithful Eloubrou, said I, arise, and look upon thy beloved Hemjunah; where is my royal father Nebenezer, and the fond Chederazade, the mother of my heart?

Eloubrou at my voice started up like one awakened from a trance.

What is it, said she in emotion, what is it I behold? Art thou the departed shade of my once loved Hemjunah!

No shade, said I, beloved Eloubrou, running to her, but the true Princess of Cassimir, whom Misnar, the Sultan of India, hath rescued from the inchantments of the wicked Ulin.

O that thy royal mother, said Eloubrou, were, like me, blessed with the sight of thy return!

What, said I, Eloubrou, what doſt thou ſay! Where then is the much honoured Chederazade! Where is the dear parent of my life!

Alas, ſaid Eloubrou, who ſhall tell the diſmal tale to thy tender heart?———

Ah, ſaid I, is my beloved mother no more? is ſhe gone to ſeek her diſobedient daughter over the burning lake!

At theſe words my ſpirits failed, and I ſunk motionleſs to the ground.

But my Lord muſt forgive me, if I haſten over the dreadful ſcene that followed. The report of Eloubrou was too true; Chederazade, the deareſt Chederazade, had been ten days dead when I was reſtored to my father's palace; and Zebenezer, diſtracted at the double loſs of his conſort, and his child, had ſhut himſelf up in the tomb of my mother.

Eloubrou haſtened to the tomb wherein my father poured forth his tears, and acquainted the guards who watched without, that I was returned.

The ſorrowful Zebenezer, although he was rejoiced at the news, reſolved not to come forth out of his conſort's tomb till the month was expired, according to his oath, and gave orders, that, during that interval, I ſhould be obeyed by his ſubjects.

My mourning was not leſs ſevere than my royal father's; I ſhut myſelf up in my apartments, and would ſuffer none but Eloubrou to ſee me.

Nine days paſſed in ſilence, our loſs affected both, and Eloubrou was as little diſpoſed as myſelf to forget the cauſe of her griefs.

The tenth morning Eloubrou
out by the grand viziar, who th
command of my father's kingdom.
She returned in haste:
Princess of Cassimir, said she
calleth himself Mahoud enquire
and the grand viziar, understandi
was instrumental in your release,
out to know your will.

At the name of Mahoud I starte
reverie.

Mahoud, said I, O Eloubrou!
notice, and the son of the Jewel
shall be rewarded for his servic
mistress.

Alas, answered Eloubrou, my
tress is distracted with her sorrow
poses the prince Mahoud to be t
of a slave.

If he be a prince, answered I,
therto concealed his circumstance
from me, or he is not that Mah
remember in the deserts of Tarap

That, answered Eloubrou, yo
discover when you see him; but
she, he desires a private audience.

Well then, replied I, introduce
brou; but let my slaves be ready
my call.

Eloubrou obeyed, and brough
chant Mahoud into my presenc
retired.

Mahoud fell at my feet, and sa
Forgive, O loveliest creation
presumption in approaching th

Caffimir, and that I have added hypocrify to my boldnefs, by affuming the title of a prince, which I confefs I have no pretenfion to take upon me, nor abilities to fupport.

What then, anfwered I fternly, has induced you to deceive my court?

Let death, faid Mahoud, falling again before me, let death atone for my crime, but firft permit me to explain the motives of my prefumption.

Proceed, faid I.

As foon, continued Mahoud, as our unnatural transformation was at an end, I perceived myfelf in the capital of Delly, near the very houfe into which Bennafkar invited me. The fight of that detefted place gave wings to my feet, and I ran forward, indifferent where I went, to avoid that fpot, till I came into the ftreet, wherein I had fpent my father's fortune. A crowd of attendants waited at the houfe, which now was poffeffed by a more fortunate inhabitant.

Sick of the fight, I flew onward, in hopes of finding in a different quarter a place of reft; but, in turning down a little alley, I came out upon the area where the cadi had condemned me to the flames.

At the fight of this place my blood curdled, and my hair ftood an end: Ah, faid I, unhappy Mahoud, the capital of Delly will renew thy diftreffes, by refrefhing thy memory with unfortunate fcenes; and as thou haft no dependence here, fince thy Sultan is with his army in the field, why fhouldeft thou not join thyfelf to the troops that daily

march

march out of the city; and when thou art arrived at the camp, throw thyself at the feet of the Sultan.

Full of these thoughts, I advanced toward the royal parade, and offered my services to the captain of one of the troops, that were drawn out in the square.

The captain readily accepted my offer, and I was enrolled among the number of my Sultan's forces.

Fortunately for me, the troop was then drawn out, in order to be sent to the main army; and being furnished with an horse, I went with my companions, and before night we joined the encampment.

Immediately I flew toward the royal pavilion, and fortunately met the viziar Horam, with his attendants, going to the Sultan.

I threw myself at his feet, and told him who I was; but the proud viziar spurned me from him with his foot, and bid the guards chastise me.

Here the Sultan looked sternly at his viziar, and Horam stood in silent amazement.

The Princess, although she saw the emotions of the Sultan and his viziar, yet still continued her Adventures without interruption.

THE CONTINUATION OF THE TALE OF THE PRINCESS OF CASSIMIR.

Mahoud, said the Princess, proceeded thus:

Seeing I had no hopes of favour or protection from the viziar Horam, I flew to the royal tent, and as the Sultan came forth to meet his viziar, I fell prostrate before him; but, alas! the pride of greatness casts a a film over the eyes of all men.

The Sultan Misnar hearing me speak of his transformation and my own, commanded his troops to cast that liar forth out of the camp.

At these words the countenance of Misnar changed, and he said, Judge, O Princess, from the actions of Misnar, whether that rebel lied before thee or not; when I heard from your mouth, that Horam had spurned him with his foot, I was enraged at my viziar, but now I am convinced he has alike traduced us both.

I will not, said the Princess Hemjunah, anticipate my Tale; the sequel will satisfy both my Sultan and his viziar.

I was immediately, continued Mahoud, carried to the extremity of the encampment, and turned out with hissings and abuse.

I fled as fast as my feet would permit, and in a few hours joined a caravan, who, fortunately for me, was journeying to Cassimir.

During my journey hither, O Princess, I lived on the alms of merchants, and at my arrival found the capital in confusion. I heard that your royal father Zebenezer was retired; that my lovely Princess saw none but Eloubrou, the partner of her afflictions; and that the viziar Hobaddan directed every thing.

Ah, said I to myself, is there then no way of seeing the Princess, but through the indulgence of her prime viziar? and what hope have I, that he will hearken to the tale of an unknown beggar, when Horam would not acknowledge the brother of his afflictions?

In this distress I knew not where to turn, but happily one saw my afflictions. A merchant who was standing in his shop, and had observed me lift up my eyes to heaven, called out, and said, Young man, what is the cause of your excessive afflictions? I looked round, and saw the merchant, and as I was going up to him, fortune inspired me with a tale that softened his heart.

I told him that I was a Prince, and well known to you, O glory of Cassimir! and that if he would, only for the space of one day, furnish me with a proper habit and attendants to appear before you, O Princess! I would pay him tenfold for his kindness.

It is not likely, said the merchant, that a Prince and a beggar should be one and the same person; but as I have taken the pains to enquire into your affairs, I will furnish you as you desire, upon condition, that if you are not what you say, you shall go before

fore the cadi, and bind yourself to me for ten years as my slave.

Being hard pressed by penury and want, I readily embraced the merchant's offer; we went before the cadi, I signed the conditions, that being properly furnished by the merchant to appear before the Princess; if the Princess of Cassimir, did not acknowledge me to be Prince Mahoud, and her deliverer in the afflictions she had lately experienced, I would submit to be the merchant's slave for ten years.

This being executed, the merchant procured me the robes in which I now stand before my Princess, and slaves to attend me, and by his interest with the viziar, I was introduced into your presence: And now, O Princess, unless you favour my innocent deceit, by which alone I was able to obtain a sight of my benefactress, I must return from your presence into the chains of slavery, and be exposed to the scoffs of ignominy.

There is no occasion, said I, of giving you a false title, Mahoud; I will send for the merchant, and buy off your ten years slavery, and give you sufficient to live creditably as a merchant.

Alas, answered Mahoud, the cunning merchant, O Princess, will never know how to ask enough for my redemption, when he finds I am favoured by the Princess of Cassimir; and if he should, I shall become the joke and contempt of the merchants, who will neither give me credit nor countenance.

Well then, said I, poor merchant, since you are so unwilling to part with your new assumed honours, be a Prince. Then clapping my hands, Eloubrou appeared, and I said, Eloubrou, let the Prince Mahoud be lodged in my father's palace, and let a proper number of slaves attend him, and do you acquaint the vizir with his quality.

Eloubrou did as I commanded, and Mahoud, full of joy, fell down at my feet, and kissed the hem of my garment.

Prince, said I, arise, and Eloubrou shall conduct you to my father's palace.

A few days experience made me repent my folly in giving credit to the falsities of Mahoud; for the insolent merchant grew proud of his new assumed honours, and soon forgot that his title was only the phantom of his own brain.

He came daily, and was introduced to me, and every time assumed greater state, till at last he dared declare his passion for me, and talked of asking my father's consent, as soon as the days of his sorrow should be accomplished.

Astonished at his insolence, I bid him depart from my presence, which he did with difficulty, muttering revenge as he went.

As soon as he was gone forth, I acquainted Eloubrou with Mahoud's story, his ridiculous and insolent behaviour, and that he had even dared to threaten me with revenge.

The threats of Mahoud, said Eloubrou, are of little consequence, though prudence should never esteem the least enemy unworthy of its notice; but care shall be taken of this insolent merchant. However, my Princess, continued the experienced Eloubrou, must suffer me to deliver the sentiments of my heart.

Our sex can never give greater encouragement to man, than by submitting to become parties in their deceits; and she who helps to exalt one of that faithless sex, must soon expect that he will debase her. Love and presumption united, cannot distinguish the valley from the mountain; and the ass crops alike the thistle or the rose. If Mahoud dared first assume honours that did not belong to him, what should prevent his more aspiring thought? They that will not destroy the weed before it produces the stalk and the pod, shall not prevail against it when it scatters forth its seeds, and gives its progeny to be dispersed by the winds.

As Eloubrou delivered this instruction before me, one of the slaves entered the apartment, and gave me notice, that Zebenezer, my father, expected me in the tomb immediately. I put on the solemn veil, and followed the guard to the tomb of Chederazade, the favourite of Alla.

I entered the lonely mansions of the dead with fear and trembling, and at the upper end of the vaulted tomb, saw my father kneeling before the embalmed corpse of the parent of my life.

Unhappy Hemjunah, said the aged form, come hither and behold the sad remains of my dearest Chederazade.

Although my heart sunk with grief, and my limbs tottered, yet I essayed to reach the place where Chederazade lay embalmed, and fell at the feet of my father Zebenezer.

Rise, said he, O daughter, and caught me suddenly in his arms, when, O fearful sight!

fight! I perceived his visage alter, and that the villanous Mahoud had seized me in his arms.

Struck with horror and despair, I essayed to cry out, but in vain; my voice was fled, and the powers of speech were taken from me.

No, said he, with a fierce air, your struggles and resistance, O prudent Princess, are all vain; for she who will join to deceive others, must expect to be deceived when there is none to help her; therefore speech, if you resist, is taken from you.

What, said I, cruel Mahoud, recollecting myself, and endeavouring to soften him, is this the return my friendship deserves, when, to save you from infamy and slavery, I gave way to your intreaties, and represented you otherwise than you really were?

They, answered Mahoud, who give false characters of their friends, should expect to find their friends as capable of deceiving them, as they have made their friends capable of deceiving others: But we must not call such intercourse friendship. Friendship, O Princess, is built upon virtue, which Mahoud has disclaimed, since he entered into the service of the sage Hyppacusan; and by her advice it was, that he told you a sham tale to deceive you to your own destruction; had you not yielded to that tale, I could have had no power over you or your father; but it is our triumph to circumvent the prudence of Mahomet's children; wherefore, seeing you would not yield openly to my wishes, I no sooner left you with Eloubrou, than by Hyppacusan's assistance, I entered this tomb invisibly, and by my inchantments overpowered

your

your father Zebenezer, and then affuming his perfon, I fent for my Princefs, and fhe came, obedient to my call.

But now, continued the falfe Mahoud, your cries will profit you but little; for Hyppacufan, who is ever hovering over Delly, to watch the motions of the Sultan Mifnar, has by this time placed us in a repofitory of the dead, where we fhall have none to overhear or difturb us.

Mahoud then fhewed me my father Zebenezer, whom by his inchantments he had deprived of all fenfation; he lay in a coffin of black marble, in an inner apartment. And after that, he vowed that he would defift from force, but that till I confented to his wifhes, I muft be content to live in the tomb.

But I will not fatigue you, O royal Sultan, with the fpecious and bafe arguments of the wretched Mahoud, when he found all in vain; he, by his inchantments, obliged me to fleep in the place from whence you delivered me, and what time has elapfed during my confinement I know not.

Princefs, faid the Sultan, we rejoice at your efcape; but as it is probable, by your account, that your royal fire Zebenezer ftill fleeps in the tomb, we will befeech Macoma to hear our petitions, and deliver him from the chains of inchantment.

The Sultan then fent officers to fearch in the tomb for the body of Zebenezer, and alfo called together thofe who were fkilled in magic, and defired them to ufe incantations to

invoke

invoke the Genius Macoma to their affiftance. But the arts of the magicians were vain, and Macoma remained deaf to the intreaties of the Sultan and his Sages.

In the mean time, while the Sultan and his viziar Horam endeavoured to comfort the afflicted Hemjunah, the ambaffadors returned from Caffimir, bringing advice, that the grand viziar Hobaddan had affumed the title of Sultan, and that the whole kingdom of Caffimir acknowledged his authority.

At this report Hemjunah funk motionlefs on the earth, and the Sultan Mifnar ran to comfort her, declaring that he would march his whole army, to recover her dominions from the rebel Hobaddan.

Horam, faid the Sultan, let us be prudent as well as juft; therefore, while you march to the affiftance of the injured fubjects of Caffimir, and to reftore that kingdom to its lawful Prince, I will keep ftrict difcipline and order in the provinces of my empire; and I truft, in a fhort time, I fhall fee you return with the head of the rebel Hobaddan.

The viziar Horam fet out in a few days from Delly, with three hundred thoufand troops of the flower of the Sultan's army, and by forced marches reached the confines of Caffimir, ere the pretended Sultan Hobaddan had notice of his arrival.

The viziar Horam's intention to reftore the Princefs Hemjunah to the throne of her forefathers being proclaimed, numbers of the fubjects of Caffimir flocked to the ftandards of Horam, and the army being now increafed to

five

five hundred thousand troops, marched toward the capital of Cassimir.

Hobaddan having notice of the increase and progress of his enemies, and finding that to engage them upon equal terms was vain, sent an embassy to the viziar Horam, assuring him that he, and his whole army, would surrender themselves up to the mercy and the clemency of his master's troops.

Horam, rejoiced at the success of his march, and desirous of regaining the kingdom of Cassimir without bloodshed, sent an assurance to Hobaddan in answer, that, if he fulfilled his promise, his own life should be saved.

The next morning, Hobaddan appeared at the head of his troops, with their heads dejected, and their arms inverted toward the ground; and in this manner they came forward to the front of the viziar Horam's army.

Horam, the more to encourage the submission of Hobaddan, had placed the troops, which he had raised in the kingdom of Cassimir, in the front of his army; and also to secure them from retreating, by the support which his own troops were to give them in the rear.

When Hobaddan was come within hearing, instead of throwing his arms on the ground, he unsheathed his cimeter, and thus spake to the troops before him.

Brethren and countrymen, whom the same fathers begat, and whom the same mothers brought forth! suffer me to speak what my affection

affection to you all, and my love for my country, require me to say.

Against whom, O my brethren! is this array of battle, and whose blood seek ye to spill on the plains which our forefathers have cultivated? Is it our own blood that must be poured forth over these lands, to enrich them for a stranger's benefit? Is it not under pretence of fighting for the Princess of Cassimir, who has been long since dead, that the Sultan of India's troops are now ravaging, not our borders only, but penetrating even into the heart of our nation? But suppose ye that the conquerors will give up the treasures they hope to earn by their blood? Will they not rather, invited by the fruitfulness of our vales, and by the rich produce of our mountains, fix here the everlasting standards of their arms, and make slaves of us, who are become thus easily the dupes of their ambitious pretences? Then farewel contentment, farewel pleasure, farewel the well-earned fruits of industry and frugality! Our lands shall be the property of others, and we still tied down by slavish chains to cultivate and improve them. Our houses, our substance, shall be the reward of foreign robbers. Our wives and our virgins shall bow down before conquerors, and we, like the beasts of the field, be drawn in the scorching mid-day to the furrow or the mine.

As Hobaddan began to utter these words, Horam, astonished at his malice and presumption, ordered the archers, who attended him, to draw forth their arrows and pierce him to

the

the heart; but the weapons of war were as straws on the armour of Hobaddan, and he stood dauntless and unhurt amidst ten thousand arrows.

Friends and brethren! continued Hobaddan, you see the powers above are on our side; the arrows of Horam are as the chaff on the plain, and as the dust which penetrates not the garments of the traveller. Halt not, therefore, your ready judgments, which incline you to embrace what nature and your own security dictate, but join your arms to the defender and supporter of your liberties and your possessions.

At these words, the recruits of Horam filed off in a body, and joined the party of Hobaddan; while the pretended Sultan, elated at his success, pushed forward to the viziar Horam's troops, and charged them with the utmost impetuosity.

The weapons of the brave were foiled by the armour of Hobaddan; for the inchantress Hyppacusan, studious of diverting the attention of the Sultan Misnar, had assisted Hobaddan with her counsel, and with invulnerable arms. Wherefore, seeing their labour vain and fruitless against the pretended and unconquerable Sultan, the hearts of Horam's warriors melted within them, and they fell away from the field of battle, as the birds of the air retreat before the whistling husbandman.

Hobaddan, sensible of his advantage, hastened after the troops of Horam all the day and all the night; and the viziar himself nearly escaped

escaped with his life, having none left behind him, to send to Delly with the unhappy report of his defeat.

But malicious fame, ever indefatigable in representing the horrors of affliction and distress, soon spread her voice throughout the regions of Delly; and Misnar heard, from every quarter, that his faithful Horam, and all his chosen troops, were defeated or cut off by the victorious arm of Hobaddan.

The Princess Hemjunah gave up herself to sighs and tears, and refused the comfort and consolation of the court of Delly; and the Sultan Misnar, enraged at his loss, resolved to assemble the greatest part of his troops, and march to the assistance of Horam.

But first he gave orders that recruits should be raised, and that the number of his troops should be increased; and then, mixing his young raised soldiers with the veterans of his army, he left one half of his troops to guard his own provinces, and with the other he marched toward the confines of Cassimir.

The viziar Horam had concealed himself in the hut of a faithful peasant, and, hearing that his master was arrived with a numerous army in the kingdom of Cassimir, he went forward and met him, and, falling down at his feet, besought his forgiveness.

Horam, said the Sultan, arise; I forgive thee, although thou hast lost so many of my troops; but I little suspected Hobaddan had been too artful for the experience and sagacity of my viziar. However, Horam, he must not expect to deceive us again; we are more

in

in number, and we are aware of his deceits.
You, Horam, forced your marches, and
weakened your troops; but I will bring them
onwards, flowly and furely. Have we, O
Horam! prevailed againſt Ulin, and Happuck, and Ollomand, and Taſnar; have we
cruſhed Ahaback and Deſra by our prudent
arts, and ſhall we fear the contrivance of a
poor viziar, who leads a few rebels among
the rocks of the province of Caſſimir? Let
us but uſe prudence, with reſolution, and
theſe enemies muſt ſoon fade away, like the
ſhadow that flieth from the noontide ſun.

The two armies of the Sultan of India, and
the pretended Sultan of Caſſimir, approached
each other; and the troops of Miſnar were
pleaſed to hear, that their number was treble
the number of their enemies. But, however
great their ſuperiority might be, the Sultan
Miſnar and his viziar kept the moſt exact diſ-
cipline among them, and behaved as if they
were about to engage a ſuperior, and not an
inferior force.

For ſome time the armies continued within ſight of each other, neither chuſing to engage without ſome ſuperiority of circum-
ſtances, and both watchful to prevent that ſuperiority.

At length, the Sultan, obſerving a weak-
neſs in the left wing of Hobaddan's army,
cauſed by ſickneſs, as they were encamped
near a moraſs, gave orders for a furious attack upon the front, but directed the main
effort to be made againſt that wing.

But

But the Sultan's intentions were defeated; for Hobaddan, commanding not in the centre, as was expected, but in the left wing (with a chosen troop he had conveyed there that very morning of the engagement), totally defeated those who were sent to oppose him.

The troops to the right of the Sultan's army giving way, put all in confusion; and the unwieldy number of Misnar's forces, instead of regularly supporting them, poured toward the right in such tumult, as destroyed the whole disposition of the army.

During this confusion, Hobaddan hewed down on all sides those who dared oppose his arms; and his chosen troop followed him over mountains of the slain, every one flying through fear at the terror of his presence.

The Sultan and his viziar Horam, finding it in vain to rally their troops, or oppose the conquerors, founded a retreat; and, amidst the general confusion, fled toward the sandy deserts, which divide the realms of Caffimir from the province of Delly.

But the prudent Sultan, in his flight, endeavoured to restore to his troops their rank and order; and, while Horam reduced the foot under their proper banners, Misnar regulated the confusion of the horse, and placed them as a covering to the rest of his forces.

In this manner they marched before the face of their enemies into the desert, without any provision or forage, but what they carried

ried with their accoutrements; and, although the Sultan and his viziar used every argument to persuade their troops (who still exceeded the number of their enemies) to turn and pursue the army of Hobaddan, yet, so great was their dread of the victorious rebel and his forces, that they threatened to throw down their arms, rather than return to the battle.

Seeing all his endeavours to inspire his men with courage ineffectual, the Sultan travelled onward with them into the desert, as one given up to certain and unavoidable destruction; and his looks on Horam were like the looks of him, who seeth the hand of death on the children of his strength.

After two days march, they halted beside several small pools; and such was the excessive drought of Misnar's army, that many perished, before they could be prevailed upon to quit the refreshing pools of the desert.

These indeed thought of little more than present relief; but Misnar, their Lord, was overwhelmed with the severest pangs of affliction and distress.

To increase their griefs, if they were capable of increase, scouts brought word, that the troops of Hobaddan, being refreshed after their fatigues, were marching toward them, intending to destroy them while they were faint with want of provision.

The army of the Sultan, terrified by the report, and seeing no hopes of escape, fell upon the wretched Sultan Misnar and his faithful viziar, and, bringing them into the centre of the troops, they demanded their blood,

blood, as an atonement for the losses they were about to suffer in their cause.

The ringleader of this general mutiny was Ourodi, the ancient enemy of the faithful Horam; who, standing foremost in the ranks, commanded the archers to bind their Sultan and his viziar to a stake.

The Sultan, seeing all his hopes defeated, and the rage of the multitude, knelt down, and recommended his cause to the all-powerful Alla.

And now the archers were about to bend their bows, and fit the deadly shafts to their bow-strings, when a luminous appearance was discovered to the eastward, and the outskirts of the army saw a female, in robes of light, travelling over the sands of the desert.

In a moment she passed through the ranks of the army, and stood in the circle who were gathered around, to see the execution of their Sultan and his viziar.

Misnar, said the favourite of heaven, arise, and fear not those sons of clay, nor the malice of inchantment: I am thy genius Macoma, sent by Mahomet to save and deliver thee, when human assistance was vain and impossible.

Therefore, continued the Genius, assume thy just command over these thy subjects, and let them all fall prostrate on the ground to Alla, and wait to see the fate of those, who fight against the Prophet of the Faithful.

But first learn, from thine own experience, the folly of trusting even to the greatest human

man power or prudence, without an affiance in the Lord of Heaven.

The world, O Mifnar! is Alla's, and the kingdom of heaven is the work of his hands; let not therefore the proudeſt boaſt, nor the humble defpair; for, although the towering mountains appear moſt glorious to the fight, the lowly vallies enjoy the fatnefs of the fkies. But Alla is able to clothe the fummits of the rocks with verdure, and to dry up even the rivers of the vale. Wherefore, although thou wert fuffered to deftroy the greateſt part of thine enemies, yet one was left to overpower thee; that thou mighteft know that thou wert but a weak inftrument in the hands of ſtrength.

I know, anfwered the Sultan Mifnar, that Alla is able to diffolve this frame of earth, and every vifion of the eye; and therefore not the proudeſt, nor the moſt powerful, can ſtand againſt him.

As the Sultan fpake this, the oppofite army of Hobaddan appeared upon the face of the fandy defert.

Although his power be infinite, faid the Genius, yet can he effect thefe changes with the moſt unexpected caufes. To him the pifmire and the giant are alike. But I will not waſte that time in words, which I am commanded to employ in action, to convince both you and your army of the fovereignty of Alla. Therefore fuffer no man to riſe from the earth, or to quit their places; but lift up your heads only, and behold thofe enemies deftroyed, before whom you fled, as th' inhabitants

habitants of the earth before the noisome pestilence.

So saying, the Genius Macoma waved her wand, and instantly the air was darkened, and a confused noise was heard above the armies of Misnar and Hobaddan.

For some hours the Sultan's troops knew not the cause of the darkness that overshadowed them; but in a little time the light returned by degrees, and they looked toward the army of Hobaddan, and saw them overwhelmed with innumerable locusts.

Thine enemies, said Macoma, O Sultan! are no more, save the inchantress Hyppacusan, who at present personates the rebel Ourodi.

The glory of extirpating her infernal race, said the viziar Horam, bowing before the Genius Macoma, belongs to my Sultan; otherwise Horam would esteem himself the happiest of mankind in her destruction.

That glory you speak of, answered the Genius Macoma, is given to another; a fly is gone forth, the winged messenger of Alla's wrath, and at this moment bereaves the vile Hyppacusan of her breath and of her life.

The viziar Horam held down his head at the just reproof of the Genius, but the words of her reproof were the words of truth; for an account was brought, that the rebel Ourodi was suddenly dead, being strangled by some impediment in his throat; and that, at his death, his figure was changed into the appearance of a deformed inchantress.

Although

Although your enemies, O Mifnar! are no more, said the Genius, yet the affistance of Alla is as neceffary for your fupport, as for their defeat; wherefore he hath given life to the fprings of the pools of the defert, and your troops will find fuch refrefhment from them, that you may fafely march over the fandy plains: And, to add to your happinefs, the old Sultan Zebenezer, being releafed from the inchantments of Hyppacufan, waits, with his daughter Hemjunah, your fafe arrival; and knows not as yet thofe wonders, which I leave your prudence to reveal to him.

The Sultan Mifnar well underftood the myfterious fpeech of the Genius Macoma; but, before he or his troops tafted of the pools, or purfued their march, he commanded them to fall down before Alla, the only Lord of the world.

The troops, having done reverence to Alla, were defirous of repeating it before Mifnar, to afk his forgivenefs; but the modeft Sultan would not permit them.

'Tis no wonder, faid he, the fheep go aftray, when the fhepherd himfelf is bewildered on the mountains. Let us make, faid he, Alla and his prophet our guide and defence, and then neither prefumption nor rebellion fhall lead us into error.

The unexpected change reached not the court of Delly, till the troops were within a few days march of the city; and Zebenezer and Hemjunah were but juft prepared to meet the Sultan Mifnar, when he entered the gates of the palace.

As Misnar advanced toward the aged Zebenezer, the good old man started with surprise, and cried out, O Mahomet! is it possible, that the Sultan of India, and the Prince of Georgia, should be one and the same!

The Princess Hemjunah was amazed and confounded at her father's speech, and she fell on his aged face, and hid in his arms the blushes that overspread her.

What you suspect, my royal friend, said Misnar, is true; I am indeed the man who passed in Cassimir for the Prince of Georgia. I beseech thee, O Zebenezer, forgive my deception!

You have no forgiveness, said the aged Zebenezer, O Sultan, to ask from me.

Indeed, answered the Sultan, my title was just; my royal father Dabulcombar, being treacherously advised by those who wished to place his younger son Ahubal on the throne, commanded me to travel, and gain renown and experience in arms; and, to conceal my importance, gave me the title of Prince of Georgia.

In this disguise I came to the royal court of Cassimir, and engaged in your service, O venerable Sultan! and Alla sent his blessing on us; your enemies were put to flight, and your subjects, who favoured me, gave the credit of the defeat to my arms.

Hearing that you intended me the honour of an alliance with your illustrious family, I resolved first to see the Princess Hemjunah, whom I heard you had confined; being warned

from

from an ancient prophecy, that a stranger should deprive you of her. I saw the princess by means of one of her slaves, and Hemjunah, my lovely Hemjunah, from that moment took possession of my heart. I was earnest therefore with you to propose the nuptials, and was to have been introduced to the princess, the very day in which I received advice, that my Lord Dabulcombar was drawing near unto his Prophet.

In expectation of demanding your daughter as the Sultan of India, and not as an obscure prince, I journeyed to Delly, and was early enough to see my royal sire ere he departed.

Son, said he, evil threatens your reign; extricate, therefore, yourself from danger before you involve others in your ruin.

Mindful of my father's words, I resolved to quell the commotions of the empire, before I made myself known to the Sultan of Cassimir; but Alla has so wound the string of our fates together, that it is needless to repeat the rest of my adventures. Only the princess must forgive me this, that hearing she had been taken away from her father's court, I was resolved to conceal my interest in her affairs, till I was sensible that the Prince of Georgia, though not blessed with her smiles, had yet no rival in her affections.

Most noble Sultan, said the Princess Hemjunah, 'tis in vain to dissemble; suffer me, therefore, freely to declare, that the Sultan of India has totally extirpated the Prince of Georgia from my heart; but whatever my own sentiments may be, assure yourself, that I shall not, at my father's commands, refuse the Prince of Georgia my hand.

The Sultan of India and Zebenezer were both delighted with the manner of the Princess Hemjunah's answer; and Horam, the faithful viziar Horam, was rejoiced to find, that his master, and the Princess Hemjunah, were desirous of rewarding each other, after their mutual fatigues.

The whole court expected the nuptials with impatience, and the good old Sultan Zebenezer staid to see his daughter Sultaness of India, and Misnar the happiest and the most thankful of the children of Alla.

The children of Alla, said the sage Iracagem (as the Genius Macoma had finished her relation), have indeed a freedom of action; but that freedom is best exercised, when it leads them to trust and depend on the Lord of all things; not that he who sees even beyond the confines of light, is pleased with idleness, or giveth encouragement to the sons of sloth; the spirit which he has infused into mankind, he expects to find active and industrious; and when prudence is joined with religion, Alla either gives success to its dictates, or, by counteracting its motions, draws forth the brighter virtues of patience and resignation.

Learn, therefore, ye pupils of the race of immortals, not to forget your dependance on Alla, while ye follow the prudent maxims of wisdom and experience; for he only is truly prudent, who adds faith to his practice; and

he

he truly religious, whose actions are the result of his faith.

But sufficient for the present hours are the instructions of Macoma and her illustrious brethren. The faithful guardians of these children of mortality will, for a time, carry them abroad, and teach them those sciences, which are justly esteemed among the sons of the earth; sciences which have been delivered in secret whispers from our race, to a few chosen minds, who, through our assistance, have broken the fetters of ignorance, and subdued the darkness of carnal infirmities: Men famous through successive generations, for cultivating and polishing the rude outlines of nature, and for instructing mankind in the elegant and social arts.

As the sage Iracagem uttered these words, the inferior Genii retired with their respective pupils, and by easy progressions conducted them through those elegant and useful arts, each of which upon earth cannot be attained, but with a steady application through life.

After these exercises, toward the wane of the moon, the whole company met again in the saloon, and Iracagem with pleasure surveyed the enlightened countenances of the pupils of his race, whose hearts and intellects seemed dilated by the pleasing progress they had made.

Science, said the sage Iracagem, may polish the manners, but virtue and religion alone can animate with exalted notions, and dignify the mind of Immortality: To neglect the first, is to turn our head from the light

light of day; but to defpife the laft, is to grafp the earth, when heaven is opened to receive us. A wife and prudent fpirit will fo ufe the one, as to improve the other, and make his fcience the handmaid of his virtue. Wherefore, noble Adiram, let us proceed in the delightful leffons of morality, and hear the wonders you are prepared to relate.

The affable Adiram arifing, thus began her much inftructive Tale.

Sadak and Kalasrade.

TALE the NINTH.

THE fame of Sadak lives yet in the plain of Erivan, where he drew the bow of the mighty, and chafed the enemies of his faith over the frozen mountains of the north.

When Amurath gave peace to the earth, Sadak retired with his beloved Kalasrade to the palace of his ancestors, which was situated on the banks of the Bosphorus, and commanded one of the most beautiful prospects in the world.

Sadak, tho' furious and impetuous in the field, was elegant and amiable in his happy retreat, where fancy and delicacy preserved their preeminence over the richest productions of unrestrained nature.

The palace of Sadak stood upon a wide-extended terrace, which overlooked the sea and the opposite shores of Europe; a deep and noble grove sheltered it behind, and on each side hills and vallies diversified the rural scene.

The gardens of the palace, though wild and irregular, yet afforded the most delightful retirement; and Sadak found in its bosom,

pleasures

pleasures far superior to the splendid pageants of the Othman court.

To increase the bliss of this earthly paradise, his favourite fair had blessed him with a numerous progeny; and as Sadak and Kalasrade sat under the shade of the lofty pines, their children wantoned and sported on the plains before them.

The spirit of their father was in the lively contests of his sons, and maternal delicacy dimpled on the cheeks of the daughters of Kalasrade.

The happy pair saw their own virtues reflected from their children; and Sadak having already earned this elegant retreat by the toils of war, was resolved to dedicate the rest of his days to the improvement of his beauteous offspring.

Kalasrade, though her charms were as yet undiminished by age, harboured not a wish in which her noble Sadak was unconcerned; all her joy was centred in Sadak; her heart rejoiced not but when Sadak appeared, and her soul, uneasy at a moment's absence, panted after Sadak her Lord. The love of Sadak equalled the affections of his beloved; he gazed every hour with new transports upon her charms; none but Kalasrade engaged his thoughts, none but Kalasrade shared in his affections.

Time, which impairs the impetuous sallies of lust, increased the holy flame of their love, and their retirement grew more and more agreeable, as they more and more experienced the purity of its joys. But Sadak indulged
not

not wholly on the sofas of pleasure, his sons required his presence with them in the chase: He led them forth to manly sports, and trained them to the exercise of arms.

His four sons followed their father Sadak daily to the plains of Rezeb, where they strove for mastery in the race, and pointed their arrows at the distant mark.

O my father, said Codan, the eldest of his children, as they were on the plain, where Sadak was drawing the bowstring to his breast, a black cloud arises from the grove, and flames of fire burst through its sides!

Sadak quickly turned his eyes toward the wood, which sheltered his palace, and saw the sparks and the flames ascending over the tops of the trees.

My children, said Sadak, with a firm countenance, fear not, continue your sports on the plain till I return: I will leave four slaves with you, the rest shall follow your father to this grove of fire.

Though Sadak was unwilling to terrify his children, he knew full well the misfortune which had befallen him. His palace was in flames, and the doating husband hastened with his slaves, to the relief of his beloved Kalasrade and her daughters.

Sadak first reached the burning palace. The slaves of the house, terrified at the fire, were flying into the woods. He commanded them back, and asked if Kalasrade and her little ones were safe.

Seeing their consternation, he flew towards the apartment of his beloved, which was situated

ated in one of the inner courts; and though the devouring flames endeavoured to bar his paſſage, the firm Sadak preſſed through the fire into the apartments of Kalaſrade.

Kalaſrade! ſaid Sadak, my beloved Kalaſrade, where art thou!

Kalaſrade anſwered not.

Sadak lifted up his voice ſtill higher, Kalaſrade, my beloved Kalaſrade, where art thou!

Kalaſrade anſwered not.

Sadak, though terrified at not diſcovering his beloved, yet ſearched every part of the Haram, till he came to the apartments of his three daughters, who, with their female ſlaves, were fallen on the earth, every moment expecting to be devoured by the flames.

Ariſe, my children, ſaid Sadak, and be comforted at the preſence of your parent: But where is your mother? Where is my beloved Kalaſrade?

Alas, anſwered the children of Sadak, we know not; ſome ſlaves forced our dear parent from her apartments, as ſhe was haſtening to our relief.

Then, anſwered Sadak, bleſſed be my Prophet, ſhe is ſafe! But come, my daughters, continued their father, you muſt not delay your eſcape, the fire makes haſty ſtrides upon us: Come, my children, to my arms, and I will bear you through the flames; but firſt let us dip in the bath, leſt the fire ſeize on our garments.

As

As they passed the female baths, they dipped themselves in the bason, and the slaves followed their master's example.

Sadak arriving at the entrance where the flames had reached, resolutely took up his two eldest children, and carried them through the flames; then again returning, I will either, said he, rescue my youngest, or perish with her.

His youngest fainted with fear as soon as her father had left her, and Sadak found her stretched on the ground, with but little signs of life.

All the female slaves following their master Sadak, had escaped out of the Haram, except one faithful creature, who rather resolved to die with her young mistress, than leave her exposed to the flames.

Sadak snatched up his dear treasure in his arms, and commanded the faithful slave to take hold of his garment, and follow him thro' the flames.

Happily the wind had turned the fire toward a different part of the palace, so that Sadak had less danger to encounter in the second effort, than in the first.

The resolute Sadak having rescued his children, enquired of his slaves where they had conveyed his dear Kalasrade; but none could give answer to the questions of their Lord.

The slaves were now all gathered together in a body; but four of their number were missing, besides those who continued with the sons of Sadak on the plain.

As little more could be rescued from the flames, Sadak left only ten slaves about the palace to recover what they were able; the rest he sent into different parts of the grove, and to the villages around, to seek for their mistress Kalasrade, and her slaves; six he dismissed with her daughters to the plains of Rezeb, commanding them with their attendants, to join his sons, and seek some shelter and refreshment in a neighbouring village, and leaving orders for his beloved Kalasrade, if she was found, to retire to her children.

Sadak then went through the most unfrequented paths, and into the loneliest parts of the wood, to seek his beloved, calling upon her as he passed along, and pronouncing the names of the slaves that were missing. This he continued, till night had thrown her sable garments on the earth, and he had compassed his palace every way around for several miles; when he resolved to turn again to his palace, and enquire of his slaves concerning his beloved Kalasrade.

He passed through the woods, guided by the red glare of light, which the clouds reflected from the fire that had nigh consumed his dwelling, and entered the farther part of the terrace, whereon stood the few remains of his once elegant building.

The flames, unsatiated with their former cruelties, seemed to rekindle at his presence. His slaves came weeping toward him, but could give no tidings of their amiable mistress; and Sadak, who in the morning had looked with the utmost satisfaction on the lively

lively scenes around him, now saw the melancholy face of nature, enlightened with the dusky gleams of his own unexpected ruin.

But yet the wreck of nature could not have disturbed Sadak more than the loss of his beloved; he doubted not but that the fire was kindled by those slaves, who had torn Kalasrade from his arms; and though he felt within himself the deepest affliction, his blood curdled with horror, when he reflected on the tenfold distresses which encompassed the pure and spotless partner of his affections.

O Alla, said the trembling Sadak, fortify my faith, and teach me, even in the horrors of this night, to believe, that mercy triumphs over evil, and that the paths of destruction are controuled by thy all-seeing power! To me all is confusion! misery! and terror! But thou seest through the dark abyss, and guidest the footsteps of the just in the vallies of desolation: Nevertheless, O thou Just One! forgive the sinking of my soul, and pour the virtuous balm of hope into the wounded spirits of thine afflicted servant.

The bounteous Alla heard the voice of his servant, and the heart of Sadak was fortified and strengthened with religious hope.

Having disposed of what effects his slaves had rescued from the flames, in a place of security, Sadak hastened to the village where his children were assembled, and disguising the severer pangs he felt himself, endeavoured to assuage the grief of his fond family for the loss of their mother.

Several

Several of Sadak's friends soon joined him in the village, and the relations of his wife offered to take care of his children, while he went in search of Kalasrade, and his villanous slaves.

Sadak with thankfulness embraced the offer of Mepiki, the father of his beloved, and having tenderly embraced his children, directed his steps toward the sea-side, and crossed in one of his feluccas to the city of Constantinople.

No sooner was Amurath seated on his throne in the Divan, than Sadak fell prostrate before him.

My brave Soldier, said Amurath, arise.

The world, Sadak, continued the Prince, talk largely concerning your happiness, and those who envy not the Othman crown, yet pant after the elegant and peaceable retirements of the fortunate Sadak. Has Sadak, then, a wish ungratified, that he comes thus an humble suppliant at a monarch's feet?

The smiles of his Prince, answered Sadak, are a soldier's joy, and in the sunshine of those smiles did Sadak live an envied life, till one dark cloud interposed, and blasted the ripe fruit of Sadak's joy.

What means my Sadak? answered Amurath.

While I led my sons to the plain, replied Sadak, to teach them the duties which they owed their Prince, the flame seized my peaceful dwelling; and ere I could return to the rescue of my beloved Kalasrade, four slaves had dragged her away, and I and my
attendants

attendants have in vain been seeking her, in woods and plains that surround my habitation; wherefore, O Amurath! I come a suppliant to thy throne to ask redress of thee.

That, answered Amurath, brave Soldier, thou shalt have; my Hasnadar Baski shall pay thee twice the value of thine house. Thou shalt have twenty of my slaves; and as to thy beloved, go where fancy leads thee, and seek a new Kalasrade.

The words of Amurath were as the arrows of death in the heart of Sadak, and he said, Let the hand of justice overtake the robbers, and let the power of my Lord restore Kalasrade to my arms.

Kalasrade, answered Amurath, has doubtless been so long in your slaves possession, that she is, ere this, contented with her lot; instead of being the slave of one, she is now the mistress of four. But why should a weak female trouble the brave soldier's heart? The chance of war gives them to our arms, and as they change their lords, our females change their love.

As the blasted oak is torn by the thunderbolt, so was the heart of Sadak rent by the words of Amurath; but he concealed the storm that shook his breast, and bowing to the earth, departed from the Divan.

He applied himself that day to enquire in the Bisisten, and public market-places, concerning Kalasrade and his four slaves; and hearing no tidings of them there, he went to the water-side, among the Levents, or watermen;

watermen; but none could give him the least account of the fugitives.

The sorrows of Sadak bore heavy on his heart, but they did not prevent him from making a regular and strict search on the opposite shores both of Europe and Asia. Several months passed in a fruitless enquiry, without the least discovery either of his slaves or the manner of their escape.

The gentle Kalasrade, in the mean time, suffered still severer afflictions.

On the morning in which she was torn from her Lord, she was seated on her sofa, with her slaves around her, when she heard from several quarters of the palace a cry of fire, and in an instant saw the blaze ascend in three different parts.

All was confusion and distress; Kalasrade forgot not her children, but was hastening to their apartment, when four slaves broke in upon her, and forced her out of the palace.

They flew with their prize to one extremity of the terrace, where a small galley, which was concealed by the trees which overshadowed the water, waited for her arrival.

The distracted Kalasrade was delivered to an old eunuch in the galley, who instantly threw a thick black veil over her head, and threatened to cast her into the sea, if she cried out or resisted.

The threats of the eunuch were vain; Kalasrade feared no greater misfortune than the loss of Sadak, and she filled the air with her lamentations.

The eunuch finding his remonstrances unsuccessful, shut up the windows of the galley, and urged the rowers to hasten away with their prize.

Kalasrade being inclosed in the galley, knew not to what shore she was carried; but ere long the vessel struck upon the ground, and ten black eunuchs entering the galley, they wrapped a covering of silk around her, and conveyed her away.

After some time they stopped, and uncovered the unfortunate Kalasrade to give her breath.

The beauteous mourner looked around her, and saw she was in a garden planted with cypress trees.

She fell at the feet of him who seemed to have the command of his brethren, and besought him to have compassion on the miseries of a distressed mother and an injured wife.

The eunuchs made no answer to the intreaties of Kalasrade; but he who commanded the rest, made a sign for them to fling the silken covering over Kalasrade, and to bear her away.

It was not long before the slaves made a second halt, and took off the silken covering again from Kalasrade, and retired.

The beauteous wife of Sadak lifted up her veil, as soon as she perceived the slaves withdraw, and found she was in an obscure room, the windows of which were guarded with iron bars.

In one corner of the room stood a small pot of boiled rice, and beside it a pitcher of water.

Kalasrade hastened to the door, but the slaves had made it fast without.

Seeing all possibility of escape taken from her, and not knowing where she was, the wretched Kalasrade threw herself on the earth, and, with tears and sighs intermixed, thus poured forth her griefs:

O whither am I carried from the arms of my beloved! Where was Sadak, the light of mine eyes, when the hand of the oppressor was on the bosom of his Kalasrade? Where was the strength of his arm, and the fierceness of his countenance, when they tore his Kalasrade from the nest of her little ones? O faithful Sadak, whither am I borne from the light of thine eyes? Whither am I carried from the smiles which refreshed my heart? Did we not, O Sadak, divide the light and the darkness together? In the bosom of Sadak I hid me from the storm; in the arms of Sadak his beloved triumphed!

Ah Sadak! Sadak! hear the voice of Kalasrade, ere the vile ravisher come and despoil thee of thy treasure! My love for thee, O Sadak, has been pure as the rain drops, and the thoughts of Kalasrade have not wandered from her Lord. In the morning I joyed not at the sun, but as he gave to mine eyes the image of my beloved. When Sadak arose, my heart was poured out in a sigh; when he led his sons to the chace, ah wretched chace! my eyes went with him to the grove,

but

but my thoughts followed him to the plain. When he returned, his presence was like the sprightly notes of music to my soul; when he smiled, he was cheerful as the light of the morning. When he spoke, his words were as the dews of heaven on the fruitful bosom of the earth; and his motion was graceful as the waving of the palm-tree on the brow of the mountain. O who has divided my beloved from mine arms! Ah, Kalasrade, thou art as the traveller among the wolves of the forest; thou art as a stranger bewildered in the snowy plain!

Kalasrade vented her sighs undisturbed for several days, no one appearing but an old female mute, who daily brought her some boiled rice and a pitcher of water, which, though but scanty, was more than sufficient for the beauteous wife of Sadak.

During this interval it was impossible for Kalasrade to guess at the meaning of her confinement; and seeing no one come to molest her, she began to bear her situation with more temper; though still, like the turtle, her moans after Sadak were every moment indulged, and her fears for her children renewed the horrors of her mind.

At length one of her own black slaves, who had assisted in forcing her away, appeared. He was dressed in a green robe, and wore a yellow turban on his head. As he entered the room, Kalasrade retired as far as she was able, but he with an horrid grin advanced, and seized her by the arm.

The

The beauteous Kalafrade, finding herself in the power of the black slave, shrieked aloud, and filled the room with her cries; but he, regardless of her tears or her intreaties, and in a rough and determined tone, acquainted her with his love, and that be intended to make her his mistress.

At these words Kalafrade redoubled her cries, and the slave proceeded to press her in his arms; when in an instant fifty eunuchs rushed into the apartment, and, seizing on the black slave, delivered Kalafrade from his embraces.

The wife of Sadak was astonished at the new scene of wonders which she beheld; but her heart soon returned to its former fears, when she beheld the mighty Amurath approach.

Let that slave, said the monarch, repay with his life the injuries he has done to this perfection of beauty.

The distressed Kalafrade, hearing the command of Amurath, fell at the feet of her Prince, and said:

Lord of thy slaves! whom Alla has sent to the relief of the distressed, behold the handmaid of thy servant Sadak before thee. As Sadak, Mighty Prince! was teaching his sons to walk in the paths of their father, four of his slaves, having set fire to his dwelling, rushed into the Haram, and bore me away to a galley, in which, throwing a blind over me, they conveyed me to this wretched hut, where, till to-day, I have been indulged in my silent woes. But a few moments ago,
this

this bafe flave entered, whom I fufpect to be the author of my misfortunes, and was about to compel me to bear his filthy love; when the guards of my Lord rufhed in, and preferved me from his villanous malice; wherefore, Mighty Lord! permit thy flave to depart; and, if it pleafe thee, gracious Prince! let a few of thefe my deliverers convey me from this flave's houfe to Sadak thy fervant.

As Kalafrade uttered thefe words, Amurath made a fign to his eunuchs to withdraw; and, taking the lovely Kalafrade by the hand, he bade her arife.

Beauteous Kalafrade! faid he, I am pleafed at your artlefs tale; yet are you much deceived; you are not in a flave's houfe, fair miftrefs of my heart! but in the garden of thy Amurath's feraglio.

At thefe words, the countenance of Kalafrade changed; a deadly palenefs overfpread her cheeks; and fhe fell to the earth, as a flower cut off from its root by the ftormy wind.

Although Amurath called in immediate affiftance, it was long before they could reftore motion and life to the miferable Kalafrade; who, as foon as fhe beheld the countenance of Amurath, again funk to the earth.

After fome time, when the diftreffed Kalafrade was a little recovered, Amurath thus began:

It is beneath the Lord of the earth to difguife his thoughts, or to wear a countenance which accords not with his heart: No, my

lovely

lovely Kalasrade! Hypocrisy is a slave's portion; the sun knows no shadow, and Asia's monarch knows no restriction: Wherefore Kalasrade shall not any longer feel the tortures of a doubt, or the shackles of fear.

Know then, lovely fair one! that I was jealous of my slave Sadak, who boasted joys superior to those which attend his Prince; and I issued forth the law of my mind, that he should be cut off for his presumption.

While the Janissaries were making ready to obey my commands, I considered that death alone was not a sufficient recompence for his folly; and therefore I determined to add suspense to the tortures which the rebel had merited at my hands.

For this purpose, I gave orders to the chief of my eunuchs to corrupt some of his slaves, who were to fire his dwelling in different parts, and to bring away his Kalasrade to my seraglio. Not that I intended, beauteous fair one! to exalt thee to my notice: No, the wife of Sadak was a personage too low for Amurath to stoop to. But, having heard that you also gloried in your Sadak, I resolved that you should live, confined in an ignominious hut, on the coarsest food for some days; which being executed, I commanded one of your slaves to go in unto you, and make you subservient to his will. But my anger was so hot against you, that this was not sufficient revenge, unless I was an eye-witness of your distress. For this purpose, a secret stand was contrived for me behind this hut, where I could unobserved behold all that passed. Hi-

ther

ther I came with the slave, just time enough to see him enter before you. But, O lovely Kalasrade! what was my emotion, when I beheld the charms which I was about to sacrifice to my revenge.

The moment I saw your irresistible beauties, I vowed the vile slave should die, who even in thought had attempted to prophane your charms. I made a sign for my eunuchs to rush in and seize him; and, ere this, his accursed blood is poured on the earth, as an atonement for his insolence.

But this is not all that Amurath will do for the mistress of his heart; and the happy Kalasrade may rejoice, that the presumption of Sadak was not unnoticed by his Lord. Your short troubles, O Kalasrade! have been productive of the greatest joy your sex can feel; for know that you have engaged the affection of the mighty Amurath; and he, who will not depart from the words of his lips, doth here call Mahomet to witness, that Amurath will make his beloved Kalasrade the Sultana of his heart.

The tender Kalasrade was overcome with the words of Amurath, and she sunk into the arms of the chief of the eunuchs who stood behind her.

Doubor, said Amurath, I perceive Kalasrade's joy has overpowered her. While she is in the trance of happiness, too great for her mortal nature to live under, let her be conveyed to the richest apartments of the seraglio, where the favourites of our race enjoy the converse of their Lords; and let all homage

be

be paid to her, who is destined to share in the pleasures of Amurath.

While Doubor, and the rest of the eunuchs, waited to perform the will of their Prince, Amurath returned to the seraglio, and entered the baths, and afterwards arrayed himself in his most sumptuous robes.

He then sent to enquire of the chief of his eunuchs, whether Kalasrade was recovered.

The chief of the eunuchs came with the countenance of sorrow.

What! said Amurath, trembling, as he saw the posture of his slave, is not the beauteous Kalasrade arisen from the slumbers of transport?

Lord of life! answered Doubor, we have used every secret of physic in vain. Our beauteous mistress still slumbers on the sofa whereon we conveyed her.

If so, replied Amurath, let us hasten to the adjoining apartment, where I may behold, unseen, the joy which will awaken in her breast, as her eyelids unfold to her the splendours that surround her.

After Amurath had been some time stationed in his secret stand, the lovely Kalasrade opened her eyes, and beheld the magnificent apartment into which she had been conveyed.

The beauteous wife of Sadak, seeing the mutes standing on each side of her, the fair female slaves falling prostrate in two rows before the steps of the sofa, and the eunuchs with folded arms and downcast eyes at a distance,

distance, shrieked aloud, and, clapping her hands together in wild despair, cried out, O Sadak, Sadak, save me from this pompous horror!

She then, in frantic haste, tore off the magnificent bracelets of diamonds, which, during her fainting, had been fastened to her arms, and the rich girdle of rubies which adorned her waist, the pearls and the emeralds which hung upon her bosom; and looking on herself, If I have any thing, said she, that may tempt the lawless to injure Sadak's love, thus will I sacrifice it to our mutual truth!

As she spake these words, she fastened her delicate hands on her cheeks, and, before the eunuch (who instantly ran toward her to prevent her intentions) could seize her, she had marked her features with streams of blood.

The disappointed Amurath could no longer contain himself, but he entered the apartment just as the blood was starting from the lovely cheeks of the wife of Sadak.

Slaves! said he, your lives shall answer this neglect; your base folly has robbed me of all my joys. Behold, my Kalafrade is defiled with blood, and Amurath must abstain from her embrace.

But, if these deserve death, what torture should await the wretched and foolish Kalafrade, who presumes to value the caresses of a slave, when the mighty Amurath hath received her into the seraglio of his pleasures?

Vol. II.   F   Alas,

Alas, mighty Prince! said the distracted Kalasrade, falling at his feet, who can absolve the plighted vow? Or——

Polluted slave! said Amurath, starting from her, defile not my garments with thy touch, nor mine ears with thy rebellion. For three days shall I leave thee, till thou art washed from the stains of this frantic deed; at the end of which time, either prepare to receive my caresses, or expect to see the head of Sadak blackening in the sun before the windows of the seraglio.

At these words the incensed Amurath left the fair Kalasrade weeping on the ground, and retired to a different part of the palace. But he gave orders that the chief of his eunuchs should attend her, to see that she was purified from the stain of her blood.

The disconsolate fair one gave herself up to perpetual grief, and refused to taste the delicacies that were set before her; although Douber on his knees besought her to consider the dreadful consequences of offending his Lord.

To these remonstrances Kalasrade answered little; her mind was full of the mighty ills which she suffered; and she could conceive nothing more dreadful than the embraces of Amurath.

As she sat the second day on her sofa, musing on her dear absent Sadak, she perceived a small bird perch on one of the windows, which looked toward the gardens of the seraglio; which, hopping from thence to her

her hand, opened its little throat, and began its artless lay.

As the bird left off singing, Kalafrade, tho' she was astonished at its tameness, yet began to stroke it, and said,

Thou, pretty chorister, art mistress of the air, and heaven hath adorned thee with the wings of liberty; thou buildest thy nest beyond the trace of human malice, and soarest abroad, where no Amurath can impede thy flight.

The moans of Kalafrade were interrupted by a small voice, which at first the beauteous wife of Sadak could scarce believe were uttered by the little bird: till, listening with attention to it, she distinguished the following words:

Startle not, lovely mistress of Sadak's thoughts, at the voice of a bird. The most trifling causes can, in the hands of strength, produce the greatest effects; as the instructions of Alla were conveyed to the holy Prophet of Mecca by the whispers of a dove.

My station appears envious to Kalafrade, because she conceives me the offspring of liberty. Her fancy represents me on the wings of pleasure and enlargement; she sees me soaring in heaven's broad path, but forgets my toils in the grove, and my labours in the field. If the light feather, which bears me on the thin surface of the air, makes me man's superior in flight, yet the artifice of human inventions again subjects my weaker understanding a prey to contrivance: But it is enough for me, Kalafrade, to know that I am the creature of Alla, who has in wisdom appointed to every thing living their proper stations and bounds.

At present, indeed, I seem to have transgressed those bounds; but it is in obedience to my mistress Adirab, who presides over the faithful family of Sadak. 'Tis she who speaks in me, and who means to speak comfort to the heart-broken Kalafrade: She it is that saith,

O beauteous mourner, and slave of the oppressor, fear not misfortunes, which are the tests of virtue, and not the rotten fruit of infirmity! The malicious shall not always triumph, the staff whereon the wicked lean shall rot and decay! When clouds hover above the fields, the drops of fatness descend; when the storm passeth over the city, the days of health are at hand. It is the glory of the Faithful to bear afflictions with patience, and to oppose the temptations of evil with fortitude and firmness.

As the bird was continuing to speak the lessons of its mistress Adirab, the chief of the eunuchs entered the apartment, and the little chorister flew swiftly away, through the window, among the trees in the garden of the seraglio.

Doubor, as he entered, approached to the sofa of Kalafrade, and fell prostrate before her.

Lovely Kalafrade, said the trembling eunuch, it is to the intercession of Sadak, the father of thy Lord, that Doubor owes the
spirit

spirit which enlivens him. When Elar, the father of Sadak, fought by the side of Mahomet his Lord, on the confines of Sclavonia, and the inhabitants of Zagrah fled before him, my widowed mother, with her family, were among the number of the fugitives; but, as she held a daughter in each hand, and was laden with me, an infant, on her back, she was soon unable to keep up with her brethren, whose concern was so urgent for themselves, that they refused to bear any part of her burthen.

My mother Idan, finding it in vain to fly with her children, and resolving not to leave them behind her to the merciless fury of her enemies, sat down by the road side, and, while I hung on the breast, embraced with the utmost tenderness her two daughters.

Ere she had completed her caresses, the outskirts of Mahomet's army appeared. Two janissaries first reached the miserable widow; they examined her features, but age had spread the veil of safety on her cheeks. The daughters of the wretched widow next excited their attention; the countenance of Liberak, the eldest, bedewed with tears, appeared like the melting snow; and the bloom of Hirab, the second, shone through the pearly drops that hung upon her face, as the rose-bud laden with the dew of night.

Be this my prey, said the first janissary, and seized on the elegant Liberak; and be this mine, said his comrade, fastening on the blush-covered Hirab.

Idan, my mother, awaking from her trance of sorrows by the rude onset of the two janissaries, called aloud on her Christian gods for relief, and held each daughter firmly by the hand, while the janissaries endeavoured to loosen her hold; which the first not effecting so easily as he hoped, drew his cimeter, and severed her hand and her daughter from the miserable Idan.

His comrade, observing the brutal success of his fellow-soldier, drew his cimeter likewise, and was about to gain his prize by the same kind of cruelty; when Elar, the captain of the band, rode up, and, seeing the accursed design of the janissary, with his uplifted cimeter hewed him to the ground.

The first janissary, seeing the fate of his comrade, fled; and Elar gave orders that Idan and her children should be preserved. He set a guard over her; and sent, with several slaves, one experienced in the knowledge of physic, to bind up her wound.

But the kind efforts of Elar were vain; my mother fainted with the loss of blood; and, before proper assistance could be procured, expired in the arms of her helpless daughters.

Liberak and Hirab, the children of Idan, fell on the face of their mother, and ceased not to mourn over their unhappy parent; neither could the attendants, which Elar had provided, prevail on them to receive the least refreshment. They continued, during the pursuit of the Turks after the Sclavonians, which lasted three days, immoveable on the

body

IDAX and her two Daughters LIBERAK and HIRAB.

body of their dear mother Idan, while I was nourished by one of the slaves of Elar.

Sorrow and fatigue soon put an end to the lives of Liberak and Hirab, the duteous daughters of the deceased Idan; and I was left an helpless infant in the arms of the slaves of Elar, who, after the return of the army from pursuing their enemies, presented me to Elar, with an account of the death of my mother and my sisters.

Elar, perceiving a liveliness in my looks, sent the slave with me to Mahomet, who gave orders that I should be admitted into his seraglio; and one of the first things I learned there, was this history, from the mouth of a slave, who was appointed to be my nurse. Wherefore be not surprised, O beauteous Kalasrade! at my affection for Sadak, the son of my Lord Elar, by whose generous intercession I became a servant of Mahomet, and was afterwards, by the favour of the mighty Amurath, exalted to this post of confidence and honour. But, alas! how will my desire to serve Sadak be believed, when it is known that I, by the command of Amurath, corrupted his slaves, and assisted them in bringing the wife of my Lord into this seraglio?

Indeed, faithful Kalasrade, my ignorance must plead my excuse. Bred up in this place, I knew no law but the will of my master; and I believed, that every female would esteem it their greatest happiness, to enjoy the smiles of the mighty Amurath.

But

But the despair of Sadak's beauteous wife, her constancy, and her contempt of every grandeur, when the price of unfaithfulness, have convinced me how much I have distressed the noble Sadak, and to what a precipice I have dragged the much injured Kalasrade; and yet, what had my refusal to obey Amurath benefited your cause? Death had been my instant reward; and some more savage heart had been procured, to direct the bloody resolves of Amurath against you. Yet I plead not my own excuse; but mean, ere it be too late, to serve the much injured wife of Sadak, the son of my patron Elar.

If you mean to serve me, Doubor, said the lovely Kalasrade (though I much suspect the integrity of your tale), lead me this instant out of the seraglio, and waft me over to the dwelling of Sadak my Lord.

What! answered Doubor, is Kalasrade such a stranger to the watchful keepers of this seraglio, that she suppoes it possible for any one to escape, unobserved, through the various guards which surround it? Know you not, beloved of Sadak! that numberless mutes and eunuchs watch it, night and day, within; and without are stationed a thousand janissaries, both by water and land? No, fair captive! there is no escape from these walls, unless Amurath consent.

Is this, base Doubor! answered Kalasrade, your promised comfort, that you officiously come to certify me of my ruin? Thou art, indeed, a Christian renegade, and no Turk; for thou delightest to torment those whom
thou

thou canst not save. O Sadak! Sadak! was it for this thy father Elar preserved this Christian's blood, that he should be the chief engine of Amurath's malice against thee? Such tales as these are fitting to drive pity from a warrior's breast, and to justify the slaughter of those, who spare neither sex nor age!

It were hard, answered Doubor, the chief of the eunuchs, to condemn the fierce courser, because he cannot fly without the assistance of the earth whereon he bounds; or to extirpate the olive-tree, because it bears not the luscious clusters of the vine. Although Doubor is unable to release the fair Kalasrade, yet he may find some expedient to drive off the completion of Amurath's designs.

Ah, faithful Doubor! said Kalasrade (convinced of her injudicious hastiness), forgive the wild sallies of a distempered mind; I am satisfied of your kind intentions, and I wait with impatience to hear your instruction and advice.

The great foible of Amurath, replied the chief of the eunuchs, is pride; and even his love is subservient to the haughtiness of his soul.

If so, answered Kalasrade, interrupting him, I will tempt his utmost anger, and merit his contempt. I will sting his proud heart with taunts and revilings, and force him to cast me forth to public scorn.

Alas! answered Doubor, you know not, beauteous Kalasrade! the fury of Amurath; such a behaviour would irritate him to invent new torments for Sadak, through whom he knows the heart of Kalasrade is soonest wounded. No, my lovely mistress! you must use far other arts, if you mean to preserve yourself unhurt in this impregnable seraglio. While Amurath thinks you love Sadak, no concessions of yours will please him; he may indeed, for a few hours, take a pleasure in your smiles; but his jealous heart will soon awake, and his rage against the unfortunate Sadak will rekindle.

O Doubor! said Kalasrade, where will your mean advice end?

Fear not, constant Kalasrade, answered the chief of the eunuchs, I seek to deliver you even from the horrors of your own imagination. In the wide ocean is a large island, surrounded by inaccessible rocks and deceitful quicksands; in the centre of which, from a rising ground, runs a small spring, whose waters are of such a nature, that whoever drinks of them, immediately forgets whatever has passed before in their lives; but these waters are beset with such unsurmountable difficulties, that no one hath ever been able to draw of that stream, though thousands have perished in the undertaking.

When Amurath then next enters, lovely Kalasrade! into these apartments, appear submissive and humble before him; and, when he presses you to accept of his love, promise to yield to his desires, on one condition, that he procures for you the waters of oblivion, that you may forget all your former converse with Sadak, and be made fit to receive the conqueror of the earth.

Ah, Doubor! Doubor! answered Kalafrade, how can I prevail upon myself, even in deceit, to speak so direspectfully of Sadak, the beloved of my soul! O Sadak, may I be indeed the tyrant's mistress, when my base heart forgets its lovely union with Sadak its lord!

Consider, faithful consort of Sadak, answered Doubor, what otherwise may be your doom; better it is to speak in terms of disgrace of Sadak, than to disgrace his love, by suffering the wild effects of Amurath's desires.

O Doubor, said Kalafrade, I had much rather submit to every lesser ill, than have my heart-strings broken by his hated embrace!

I had not dared to have staid thus long at the feet of Kalafrade, answered Doubor, unless Amurath had sent me to soften your heart. I will now return, and prepare him to be deceived by the request of his Sultana.

Ah, Doubor, said Kalafrade, if you mean to serve me, never again let me hear that detested name: Sultana! to me is a worse sound, than poverty and contempt can frame!

The chief of the eunuchs bowed to the earth, and withdrew from the presence of Kalafrade.

The tale of Doubor, said Kalafrade to herself, as the chief of the eunuchs left the room, may be only a fertile invention to amuse, and soften the rigorous sorrows of my heart;

heart; but as they cannot change my fixed resolves, I will act as though I believed them. If there is truth in his words, his device may at worst put off for a time the misfortunes I have too much reason to dread.

The mind of Kalasrade was so greatly eased by the instructions of the bird of Adiram, and the devices of Doubor, the chief of the eunuchs, that on the third day she suffered the slaves to adorn her, and partook of the delicacies which were set before her.

In the evening the slaves of the seraglio warned Kalasrade of Amurath's approach, and as he entered, the beauteous wife of Sadak fell with her face to the earth.

Kalasrade, said Amurath, let me know, ere you rise from the earth, to the blissful paradise of these arms, whether you have well weighed the difference between a slave's love and a monarch's favour, or is it necessary to compel you to be happy?

Light of the faithful, and Lord of the earth, answered the prostrate Kalasrade, the preference you have shewn an object unworthy of your notice, can never be sufficiently acknowledged by your slave. But, O my Lord, mention not the mighty honours you mean to heap upon me, lest my dazzled fancy totter with the towering thought, and my overcharged reflection sink into the long slumbers of eternal night.

Blessed and unexpected change, said the transported Amurath, raising up the trembling Kalasrade in haste, what were those
sweet

sweet words that I suffered to fall so soon to the earth, words valuable as the wide empire that I hold! Repeat them, beauteous Kalasrade, ten thousand thousand times in mine ears, and ask your own reward for the sweet labour I have imposed upon you.

THE CONTINUATION OF THE TALE OF SADAK AND KALASRADE.

ALAS, alas, continued Kalasrade, what has my weak heart uttered in the ears of my Prince! Can the mighty Amurath stoop to raise a peasant's daughter! shall the age-stricken wife of Sadak, shall the mother of a numerous family, shall the mean inhabitant of a cottage on the banks of the Bosphorus, become the favourite of Amurath, and the Sultana of the Othman court! No, Kalasrade, foolish Kalasrade, Amurath laughs at thy folly, and has raised thee to this height, to make thy fall more terrible.

As the humble tortoise is lifted up and borne on the pinions of the eagle, till his giddy sight swim at the wide prospect round him, and then hurled suddenly downward to the pointed rock, so shall Kalasrade be raised by the mock pageants of power, till it please those who delight in her miseries, to cast her forth to infamy and scorn.

By the sacred blood of that Prophet which animates me, I swear, O Kalasrade, I mean to fulfil the word I have spoken, and thou alone shalt be the Sultana of my heart.

But

But will the mighty Amurath consent to one request of his slave; will he bear with his Kalasrade in one petition, in which her happiness is concerned?

Ah, Kalasrade! said Amurath starting, beware of all past reflections, for if the hated Sadak be the subject of thy request, thou shalt indeed be cast to infamy and scorn.

The name of him who has deserved Amurath's hatred, replied Kalasrade, be far from the tongue of Kalasrade! O gracious Prince, dismiss such ungenerous suspicions from your mind!——But that, alas! is vain to hope, and I must still be wretched. No, mighty Amurath, expect no happiness with her, who must ever disturb thy joys with the mean thoughts of what she once has been. How shall I meet my Prince with the noble ardor he requires, when my poor mind shall be weighed down with the remembrance of my former meanness?

Ten thousand pleasures, replied Amurath, shall hourly surround you: The sun and moon shall alike be witnesses of our eternal festivals: The dance, the song, the sprightly music, the masque, the feast, the public shew, the private transport, shall all succeed in quick rotation, and drive from your pleased fancy every former thought. Each wish of your heart shall be so quickly gratified, your fertile mind shall toil to recollect its wants.

Prince of my life, answered Kalasrade, though I must not doubt your power, nor your desire to please, yet will the mind,

stretched

stretched out by the long scenes of pleasure, oft recoil upon its former self, and the sense of my unworthiness embitter the undeserved joys my Prince shall fondly heap upon me.

To prove my sincerity, and to shew you how soon I mean to gratify every thought Kalasrade forms, said Amurath, let me hear the request of your lips; but see it glance not upon Sadak's love.

Gracious Amurath, said Kalasrade, forgive a slave's presumption, and I will speak.

Speak the whole wishes of your heart, replied Amurath; and if they are subservient to our love, though my empire were the price, I would purchase fair Kalasrade's peace.

There is, my Lord, said Kalasrade, as I have heard, a spring, whose waters are of such a nature, that whoever drinks of them immediately forgets whatever has passed before in their lives. Let my Lord then swear unto his slave, that ere he takes her to his arms, he will procure her a draught of that pleasant stream, and then Kalasrade shall be wholly, both in body and mind, the slave of Amurath's desires.

Rather, said Amurath, the mistress of his heart. Yes, lovely Kalasrade, I will swear by Mahomet, our holy prophet, never to come in unto you, till I have procured you a taste of that stream, provided you can find any one within two days who can describe to me the place where it rises.

Kalasrade then fell at the feet of Amurath, and said, Thou hast made the heart of thy slave to rejoice; thou hast not only lifted her

from

from obscurity, but thou hast renewed the streams of her life; that having lost all memory of the past, she may seek to please her Lord, without diffidence at the mean thoughts of her former state.

Beauteous Kalasrade, said the fond Amurath, arise. Ah, said he, looking with transports upon her, what have I done? I have prolonged my expectations, perhaps for a week, but I have sworn by Mahomet, and I will hasten to gratify the desire of my Kalasrade.

At these words Amurath left the fair Kalasrade, inwardly rejoicing at the success of Doubor's advice, and hastened to call unto him the sage Balobor, who was acquainted with every natural production of the earth.

Balobor, said Amurath, as the sage came into his presence, can you describe to me the place where that spring may be found, whose waters are of such a nature, that whoever drinks of them, immediately forgets whatever has passed before in his life?

If the mighty Amurath, answered the sage Balobor, will permit me to retire to my books, I will, ere the morning's sun, discover to my Prince, if the earth produces such a spring, where it may be found.

As soon as Balobor was gone forth from the presence of Amurath, the impatient Prince sent after the chief of his eunuchs, and enquired of him, where the spring of the waters of oblivion might be found.

Doubor perceived by the questions of his Lord, that Kalasrade had succeeded; but the prudent

prudent eunuch cared not to confess his knowledge of that spring, he therefore disguised his words, and said:

Son of the faithful, thy slave has never been bred in the natural sciences; but if my Lord will permit me to go in quest of the wise philosopher Balobor, he will doubtless unfold to my Prince the secret springs of the waters of oblivion.

It is enough, said Amurath, faithful Doubor! Balobor has promised by to-morrow's sun, to reveal to me the fountains of oblivion.

While Amurath was in search of the waters of oblivion, the gentle Kalasrade was in secret praising the bounteous Alla, who had for a time preserved her from the tyrant's will.

The next morning the sage Balobor appeared in the presence of Amurath, and said:

The waters of oblivion, O mighty Amurath, are preserved by a watchful race of Genii, in a wide-extended island, in the southern parts of the Pacific Ocean. The island itself is fortified by inaccessible precipices, and beset with pointed rocks; and around it are spread insidious quicksands, to prevent the approach of any vessel, and which sinks with the weight of those who attempt to venture upon it. What dangers surround the spring, which is situated in the centre of the island, none can tell; for although thousands have attempted to seek after it, none have ever succeeded, but destruction has overwhelmed them in the very entrance of their toils.

At the words of the sage Balobor, the countenance of Amurath was overcast with frowns, and the tempest which raged in his breast, strove for utterance in his face; but the disappointed monarch endeavoured to conceal his discontent, and retired from the apartment whither Balobor had been ordered to attend him.

Amurath, vexed and enraged at the contrivance of Kalafrade, hastened to the female seraglio, meditating vengeance on Sadak and his wife. But as he went along, a thought glanced across his imagination, and he stopped to pause on the malice his heart was framing against the innocent victims of his wrath.

Sadak, said the monarch to himself, the proud Sadak, still pursues his enquiries after Kalafrade; I will command him to appear in my presence, and heap the vengeance due to Kalafrade's falsehood on his head.

Amurath then gave orders for his janissaries to bring Sadak before him, not by compulsion, but to consult with him, as one who had formerly experienced the favours of his Lord.

The janissaries found the melancholy Sadak instructing his little ones, in the village whither they had retired from the flames of his palace. They shewed him the signet of Amurath, and required his immediate attendance.

Alas, said the afflicted mourner, doth Amurath again mean to jest with his slave, that he calls me from this poor recess? Unless the trumpet sound, what call hath Sadak to the courts of kings? But I obey. Obedience and

and submission are the most welcome tributes that a slave can offer.

The janissaries having brought the wretched Sadak into the presence of Amurath retired.

Brave soldier, said Amurath, hath the peaceful sloth of retirement yet unstrung your manly heart, or are you still the undaunted warrior I once knew you? Can the shrill trumpet's sound, and the hollow murmurs of the brazen cymbal, rouze the fire of war in all your soul, or are you relaxed by the soft voice of love into the inactive slumbers of a life of ease? Say, brave companion of my former toils, were Amurath again to take the field, would Sadak headlong plunge into the rapid stream? Would he, laden with war's heavy trophies, again climb the ragged precipice, or sleep on beds of snow, or stand undaunted in the bloody struggle of contending armies?

Dead as I am to pleasure, noble Amurath, said Sadak, yet were my Prince's voice to call me to the field, Sadak again should live in arms, and court the toils and horrors of war's bloody stage. Yes, Amurath, at thy command, this arm should fix the standards of our faith on Russia's frozen bounds, or on the burning sands of Afric's distant shore.

Brave, noble Sadak, said the false Amurath, embracing him, I cannot doubt your truth, though the base minions of my court have stained that name they long have envied, with their mean surmises.

A courtier's malice, mighty Amurath, replied Sadak, is beneath a soldier's notice; and

best

best is answered, when occasion calls, by deeds, at which their dastard minds shall shudder to relate.

Such deeds, replied the artful monarch, Amurath hath in store for Sadak's arms to execute; deeds which wear the fiercest countenance of danger, and which none but Sadak dare to undertake.

My Prince, answered Sadak, Sadak is ready to receive your commands; but the day is ill spent in words, when action only can approve my worth.

Sadak, answered Amurath, the malicious whispers of my courtiers concerning your worth, have much disturbed me; and I mean to-morrow, in the public Divan, to give you a glorious opportunity of convincing their little souls, how greatly the soldier towers above the safe advisers of the cabinet. Fail not, generous Sadak, to be present, and I will, in the sight of my whole court, require some one to stand forth, and undertake a voyage in quest of the waters of oblivion, which are guarded by every natural barrier, and the united efforts of a race of evil Genii. Then, when a tame silence follows my proposal, and the base courtiers hang their coward heads, my brave Sadak shall arise, and challenge to himself the glorious undertaking.

Sadak bowed at the words of Amurath, and said: Lord of the faithful, far be it from Sadak to prove unworthy of his Master's love!

The artful Amurath having thus prepossessed the mind of Sadak, went not into the apartments

ments of Kalafrade, but waited with great folicitude the arrival of the next day.

As the all-diffufive light of morn appeared, which fhines alike upon the care-worn countenance of the guilty wretch, and on the open face of artlefs innocence, Amurath arofe, impatient till the hour of public audience came; when, being feated on his throne, amidft the nobles of his court, and feeing the faithful Sadak at the extremity of the Divan, he thus began his deceitful fpeech:

Nobles, and warriors, who, by your councils and exploits in arms, caft various luftres on my throne, fay, where fhall Amurath find that brave refolved heart, who will engage to procure for him the waters of oblivion, which are preferved in a far diftant ifle, defended by quickfands, monftrous rocks, the perils of the waves, and flames of fire? Genii are its guardians, and all nature is combined to fave it from man's poffeffion.

Such an acquifition, nobles, would manifeft to all the earth the fuperiority of your monarch, and the bravery of his fubjects: who is there then among your ranks, dare hope to add fuch luftre to my throne, and fuch honor to himfelf? But fpeak not, nobles, unlefs a fixed refolve attend your fpeech. To undertake, and not fucceed, would wither, and not increafe, the laurels we have already won in arms; wherefore be thefe the terms on which the noble adventurer iffues forth:

Let him be fworn not to turn back till he have the water in poffeffion. Let him likewife forfeit his life, if he depart not in search

of

of this water, ere the remainder of this moon be worn away.

As Amurath left off speaking, a general silence succeeded, and the eyes of all were turned upon Sadak.

The noble Sadak perceiving no one offer, stood up and advanced toward the throne.

Descendant of Mahomet, and lord of thy creatures, said Sadak, and bowed before Amurath, behold the hand of thy slave is prepared to execute the desires of thy heart; and here I swear, in this august assembly, never to turn back till I have procured the waters; and ere three days be passed, shall the face of Sadak be set toward the dangers that surround the fountain of oblivion.

Thanks, noble Sadak, said Amurath aloud, thanks for this proffered service which my nobles feared to undertake: and thus I swear before the face of heaven, that when Sadak returns, I will make either him, or one of his family, the second in honor throughout all my dominions.

The beguiled Sadak understood not the base meaning of his Lord, but he fell at his feet, and kissed the earth whereon Amurath stood.

The chief of the eunuchs seeing the noble Sadak in the Divan, passed by his side as he was retiring, and whispered, Wait a few minutes, much injured Sadak, and I will convey into your hands the words of comfort.

Sadak was astonished at the speech of the eunuch, and now his heart began to misgive him, and tumults arose in his breast.

Before

TALES OF THE GENII.

Before the crowd were diffipated out of the Divan, the eunuch flipped a note into Sadak's bofom, and the much afflicted warrior retired with it to the rocks which are behind the city, and there read as follows:

"Doubor, who oweth his life to the generous interpofition of thy father Elar, is diftreffed for his friend: Alas, noble Sadak, Kalafrade is in the royal feraglio, and Amurath is—— what my hand dare not write! He alone who has undertaken to procure the waters of oblivion, is able to enter the feraglio of Amurath. Doubor has no command without; but fhould Sadak efcape through the janiffaries, and fcale the wall at the eaftern part of the gardens, Doubor will this night watch his approach, and convey him to the apartments of the wretched Kalafrade. May Alla forbid, that the life which Elar faved, fhould be facrificed by the imprudence of Sadak!"

O Mahomet, the prophet of the juft! faid Sadak, as he read the fcroll of Doubor, the chief of the eunuchs, is it poffible that Amurath hath done this wrong to the hand which raifed him! Was it for this I covered him with the fhield of ftrength in the day of battle? Was it for this I plunged into the rapid ftream, and bore him breathlefs to the diftant rock, when he fled from the face of his enemies to the fea of Azoph? Who reconciled Amurath to his mutinous janiffaries, when, offended at his avarice, they demanded the plunder of Lepanto? Who preferved him from the fury of Irac, the rebellious fon of Porob, who endeavoured to depofe him in the

feraglio

seraglio of his ancestors? Who, but that man whom he hath basely robbed of all his substance, plundered of heaven's best treasure, the lovely Kalasrade, and betrayed into a rash vow to leave the Othman empire and his just revenge, to seek in distant seas the various countenance of death. But what revenge could Sadak meditate against the blood of his prince; would he wish to make his private injuries the cause of public shame; would he strive to glut his malice on the ruins of the faith of musselmen, and the Othman majesty! And yet, O soul of life, O beauteous and constant Kalasrade, shall Sadak undisturbed behold the afflictions of his love? Shall Kalasrade lift up the hand of supplicating virtue, and pour forth in vain the tears of constancy, and Sadak stand unmoved at the voice of the beloved? O Prophet, holy Prophet, whither must I turn? not against my Prince, for whom his slaves live; not against thy truth, which the blood of the faithful hath planted and nourished on the fertile plains of Europe and Asia! Must I then bear the curses of Amurath? Ah! that is tenfold death! Must I rebel against one who was once my friend, and is still the lord of his slave?—But doubts are vain. The vows I have made in the Divan bar all other views; yet ere I go a voluntary exile from the plains of the faithful, I will see Kalasrade, or perish by the hands of the slaves which surround her. She is mine, though the arm of power oppress her, and Amurath, who once held the sacred vow most solemn,

solemn, cannot blame that love which leads me to my lawful treasure.

These reflections fixed Sadak in his resolutions of attempting to enter the seraglio, and he returned to the city, in order to procure such things as might be necessary to assist him in his undertaking.

Going to the Bezestein, he ordered an iron to be made with five hooks, and an eye in the center, and at the silk merchant's bought a cord of silk, fifty feet in length; he also purchased a small iron trowel and a poignard.

Having these things in his possession, in the evening he went down to the water side, between Pera and Constantinople, and suddenly unloosing a small boat, he launched it into the gulph Keratius, and swiftly rowed to Riscula, which is on a rock, near the shore of Asia, facing the eastern part of the seraglio.

Here the determined Sadak rested on his oars, till the clouds of night had shortened the vigilant sight of the janissaries, and the tide was fallen from the walls of the palace, when paddling toward the seraglio, he advanced in his boat within six hundred paces of the shore.

A part of the guard, who were then going round on the beach, to examine the walls, halted at the noise of Sadak's oars, and made a signal for a galley which lay near them to come up.

The slaves in the galley obeyed the janissaries, and coming along-side the shore, took them on board.

The janiffaries directed them to row toward the place where they imagined they had heard the paddling of oars, and in a few minutes Sadak perceived one of the Sultan's galleys advancing toward him.

The bold Sadak, pleafed at the fuccefs of his ftratagem, gently glided out of the boat into the water, and diving wide of the galley, fometimes rifing for breath, and at other times continuing to ftrike forward under the water, he in a fhort time reached the fhore, and landed between Sera Burni and the gate Topcapu, through which his beloved was hurried by the flaves of the feraglio.

Sadak knowing his time might not be wafted (as the janiffaries finding no one in the boat would foon return to the fhore), immediately pulled out the iron with five hooks, and the filken cord, and faftening them together, he threw the hook over the wall, which catching on the top, by means of the filken cord, Sadak raifed himfelf up on the wall; then again fixing the hook on the inner fide, in fuch a manner as he might loofen it from the wall, by fhaking the cord backward and forward, he quickly defcended into the gardens of the feraglio, and unhitching the iron from the wall, with a few fhakes of the cord, he took out his trowel, and buried them in the earth; then haftening toward a thicket of fmall trees and fhrubs, he hid himfelf therein.

Here Sadak had time to recollect his thoughts; but he was hardly covered by the bufhes, before he heard the galley on the oppofite posite side of the wall strike against the shore, and could distinguish the voices of the janissaries descending from its sides.

By their conversation he learned, that they were alarmed at finding a boat without any one in it; and as they hastened toward the gate Topcapu, he doubted not but they would shortly raise the guards of the seraglio.

In the midst of these thoughts Sadak heard the fall of feet approaching toward him, and presently one drew near the bushes, and was entering into the very place where Sadak was concealed.

Although the frame of Sadak was more disturbed at the approach of the stranger, than it had ever been in the field of blood, yet he neglected not to draw his poignard; and as the stranger entered among the bushes, he seized him, and was about to strike the steel into his heart, when Doubor cried out, O Sadak, destroy not thy friend.

The spirits of Sadak having been hurried by the noise of the janissaries, made him forget the appointment of Doubor to meet him in the garden; but when he perceived it was the grateful eunuch, he dropped the poignard on the earth, and said,

O friend of my bosom, forgive the fears and the distraction of the miserable Sadak, who in mad fury had nearly sacrificed his comforter, and driven the poignard of suspicion into the breast of the tender-hearted Doubor!

Noble Sadak, answered the chief of the eunuchs, I wonder not at your suspicions; it is an hard task for the brave to dissemble, or for the generous warrior to defcend to the dark deeds of a midnight robber: But let us haften toward the feraglio; yet before we iffue forth out of the thicket, let me help you to drefs yourfelf in the habit of a mute; the garments are hidden in the thicket behind, and I was coming to feek whether they were fafe againft your arrival, when you feized me by the arm.

Sadak was pleafed at the propofal of the chief of the eunuchs, and ftripping himfelf, he left his own garments concealed in the thicket, and putting on the mute's habit, followed Doubor toward the female feraglio.

Doubor advancing toward the feraglio, made a fign for the eunuchs which were placed at the gates to retire; and entering he bid his mute follow him to the apartments of Kalafrade.

The joy of Sadak, at the thoughts of again viewing his beloved, and his fears left any unfortunate difafter fhould difcover him, raifed alternate ftorms in his breaft; but the mighty warrior concealed in his countenance the ftrong paffions which befet his heart.

After paffing through feveral galleries, the chief of the eunuchs arrived at the apartment of the beauteous Kalafrade, and was about to enter, when he perceived the royal fandals at the door.

Doubor ftarted back at the fight.

O Mahomet, faid he in a whifper, Amurath is rifen in the dead of night, and entered into Kalafrade's apartment.

The words of Doubor were as deadly poifon to the heart of Sadak, the cold hand of death chilled

chilled his astonished blood, and his weak nature could scarce sustain the mighty shock.

Oh! Doubor! Doubor! said the wretched son of Elar, support my conflicting frame; O Doubor, I am unable to bear this tenfold death!—Ah, tyrant! Ah, my friend! If I strike, thou must perish; if I with-hold my arm—O wretched. Sadak, wander not into that hell of thought. O Mahomet! O Alla! have I deserved this torture? If I have, strike with thy merciful thunder this rebellious heart: If not, strengthen and support the wretch whom thou art pleased to load with ills past human thought! O that I were a worm, to be trodden under a Giaurs foot: O that I were a toad, and my food corruption: That I were a camel in the desert, or an ass in the mill: That I were ought but Sadak, the accursed of his Prophet!

As the miserable Sadak thus poured forth his griefs in the bosom of his friend, the affrighted Doubor pressed his head, and covered it with the folds of his garment, that the voice of the wretched Sadak might not pierce the walls of the apartment, and raise the suspicion of Amurath: But his utmost precaution could not prevent the sighs of Sadak, whose wounded and afflicted soul was as the wearied boar of the forest, when pierced with the darts and javelins of a thousand hunters.

In the midst of his sighs the door of the apartment opened, Amurath came forth, and Sadak leaving the bosom of Doubor, fell with his face toward the earth.

Doubor, said the Sultan, where hast thou been? and where are thy guards? Who is that mute whom thou didst cherish in thy bosom? and why art thou here in the dark noon of night?

Lord of princes, answered Doubor, when my master retired to his sofa, I went to examine the guard of eunuchs, and to see that thy slaves were faithful to their trust; and at my return, perceiving that my Lord was arisen, I called this mute to me, as I was unwilling to disturb my Sultan with the feet of his guards, and followed thee to the apartment of the ever-blooming Kalafrade. But as I tarried here, waiting lest my Lord should have any command for his slave to execute, the poor mute fell sick, and in pity I took him to my bosom; as I have learned from the kindness which my Lord shews his slaves, to copy as far as my poor and weak capacity will permit, the bright virtues of the favourite of Alla.

Doubor, said Amurath, I commend your care, but since the slave is ill, let him be sent to Kalafrade to nurse; the haughty fair one despises my condescending love, and the embraces of the son of Othman are grievous to the slave of Sadak: Wherefore, Doubor, see you place this slave on the sofa of Kalafrade, and let her fancy him her lover, till she fling her proud arms around him, and call him Sadak and her lord.

The heart of Doubor rejoiced at the words of Amurath, but he concealed his joy, and said:

Will

Will the glory of the Othman race first suffer me to attend him to the apartments of my Sultan?

Doubor, said Amurath sternly, have I said, and shall I recal my words? Slave, obey me instantly, and force this wretch into Kalafrade's arms.

The chief of the eunuchs laying his hand upon his breast, bowed down and said,

The will of Amurath is the law of his slave.

No sooner was Amurath gone, than the chief of the eunuchs raised up Sadak, and said,

Son of Elar, friend of my bosom, first in my esteem, arise, and perform the commands of Amurath.

Yes, faithful, generous Doubor, thou balsam of peace to my wounded soul, thou ray of heaven on the spirits of the afflicted, I will arise, and bless the great fountain of happiness, for the merciful change he has wrought in my favour. Now, Doubor, I am more than Amurath! I am about to enjoy a paradise, from which, O Alla, grant the blood of Othman be for ever barred! While the emperor of the world retires to a discontented sofa, Sadak shall revel in the rich pastures of unsatiated pleasure.——But why do I delay to seek Kalafrade? if life is short, how fleeting are the joys of life!

At these words Doubor interposed.

Permit me, O fortunate Sadak, said he, to go first in to Kalafrade, and prepare her delicate frame for your reception, lest the strong tide of returning happiness overpower her nature, and faintness, or death, again snatch her from the embrace of her beloved.

The tender Sadak acquiesced in the reasons of the chief of the eunuchs, and Doubor hastened to impart to Kalasrade the arrival of her beloved.

After a few minutes Doubor returned, and entered with Sadak into the female apartments.

As the happy Kalasrade beheld the features of her lord under the disguise of a mute, she sprang forward; her eyes enlivened by the transports of her heart, and with a fond surprise, half fearful, half overjoyed, she pressed him in her arms.

Ah, lovely Sadak, said she, joy of my soul, master of my thoughts, life of my heart, and guardian of my honour, how have I panted for this blessed embrace! O how has thy Kalasrade sighed and despaired at thy absence! I have been, my Sadak, like the shriek owl in the wilderness; I have been, my Sadak, like the widowed dove; but now am I as the deer, which bounds on the sunny plain; as the bird, which sips the dew of the morning among the blossoms of the orange grove.

O fond and constant Kalasrade, answered Sadak, how has my heart sought thee in solitude and found thee not! I have been, my Kalasrade, as the coward in the day of battle; as the warrior disarmed by the treachery of his foe; as the lion in the toils of the hunters; as the leopard surrounded by the flood. But now am I like the man of valour who bestrides his foe; like the conqueror in the day

of

of triumph: But now am I as the tyger springing on his prey; as the lusty eagle on the clouds of heaven.——Ah, what have I said in the fulness of my heart! Amurath is now the master of Kalasrade, and perhaps I am enfolded in those arms, which are yet stained with the embrace of thy Sultan! Kalasrade is no more the wife of Sadak, but the Sultana of the Othman race.

Unjust and cruel Sadak, replied the fond Kalasrade, how has thine heart invented the accusations of falshood! Can I, O Sadak, be false to my lord! Had Kalasrade ever a wish, in which her Sadak held not the chief account!

But how, O Kalasrade, said the suspicious Sadak, how has female weakness been capable of withstanding the glittering tyranny of the son of Othman? who, if he failed to draw thee to his purpose by the costly parade of his seraglio, could yet compel thee to receive his embraces.

Lovely master of my thoughts, answered Kalasrade, our Prophet hath heard my prayer, and the bird of Adiram hath poured the balsam of comfort into my afflicted soul. Nay more, the generous and grateful Doubor also hath whispered in my ears the words of consolation, and by the advice of him whom Elar, thy father, preserved from destruction, hath Kalasrade triumphed over the wiles of Amurath.

As the beauteous Kalasrade uttered these words, the countenance of Doubor, the chief of the eunuchs, fell; but Kalasrade was so intent

intent on contemplating her long loſt lord, that ſhe perceived not the anxious face of the generous Doubor.

And by what ſtratagem, ſaid Sadak eagerly, hath Kalaſrade reſcued herſelf from the power of Amurath?

Monarch of my affections, anſwered Kalaſrade, I challenge not the honour of the device, it is to Doubor's prudence that I owe my ſafety; he opened to me the cauſe of his friendſhip for the ſon of Elar, and adviſed me, when Amurath ſhould again return to me, that I ſhould uſe him deceitfully, and engage him by a vow not to come near me, till he ſhould procure for me the waters of oblivion.

And what conceſſions, ſaid the ſtern Sadak, has Kalaſrade made the Sultan Amurath, to obtain from him this mighty and important vow?

Alas! noble Sadak, ſaid Doubor interpoſing; the wary Sultan hath turned our toils upon ourſelves, and we are caught in the ſnare which was laid for the foot of Amurath.

What, Doubor, replied the aſtoniſhed Kalaſrade, what doth thy ominous tongue, and the ſtern front of my offended lord portend? Ah! ſaid you not that Amurath hath entangled us? Hath he then, faithful Doubor, made a falſe uſe of my ſoothing words? Hath he defiled my honour by looſe hints? Now on my ſoul, brave Sadak, the tyrant lies; never, never, in word or thought hath Kalaſrade injured her lord; and I call the great Alla, and the ſpirits of the juſt to witneſs, Amurath,
the

the vile Amurath, hath never approached the arms of Sadak's wife.

Peace, gentle and much injured fair one, said Doubor, and diſſipate, brave Sadak, the cloud on thy brow. Kalaſrade never has, nor can yield to Amurath's deſires, nor hath the Prince pretended to boaſt of joys he never knew; no, conſtant pair, Amurath, though furious in his revenge, is juſt and perfect in his ſpeech, and would as quickly throw off the ſtate of his empire, as falſify his oath. But briefly thus it is, ſweet miſtreſs of brave Sadak's heart. The Sultan, nettled at your requeſt, when he found it would prevent him for a long ſeaſon, from uſing force to compel you, caſt about how he might make your imagined ſecurity as irkſome to yourſelf as it was forbidding to him; and therefore he has engaged thy unſuſpecting lord, by a firm oath, to ſeek for him the waters of oblivion, and never to return to the Othman empire, till he bring with him the produce of that inacceſſible fountain.

What, ſaid the affrighted Kalaſrade, what are the words which have eſcaped the lips of the generous Doubor? Look on me, O Sadak, thou much injured lord! Look on her, who, by a mean device, hath heaped eternal afflictions on thy heart! O curſe on this tongue, on this heart, on this head, which have all been the wretched inſtruments of Sadak's baniſhment! Ah, bird of Adiram! Ah, ſweet ſpoken Doubor! ſee you not the poiſon that lurks under the tongue of the adder! ſee you not the flames which lie beneath the verdant surface of the burning Santorini?

O Sadak, Sadak, rather let me run to Amurath, and satisfy his brutal appetite, than Sadak shall wander amidst ten thousand deaths. The treacherous sands, my love, will sink with thee; evil Genii will hurl thee from the summit of their rocks; thy wretched carcase shall be cast upon an unknown shore; the vultures of the air, and the monsters of the deep, shall feast on my beloved, and the wild ungoverned Amurath, fearless of thy arm, ravage the poor remains of thy Kalafrade's beauty.

Rather, said Sadak, shall this arm hurl instant vengeance on the tyrant's head, and all the blood of Othman perish, than ever Kalafrade shall be stained with Amurath's unhallowed touch.

Ah, furious Sadak, answered the chief of the eunuchs, what mean the black resolves of thy rebellious heart? But think not Doubor intends to stand a tame spectator of thy malice; faithful to my lord in every just command, through me must the base Sadak reach the heart of Amurath. But moderate your rage, bold man, and know, though Doubor love not every deed of Amurath's, yet will he never prove a traitor to his life. While Sadak means no more than to recover his Kalafrade, I am bound by gratitude and justice to espouse his cause; but if his murderous, traitorous heart aim at his Prince's life, both gratitude and justice call me then to Amurath's defence.

Generous Doubor, answered Sadak, I justly stand rebuked; I were indeed a wretch, when

holy

holy Othman's race is near extinct, to rob our faith of its last royal leader; no, faithful eunuch, the man who out of private malice gives confusion to his country, and subverts its peace, deserves nor pity nor relief.

Are these then, replied Kalasrade in tears, the virtuous resolutions of a patriot, to give up private happiness to publick tyranny? For what were Othman's race decreed to rule, but for the safety of the faithful? And if a tyrant violate unchecked each social duty, 'tis he first robs his subjects of their peace. But thou, O Sadak, art a noble patriot, thou canst unconcerned behold thy palace flaming, and thy wife torn from thy arms to sate a tyrant's palate; thou canst with meanness crouch before a puny lord, in ought but pomp inferior to thyself, and call his vile unhallowed lust, the unalterable law which Alla sanctifies, and Mahomet approves. Such then be Sadak's love, and such his vowed protection of Kalasrade's honour; but hear me, Prophet of the just, and thou pure, heavenly being, spotless and holy God! Thou who canst protect the weakest with thy mighty arm, O give me strength to save that chastity, which cruel Sadak dares not justify, and make thy trembling votary the instrument of vengeance on the tyrant's head.

O beauteous, and much injured Kalasrade, answered Sadak, rather pray that Mahomet would fortify thy Sadak's heart, and teach him in this doubtful path, his duty to Kalasrade and his prince.

Alas,

Alas, interrupted Doubor, the chief of the eunuchs, I hoped this interview would have administered comfort to the hearts of Sadak and Kalafrade; but passion, alas, has consumed the short moments that belonged to love, for now in the East are hung the banners of approaching day, and the faint purple light, reflected from the distant clouds, warns our retreat. Come, noble Sadak, let us leave the beauteous fair, in full assurance, that Alla will prevent the worst ill you dread, and save Kalafrade spotless till her lord's return.

Leave her! O Doubor, answered Sadak, looking with wild extacy on his beloved wife, whom am I to leave?——

Brave and resolved chief, interrupted Kalafrade, thy master wants thy wife, and thou must yield her to his furious will; retire then, noble Sadak, for Amurath approaches with the wild eye of lust, and passion heats his blood to fold Kalafrade with his warm embrace; retire, my Sadak, to some convenient spot, where safely hidden from the flashes of thy Sultan's amorous rage, thou mayest be a duteous and submissive witness of thy master's pleasures. Yes, continued the distracted Kalafrade, thou shalt view my tender frame convulsed, and see these arms, which oft have folded Sadak, stretched beneath the imperial rack of *righteous* Othman's power.

O Sadak, interrupted Doubor, one moment more and all is lost; O Kalafrade, if Sadak ere deserved thy love, dismiss him hence, and save thyself, thy lord, and me, from instant ruin.

What,

What, replied the wild Kalafrade, folding her noble Sadak in her arms, wilt thou bereave me of this polished shaft on whom I twine, and after crush me with the ponderous mass of Amurath? No, base eunuch, 'tis here alone Kalafrade lives, and Sadak lost, my own weak female arm will set me free from Amurath's embrace.

To leave thee now, replied Sadak, were to give thee up a prey to tyranny and lust: No, Kalafrade, let the tyrant come, we'll disappoint his malice, and both at once seek peace beyond the gates of death.

It was in vain that Doubor attempted to interrupt the vehemence of Sadak and Kalafrade; forgetful of themselves, or of the hazard of their friendly eunuch, they folded each other in mutual embraces, and seemed resolved that nothing more should part them.

The distressed eunuch finding every remonstrance in vain, departed from the apartments of Kalafrade, and hastened to the chambers of the Sultan.

Sadak and Kalafrade, without perceiving the chief of the eunuchs had left them, continued entranced in each other's arms, and calling Alla and Mahomet to witness their mutual constancy and truth.

In the midst of these passionate expressions, the bird of Adiram entered the windows of the palace, and perching on the shoulder of Sadak, thus delivered the message of his mistress to the astonished pair.

" To comfort the afflicted is the delight of our race, and the inhabitants of heaven stoop

with

with pleasure to the children of earth, when mercy calls them down: For this cause came the voice of consolation to Kalasrade; when the evils of tyranny beset her, Adiram also, the servant of Mahomet, watched over the afflicted fair one, and gave to Doubor the feelings of compassion. By his counsels was Amurath engaged in an inviolable oath, to abstain from his base purpose, till the waters of oblivion were obtained, and Sadak, by his assistance, was again blessed with the sight of his Kalasrade.

"How have ye, wretched pair, perverted these kind purposes of Adiram! And where is that fortitude which first recommended you to the tutelage of our immortal race! By an ill-judged perseverance, you have changed a virtuous constancy into a vicious passion; and neglecting both the bonds of friendship and the commands of Mahomet, you have nearly sacrificed Doubor to your folly, and yourselves to the idle dreams of uncurbed love. Love is an heavenly appetite, planted in the human species, to beget in them social harmonies; it melts and subdues the savage heart, as the stubborn ore is softened in the refiner's vessel; and when regulated by religion, it is ever protected by Alla and his Prophet; but blessings in the cup of the unrighteous, are as the dregs of heaven's wrath; and appetite, when it overcomes reason and religion, is as the vassal of sin; though Alla hath taught you to submit, and bear with patience the evils of life, ye have listened to the fantasies of love, and in the bravery of your hearts, resolved

solved to pass together to the gates of death. What then are ye, foolish pair, that ye should have dominion over that life, which Alla breathed into the clay-formed tabernacles of your unanimated flesh? Or where is the fortitude of flying like cowards from the face of danger, to the silent grave? Yet know, while Alla reigns, no evil shall befal the sons of infirmity, but such as, patiently endured, may work their future good; and therefore, to the just one alone, it appertaineth to dismiss from the service of life, or to continue his children in the trials of affliction.

"Thus, saith Adiram, the Genius of Sadak and Kalasrade, who is now compelled by the law of fate, to leave her pupils to the miseries they have entailed upon themselves."

The bird of Adiram uttered no more, but flew on the elastic surface of the air into the gardens of the palace, while the tender Kalasrade sunk in tears on the bosom of her astonished Sadak.

The bird was no sooner gone forth, than Sadak heard the feet of a multitude in the gallery; and the doors of the apartment immediately bursting open, the guards of the seraglio entered, and seized on the unhappy pair.

Sadak, unmindful of himself, endeavoured to defend his beloved; and though oppressed by numbers, yet he fell upon the eunuch who held his Kalasrade, and tore him to the ground.

But the resistance of Sadak was vain, the guards parted him from Kalasrade, and loaded him with chains.

As soon as Sadak was secured by the guards, the chief of the eunuchs appeared at the door of the apartment.

Slaves, said he aloud, is the vile miscreant Sadak, who hath entered the sacred walls of Amurath's seraglio, seized?

He is, great Doubor, answered the guards; the chain of death is on him, and we wait but for your commands to send his soul among those who rebel against their prince.

Hold, slave, replied Doubor, and secure him unhurt, till the mighty Amurath approach.

Sadak was confounded at the appearance and behaviour of Doubor, and Kalasrade wished to load him with reproach; but she feared she might incur the censures of Adiram, as she knew not as yet by what means her lord was discovered.

Ere long the music of the seraglio sounded, and Doubor, the chief of the eunuchs, perceiving that Amurath was near, hasted to receive him.

Prince of my life, said the chief of the eunuchs, as the royal Amurath came forward with the deadly frown on his brow, thy slaves have secured the enemy of thy peace.

Faithful Doubor, replied Amurath, I commend thy zeal: But where is this vile miscreant, who presumes to invade the recesses of Amurath's seraglio?

Here, tyrant, said the stern Sadak, if the oppressor dare look upon his injured——

The guards who had secured Sadak, perceiving by his speech that he meant to insult their Sultan, stopped with their hands all farther

ther utterance, and gagged him with a bit of iron.

The wretched Kalafrade seeing her lord in such distress, broke from the guards (who held her but slightly, fearing the same fate which befel the black slave, should Amurath relent) and clasping the much injured Sadak in her arms:

Vile slaves, said she, unhand my lord; then bursting into tears, O Sadak, noble Sadak, continued she, joy of my soul, and fountain of my life! How have these wretches dared deform thy noble image with their bonds of iron! Why didst thou not frown, my love, and fix them motionless with awe and fear! What is this puny Amurath, and all his guards, against the noble effort of thy uplifted arm! Alas, alas, my Sadak, they have bound you while you slept with ignominious chains, and now the tyrants laugh at your distress.

As the wild Kalafrade uttered these incoherent words, the guards and Doubor stood in fixed amazement, fearing to interpose, or use the fair one roughly, and yet alarmed at her bold speech.

Nor was the Sultan less confounded than his guards; each word she uttered stung him to the soul, and yet her glowing beauties, enlivened by her distress, and the tumultuous workings of her lovely frame, so strongly affected Amurath, that his lips refused to give forth the commands of his heart.

But seeing the beauteous Kalafrade endeavouring to embrace her lord, his fury returned, and he cried aloud,

Base

Base eunuch, secure the mad female from polluting herself with that wretch she dare prefer to Amurath. And, slaves, continued the enraged Sultan, your lives shall answer for your base neglect, in not destroying the rebellious Sadak.

The chief of the eunuchs having secured the distressed Kalasrade, gave her into the custody of the eunuchs, and then he commanded the guards to put the bow-string upon Sadak.

The wild, miserable Kalasrade, at sight of the bow-string screamed aloud, and fell into the arms of the eunuchs; her fixed eyes were dilated with madness, and her teeth shook with the agonies of death.

Amurath saw the affecting change with wild emotion, and fearful lest the soul of Kalasrade should escape, ordered the slaves to release Sadak from the bow-string.

Slothful Doubor, said Amurath, hasten to my Kalasrade's assistance; for by the Othman faith I swear, ye all shall follow if my fair one perish.

The attempts of Doubor and his attendants were vain; Kalasrade continued entranced, and Amurath in despair ordered Sadak to be released, that he might endeavour to recover his Kalasrade from her alarming trance.

As soon as the guards had unbound Sadak, and released his mouth, they signified to him the Sultan's orders, and led him toward the motionless Kalasrade.

Happy Kalasrade, said the brave Sadak, I trust ere this the Prophet of the faithful hath delivered thee from the tyrant's power; if not,

Sadak

Sadak will not disturb thy fleeting spirit: Proceed, thou divine spirit of innocence and virtue, toward thy eternal mansion, and let not the rude breath of Sadak's voice divert thee from thy righteous course.

Ah, blessed Alla, said the faint Kalasrade (reviving at her Sadak's well-known voice), where am I? in what blissful seat hast thou placed me? where the sweet music of my Sadak's voice sings comfort to my soul. Ah, surely the trance of death is passed, and I am far removed from Amurath and all his curses!

Unfortunate Kalasrade, said Sadak, starting, art thou again returned from the sweet sleep of death, to new-invented scenes of misery! Then bind me, slaves, again, and fix the bow-string to my neck: Once more, thou virtuous partner of my heart, I call thy faithful soul away. Tyrant, release me from the world, for now I know Kalasrade will not stay behind.

No, proud rebel, said Amurath, when Kalasrade's life's at stake, thy being is of trivial moment: At present live, that she may live for whom life's only sweet. But I demean my royalty, in holding speech with such a slave. Doubor, separate these stubborn spirits, and, for Kalasrade's sake, let Sadak, though confined, want not life's comfort. But, eunuch, watch with steady eye my beauteous Sultana, supply her wants unbidden, yet on your life take care, her frantic wildness is not suffered to prey upon herself: and, Doubor, when these things are executed according to
the

the will of thy lord, let me see thee in the palace of pictures.

At these words the Sultan Amurath retired, and Doubor, having executed his commission, hastened to meet his lord.

Faithful eunuch, said Amurath, as he entered, I am pleased at thy contrivance; it had been dangerous, as thou well observest, to have seized on Sadak, the favourite of the Janissaries, in the public face of day; but now, by thy artifice, his life is forfeit, and the silent bow-string will, unheard, release me from this enemy of my love. Wherefore I mean, that ere to-morrow's sun survey the wide-extended Othman empire, my faithful Doubor, with a few attendants, seize on his forfeit life.

Lord of the Othman empire, answered Doubor, I shall obey the law of thy mouth.

But, Doubor, said Amurath, one circumstance still hangs upon my doubtful mind. You say this Sadak entered the seraglio by your advice; yet, Doubor, what need was there to bring him in the silent hour of midnight to Kalafrade's apartment? to have detected him in our royal gardens were sufficient: Doubor, the thought breeds anguish in my soul; besides, traitor, thou leddest him as a mute into Kalafrade's arms; slave, slave, thou liest, and Amurath's betrayed.

Most enlightened of Mussulmen, answered Doubor, the slave that dared attempt to deceive my lord might justly tremble, as nothing can escape thy penetrating eye. Alas, had ignorant Doubor the judgment of the

Father

Father of the faithful, I had assuredly done as thou hast said; but foolishly hoping to do more, I have nearly forfeited the esteem of my Sultan.

What more didst thou mean, vain man, to execute? said Amurath, somewhat softened.

Mighty Amurath, answered the chief of the eunuchs, when first I brought the disguised Sadak from the gardens of the seraglio, I asked the deceitful slave, whether he would yield Kalasrade to thy arms, if Amurath would vest him with a Viziar's honors; to which he yielded a pretended assent, and assured me he would engage Kalasrade to receive thy embrace, the moment she was convinced of his exaltation.

Allured by this promise, I led him to the fair one's apartment, and as I hoped the consequence would be grateful to my Sultan, I neglected to inform thee of Sadak's presence, till I had heard the issue of his conference with Kalasrade. But when I had brought the deceitful slave before her, unmindful of his promise, he attempted to pour forth a love tale at her feet; upon which I hastened to inform thee of his presence, and the guards of the seraglio soon secured the deceitful wretch.

Since then he values love beyond the honours of the Othman State, said Amurath, let him fall a sacrifice to love. Doubor, dispatch him instantly; each moment that he lives increases my disquiet; but remember, his breath in secret pass, that not a sigh contaminate the air to wound Kalasrade's peace.

No sooner was Doubor gone, than the wavering Amurath began to repent that he had sent him.

How am I divided, said he, by love and honour! Without the waters of oblivion are obtained, my sacred oath prevents all intercourse with Kalasrade! And if Sadak dies, who shall be able to surmount the dangers that environ the fountains of oblivion?

Guards, said the anxious Sultan, call back the slave Doubor, stop his officious haste, and bring him here before thy prince.

The chief of the eunuchs returned!

Peace, said he, be to the mighty Amurath, and may all his foes perish from before him!

What, wretched eunuch, said Amurath hastily, is Sadak numbered with the dead?

The word of my lord, replied Doubor, was pressing, and thy slave hasted to obey thy command; but being recalled so suddenly by thy guards, I stopped the slaves who drew the bowstring, and Sadak on his knees expects his doubtful fate.

Then all is well, replied Amurath, for I mean not, Doubor, to destroy the doating wretch, through whom alone (such has been thy master's folly) must Amurath hope to reach Kalasrade's beauties.

Alas, replied Doubor, the chief of the eunuchs, thy slave doth oft reflect upon the oath, which robs my Sultan of the haughty fair one.

Yet,

Yet, Doubor, think not, continued Amurath, that, Christian like, I mean to break my faith, where interest or occasion tempt; no, I have bound this happy and luxurious Sadak, to draw his own destruction from the fountains of oblivion; and now, if he fail to execute the vow, his life is justly forfeit, and Kalafrade at our own disposal. Wherefore, Doubor, let a ship be prepared, to convey him to that distant island, where the waters of oblivion are concealed.

Lord of the Othman race, answered Doubor, I shall haste to obey thy will; nevertheless, if the weakness of Doubor's understanding might be permitted to unfold itself in the sight of my Prince, I would wish my lord appointed some one on whom he might depend, as master of the ship in which the rebel Sadak sails. For well thou knowest, mighty Father of Mussulmen, that Sadak is beloved in the army, and the admirals of the fleet look on him with partial eyes. Was it not, O Light of the world, in the insurrection of janissaries, in the month Muharrem, that Sadak only was sufficient to appease the tumult? He then was faithful to his lord; but now he leaves Kalafrade in thy possession, I fear his fierce unconquerable soul may easily be led aside from his obedience.

Then, Doubor, answered Amurath, let him perish; for I will bear no rival in my power, or in my love: Yet surely, Doubor, the soul of Sadak will not break through those bonds his faith hath formed; ere to-morrow's sun new gilds the Hellespont, his vow must urge him to depart.

True, Prince of the faithful, answered Doubor; nor need you fear a rival in this Sadak, whose pale glimmering glories are enlivened only by the favour of Amurath.

Well then, replied the Sultan, since his courage is necessary for our repose, to your care, faithful eunuch, I commit him; and let him haste away, for Amurath's love ill brooks the tortures of suspense.

The chief of the eunuchs hasted to obey the command of Amurath, and returning to the dungeon where Sadak expected the end of his fate, he ordered the mutes to release him.

Sadak, amazed at the order of Doubor, arose, and the mutes having released him, retired.

Sadak, said Doubor, as the mutes retired, behold the messenger of thy Sultan's mercy, who spares thy forfeit life, because thy vow hath dedicated it to thy master's service!

If by thy master's gift alone, O treacherous eunuch, I am to possess my life, said Sadak sternly, he sends his mercy to a thankless slave. Mercy! dare the tyrant thus miscall the malice of his heart? Is it mercy then to defile my better life; and send the poor remainder an outcast vagabond upon a pandar's errand? Go, obsequious eunuch, return to thy proud pampered master, and tell him, Sadak wants not his life upon such slavish terms.

Alas,

Alas, unfortunate Sadak, anſwered the chief of the eunuchs, what will the big word avail thee? When Amurath perceives you mean not to execute the vow you have made, he will hold himſelf no longer bound by that oath the duteous Kalaſrade has extorted from him.

Slave, returned Sadak, I underſtand thee not; there is a ſhew of friendſhip in thy ſpeech, and yet methinks I have more to fear when the wily ſerpent glides beſide me, than when his angry hiſs timely proclaims a generous defiance.

The friendſhip of humanity, ſaid Doubor coolly, I owe to all; nor is my heart ſufficiently revengeful, even to cruſh the ungrateful adder that ſtings me while I cheriſh him. But, Sadak, I mean not to gall thee with reproach, but as a friend adviſe thee to ſubmit, where ſubmiſſion only can yield thee hopes of comfort.

Friendly Doubor, anſwered Sadak pauſing, I ſubmit; but the time preſcribed is near elapſed——

Fear not, anſwered Doubor, already orders are given to equip you; and ere night you ſhall be conveyed to one of the Othman ſhips, with an able commander to ſteer you to the deſtined ſpot. But I can ſay no more; Amurath expects your anſwer, and I haſte to proclaim your obedience.

Sadak now began to relent, and he accuſed his heart, in ſuſpecting the integrity of the chief of the eunuchs. But Doubor was fled,

and

and Sadak left alone in the dungeon of the seraglio.

O Alla, said the wretched Sadak, to thy all just protection I commit my faithful Kalasrade; thou, who over-rulest the princes of the world, canst secure her in the fiery trial: relying on thy arm, she shall stand as the water fowl on the rock, and see the tempestuous billows of the ocean spend their vain force beneath her, unable to wash with their rude waves the surface of her dwelling-place!

The chief of the eunuchs having declared to Amurath the obedience of Sadak, waited till the evening, when entering the dungeon with the guards of the seraglio, they conveyed Sadak through the water-gate, to the ship which was prepared to sail in quest of the waters of oblivion; neither had the noble Sadak, by reason of the attendant guards, any opportunity of expressing his gratitude to Doubor, the chief of the eunuchs.

As soon as Sadak was embarked, the ship set sail, and the noble son of Elar found that the captain of the ship was a Christian renegado; for Doubor had in vain sought after one of his own nation, who was sufficiently skilled in navigation to perform the voyage.

For several days the ship ran swiftly before the wind, and hurried the unfortunate Sadak from the place of his beloved, as the vulture bears in his talons the panting lamb from its mother's teats.

But

But these winds were after a short time succeeded by a calm, in which, being detained from their purpose, and a small gale afterward arising, the captain of the vessel put into the island of Serfu, and there continued for two months, neither suffering his men to land, nor permitting the natives to enter his ship.

Sadak, though astonished at the behaviour of Gehari, the captain, yet attempted not to leave the ship, but spent his time chiefly in solitude and contemplation.

A small vessel arriving from Constantinople, at length brought the captain the orders he expected; and the wind being favourable, he hoisted his sails, and steered for the Atlantic ocean.

And now they were passing the island of Kirigou when a storm arose, and after many days buffeting against the wind, obliged them to sail into the bay which embosoms the city of Koron.

It was in vain the citizens made signs for the ship to steer away from their port; the swelling ocean, and the fierce winds united, drove them precipitately on the beach, and every one being terrified with the storm, they hastened on shore, leaving the ship at anchor near the beach.

Unhappy mariners, said an aged citizen to them, as they walked up the beach, you have escaped the womb of the sea, to be buried in this contagious city.

The mariners hung down their heads at this dreadful declaration, and Sadak perceived

that

that the plague was raging in the city of Koron.

The captain, whose Mahometan name was Gehari, ordered his crew to seize on Sadak; at the same time sending notice to the governor of the city, that he bore the commission of Amurath, and had a state prisoner under his care.

Sadak was amazed at the captain's behaviour, for he knew not before that he was looked upon as a prisoner, or that Gehari had any command over him.

My Lord, said Gehari, be not alarmed, I have no commission to treat you ill, and if I had, your noble behaviour would prevent the execution of it; only I was commanded, if possible, not to land in the Othman empire, and if necessity drove me ashore, I was to look upon you as my prisoner.

Gehari, said Sadak, use me as you please; you have the commission of my Prince, before whose lawful will I shall ever prostrate my obedient spirit.

It was happy for Gehari that his prisoner was of a noble temper; for such was the confusion of the city, that the governor had neither guard nor authority among his miserable subjects.

Alas, said Gehari to Sadak, as they entered the city, to boast a power over you here, were to carry human vanity even beyond the grave. Death and destruction are the rulers of Koron, and desolation tyrannizes over the children of Alla.

Not so, noble Gehari, answered Sadak, thou hast yet but a Christian's faith, or thou wouldst learn to acknowledge Alla, the father of his children, even in the grave of death. His hand, O Gehari, is on the famine and the plague; where he suffers, they spread the dark wings of fate, and where he stops, the mighty conquerors fall appeased. But let us boldly enter these gates of sickness, and while we have strength, administer to those over whom the dark fiend hath thrown the purple mantle of contagion.

The mariners, animated by the words and the example of Sadak, boldly entered the city of Koron; and while the ghastly inhabitants sat trembling and inactive in their houses, Sadak and his companions exercised the compassionate offices of humanity on the miserable objects that surrounded them.

But his laborious and dangerous employment soon overwhelmed the noble Sadak, and he found the plague had seized his distempered blood.

Listless, and unable to serve others, or to help himself, the wretched son of Elar fell between two carcases, to preserve whom his utmost endeavours had proved abortive.

The miseries that succeeded, Nature kindly hid from his remembrance; the disorder possessed his brain, and he lay entranced on the ground in the streets of Koron.

After two days he arose from the ground, his knees tottering with the weight of his emaciated body; he cast his hollow eyes around him,

him, and on every side saw the dismal marks of the all-destructive plague.

But what engaged his chief attention were two youths, who were kneeling on the ground beside an aged body, which was just sending forth his last pestiferous breath, as a deadly legacy between his children. Their pious tears, and their duteous attention to the expiring sage, mixed with a submissive resignation to the will of Alla, struck the soul of Sadak, long before he perceived they were the sons of his strength, who were performing the last sad offices to Mepiki, the father of Kalafrade.

My children, my duteous children, said the enervated Sadak, crawling with trembling limbs to their assistance, may Alla bless your pious care! You are indeed the sons of Sadak, and the offspring of Kalafrade, and your father is better pleased to see you thus active in this vale of death, than crowned with the conquest of unnumbered foes.

The astonishment of Codan and Ahud at the sight of their father, did not prevent their attendance on the dying Mepiki; they closed the eyes of their departing friend with pious tears, and embraced with reverence the dead body of their honoured ancestor.

The soul of Sadak was overcome by the piety of his children, and he, whom embattled armies could not move from his post, became the tender victim of paternal affection.

Codan and Ahud perceiving their father fainting, ran to his assistance; new cares succeeded

ceeded to increase their affliction; and the dying groans of Mepiki were scarce remembered, while Sadak continued to faint in the arms of his children.

Thanks, gentle Codan, thanks, tender Ahud, said Sadak to his children, as he arose from the bondage of weakness, though nature is exhausted, my soul is revived by the behaviour of my sons, and Sadak rejoices to see the tenderness of Kalasrade triumphant over thy father's fierceness.

Fountain of our life, and leader of our thoughts, answered Codan, thy children lift up their hearts to Alla, and bless him for the comforts he has given us in this scene of terrors.

Ah, my sons, said Sadak, why should I complain of bodily weakness, when the weakness of my mind is superior? Unsatisfied with the presence of my children, I burn to know what strange fatality has brought you to the city of Koron.

Author of our being, answered Ahud, thy children have not been exempt from the misfortunes of their parents. Soon after our father left us under the protection of the affectionate Mepiki, a slave hastened toward the hut, whither thy offspring had retired from the rage of the flame.

Aged Mepiki, said the slave, retire with the children of Sadak, for behold the royal janissaries are advancing, and Amurath hath commanded the progeny of Sadak to be brought before him.

Our aged parent wrung his hands at the relation of the slave; the janissaries were in sight, and Codan and myself only with thy father Mepiki.

Alas, said the parent of our honoured mother Kalasrade, five of my daughter's children are with the eunuchs, at the extremity of the garden, and to us there are little hopes of flight, to them is the certainty of condemnation.

Venerable sire, answered the slave, it will be vain to attempt the rescue of those who are absent from my Lord; but if you and the children of Sadak will follow me into the forest that overshadows the village, I will engage to lead you in safety from the malice of your pursuers.

Lead me then, replied our sire Mepiki, lead me, faithful slave, from the tyranny of Amurath! For myself indeed it little matters whether I perish by age, or by the sword, but these may live to revenge the blood of their ancestors.

Thus saying, Mepiki leaned on the slave, and Codan and myself drawing our cimeters, we issued forth, and covered ourselves from the sight of the janissaries among the cedars of the forest.

Here we continued till night, when the faithful slave besought us to follow him through the forest, to a town about four leagues from the habitation of Mepiki.

Thinking ourselves too near the arm of Amurath, we departed thence the following night to Barebo, and there continued, till a vessel,

vessel, which was trading to Ismir, took us on board, and carried us to that pride of Asia.

We continued in Ismir but a few days; the plague broke out in the suburbs, and raged with such violence, that Mepiki resolved to embark in the first vessel that left the city of Ismir.

This happened to be a merchant's sloop, bound for Koron, in which we came with favourable gales, and landed not long since in this miserable city.

The mariners who came with us, escaped not the pestilence, although they had left the city of Ismir; they were seized with the contagion as soon as they landed, and the disorder raged with such violence, that ere half the moon was elapsed, the whole city groaned under its wretched influence.

The aged Mepiki for some time shut himself and us up in an inner apartment, hoping to escape the contagion; but when he found the deadly disorder had seized him, he commanded us to carry him forth into the open air, which, in obedience to his will, we performed this morning.

And have ye, my children, said Sadak hastily, overcome the contagion, or hath it yet delayed to seize on your youthful frames?

We have hitherto, answered Codan, experienced a doubtful life; but seeing our parent has escaped from the danger of the plague, we shall no longer accuse our stars of leading us to the horrors of this place.

Son, answered Sadak, to accuse fate is to rebel against Alla; and no circumstances can justify our imprecations, while our faith must assure us, that he is the merciful governor of all our fortunes.

Codan, abashed at the reproof of Sadak, covered his breast with his declining head.

As Sadak held this converse in the desolate streets of Koron, he perceived the captain of the ship drawing near him; but the fire of his countenance was extinguished, and the lamp of life glimmered but palely in the cheeks of Gehari.

Noble Gehari, said Sadak, turning toward him, I perceive that equal misfortunes have oppressed us; yet in this victory of the grave, how much are we indebted to Alla for our wonderful escape!

That I should bless Alla, answered Gehari, is not wonderful, for my enjoyments will probably be restored with my life; but surely to the much injured Sadak, death had been a welcome guest.

Gehari, answered Sadak, it is by the gracious Alla's appointment, that I bear the standard of affliction, in which post if I fall, blessed be his will; but while I live, I mean not cowardly to lament my situation.

Well, replied Gehari, dost thou unite the determinations of the brave with the submissions of the pious; nor are your virtues useless, for Amurath means to try their utmost strength, and I come an unwilling slave to urge your departure from the city of Koron.

If

If Gehari will point out the means of my departure, anſwered Sadak, I am prepared; but ſuffer me to take theſe my children, as companions in my toils.

Ah, replied Gehari, ſtarting, are theſe the ſons of Sadak, on whoſe lives the Sultan ſets ſo high a price? Now, Sadak, teach me the duty that I owe my Prince, conſiſtent with my friendſhip to thy noble nature: On pain of Amurath's diſpleaſure, is every one who owns the Othman ſway, bound to diſcover their knowledge of thy children; and yet ſooner ſhall Gehari periſh, than bring ſuch exquiſite diſtreſs on Sadak's generous ſpirit.

Gehari, anſwered Sadak, obey thy Prince, and let not friendſhip breed rebellion.

What, my father, interrupted Codan, will you tamely yield your ſons a prey to tyranny? If ſo, Mepiki's life is ſpent in vain; we better had fallen with our brethren, beneath the cimeters of the janiſſaries, than met at Koron with our father's friend.

Codan, anſwered Sadak ſternly, it ill becomes the ſucker to vie with its parent ſtock; as a father, in tenderneſs I ſhould forget your want of filial duty; but rebellion, ſon, ſhall meet with Sadak's curſe, though his uplifted dagger pierce his Codan's heart; and yet, my ſon, I would this mighty Amurath, for whom the ſlaves of Othman live, did weigh in equal balance his own impetuous pleaſures and his people's comfort. Surely, Alla, thou gaveſt not our lives to be the tyrant's ſport, but didſt intend the Ruler of the faithful ſhould be his ſubjects' joy! If thou ſhalt judge hereafter

the

the princes of the earth, for every life in wantonness destroyed, there is not a prince but gladly would exchange his nature with a peasant!

Generous Sadak, said Gehari, dispel the gloom that overwhelms thee, for Gehari means not to betray thy sons: The spirited Codan, and his more submissive brother, shall, if it please thee, partake of their father's fortune. Of all our mariners but seven have escaped the plague. Codan, therefore, and Ahud, shall supply the place of two of my officers, and the rest we must seek for in some neighbouring port.

Friendly Gehari, answered Sadak, how shall I repay thy generous services! Permit us only to hide the corpse of our dear parent in the earth, and we will attend thy will.

At these words Gehari left Sadak and his children; and calling together his scattered mariners, returned to the ship.

Sadak in the mean time assisted his sons in their melancholy office, and having covered up the body of Mepiki, he led them to the vessel which Gehari commanded.

The wind blowing from the land, soon wafted them from the city of Koron, and Gehari, unwilling to return toward Constantinople, sailed to Medan, and there recruited the number of his mariners.

From Medan, after a tedious passage, they reached the island of Gomerou, where refreshing themselves a short space, they steered to the south, through the wide Atlantic, and approaching

proaching toward the sun, they encountered the sultry heats of the torrid zone.

Sadak, though unacquainted with the sea, was not indolent; the day was spent in instructing his sons, and in the night he strove with manly courage to surmount the oppressions of his mind, which were aggravated by the thoughts of Kalasrade's distress.

Having passed the warmer climates, they drew near to the cold regions of the south, and Gehari perceiving land, steered his vessel toward the shore, and anchored at a small distance from a beautiful island.

Here they found the blessings of plenty, and the mariners quickly recovering from the disorders of the sea, were enabled to pursue the directions of the bold Gehari, who stayed no longer than was necessary to refit his vessel and renew his stores.

From this island they sailed toward the straits, which divide the Atlantic from the Pacific Ocean. But as they approached the land, the wind arose, and the sea beat in tempestuous billows against the vessel of Gehari.

The mariners in vain pointed their vessel to the west, her sides shook, as fearful of the storm, and the ship started from the face of the tempest, as the war horse trembles in the day of battle.

Sadak beheld the conflicting elements with patience and calmness; but Codan was terrified at the black mountainous ocean, which rose in broken precipices above the masts of the ship.

As

As the vessel sunk embosomed in hollow sounding billows, so sunk the heart of Codan, and Sadak in vain attempted to give to his son a courageous mind.

Is this Codan, said his father, as he saw him dissolved in tears, and trembling at his fate? Is this the descendant of Elar, who so nobly supported the dying Mepiki? Where, wretched son, is that undaunted mind, which formerly endeared thee to thy parent?

Pardon, O Sadak, answered Codan, the misgivings of my soul: 'Tis not for myself, O Parent of my life, but for thee my heart pants, and my strength flies from me; was it not sufficient that Amurath bereaved thee of Kalasrade, without sending thee hither amidst conflicting elements!

Codan, answered Sadak, thy fears for me discover a noble soul, and Sadak thanks thee for them; but dismiss them quickly, Codan——

As Sadak was uttering these words, a tremendous swell broke over the ship, and the wave overwhelmed both Sadak and his son.

The father instantly secured himself by embracing a part of the ship, which saved him from the efforts of the wave; but Codan became a sacrifice to its violence, and was driven over the sides of the vessel into the tumultuous ocean.

It was some time before Sadak recovered from the confusion around, as the sea had nearly stunned him in its passage; but when he found his son was torn from him by the swell, and saw him tossed on the billows, the

un-

undaunted Sadak leaped forward, and was about to follow, had not Ahud caught his father in his arms, and prevented his intentions.

Wretched Ahud, said Sadak sternly, art thou jealous of Codan's better spirit, that thou hast dared prevent thy father in rescuing his first-born from the womb of the sea?

Protector of thy children, answered Ahud, forgive my presumption, and let Sadak be reserved for the arms of his Kalasrade; Ahud either will deliver his brother, or perish beside him.

The Continuation of the Tale of Sadak and Kalasrade.

NO, replied Sadak, preventing the intentions of Ahud, as his son struggled to fling himself into the tempestuous ocean, I now am satisfied, and Sadak, thy father, shall restore thy Codan to his brother's arms.

In this tender struggle between Sadak and his son, Gehari advanced, and taking each by the hand,

Alas, noble friend, said he, will you increase the misfortunes of Gehari? The good Codan is already the prey of our boisterous enemy, and will you likewise desert me in this perilous storm?

We mean, answered Sadak struggling, to rescue Codan, the beloved of our heart.

Though

Though I admire your affection, replied Gehari (still preventing the purpose of Sadak), yet I must not suffer it to overpower your reason; to sacrifice our lives in madness to the memory of our friend, is neither prudent nor courageous; and greater fortitude is exercised in forbearance, than in the vehement sallies of distempered passion.

The words of Gehari, answered Sadak, are as oil to the wounded on the plain; and we must learn, Ahud, to submit, where Alla hath denied us the conquest of aught but ourselves. Yes, Gehari, to see my breathless son extended on the wave, and yet stand motionless beside him, is far more difficult than to seek his embrace among the roarings of the ocean: But Alla, O Codan, is present with thee, and Mahomet hath taken charge of thy duteous body; 'tis we are afflicted by the storm, while thou art wafted from this scene of misery to the mansions of the faithful!

The gentle Ahud yielded to the wise dictates of his father, and Gehari prevailed on his friends to desist from their frantic purpose, as the sea was so fierce, that the ship could scarce bear the billows that broke around her.

After some time the storm abated, and Gehari prepared to run through the straits into the Pacific Ocean.

The rest of the voyage passed uninterrupted by the wind or the sea, but the serenity of the weather did but ill compensate to Sadak the loss of his first-born.

After

After fifty days sailing, Gehari discovered a great smoke; and in the night could distinguish at a distance flames of fire. These increased every hour, and so greatly terrified the mariners, that Gehari was fearful they would rise up against him, and refuse to proceed in their voyage.

Nor were the fears of Gehari groundless; for at their nearer approach, the curling foam of the waves each night appeared as liquid fire, and the ocean glowed like the melting-pot of the refiner. The mariners aghast viewed with despair the horrid scene, and the fears which were expressed in their countenance, seemed to gather strength from the pale deadly light, which flashed on the broken surface of the sea beneath them.

Overpowered by the gloomy terror, they fell with their faces on the deck, and their captain in vain addressed them with alternate promises and threats.

Sadak perceiving the distress of Gehari, and that their purpose would prove abortive, if they were suffered to persist in their fears, obtained from Gehari permission to arouse them, and with his drawn sabre, walking into the midst of the prostrate mariners, he thus addressed their coward spirits:

"Sons of Mahomet, and brethren of the truth, why fall ye thus as the leaves of autumn on the sandy plain? What conquering enemy cometh against you, whose terrifying aspect you dare not behold? Or, what dangers are these which have subdued the soldiers of our Prophet? Come the infidels of Europe against us; or is the all-battering Christian arisen up in arms to oppose our passage? If these were in sight, my friends would doubtless arise, and vindicate the faith of Mussulmen; they would start from the slumbers of fear, and put on the manly countenance of war. Shall then the harmless wave affright you, when in sportive gambols he imitates the brisk flashes of a livelier element? Or shall you, who have undaunted seen the ocean's hollow womb, and all its watry caves, now sink in terror back, when the heavy sea casts its languid smiles upon you? These, my friends, are omens of our safety, and assure us of success. But rise, and see me pour this harmless lightning on my hands, and thank our Prophet, that, in the starless night, he makes old ocean light us on our destined course."

Thus saying, the bold Sadak drew from the surrounding waves a bowl of water, which sparkled as it rose, and poured on his hands: The trembling mariners raised up their fearful heads, and viewed with wonder the innocent effect of Sadak's trial, till, satisfied by the experiment, they again ventured to arise, each blushing at his causeless fear.

But a few days sailing again recalled their fears. The island was now discovered, and in the middle of it an huge mountain, whose summit reached far above the fleeting clouds, where an uncommon volcano vomited forth a wide deluge of liquid fire, which broke forth from the mountain, with terrible roarings, and a mighty sound, as of winds bursting from the deep caverns of the earth.

The

The glowing deluge descended down the mountain in a sheet of fire, and rushing violently into the sea, drove back the affrighted waves in dreadful hisses from its surface, and for a long time preserved its fiery course beneath the waters that foamed above it.

The countenance of Gehari was now fixed with astonishment and dread, and he confessed to Sadak, that he dared not trust his ship any nearer the island.

Give me then, answered the undaunted warrior, a boat, and a small portion of your provision, and Sadak will alone risk the dangers that surround the fountains of oblivion.

No, my father, answered the duteous Ahud, there is yet one left that is ready to share with thee the dangers of this horrid place.

My son Ahud, replied Sadak, Codan is no more, and the javelines of Amurath have doubtless, ere this, pierced the heart of thy brethren: If Sadak perish, yet shall his name live in Ahud, and Kalasrade shall yet have one to revenge her wrongs!

'Tis not revenge alone, answered Ahud, that thy Kalasrade will require from her Ahud; she will ask me also for thee, O Sadak; and when she hears, that I refused to share in my father's toils, she will pour on me the imprecations of an heart-broken parent.

O Sadak, interrupted Gehari, yield to the duteous voice of Ahud, whose presence with thee,

thee, may haply be the means of both your future safety.

Sadak, at length overcome by Ahud and Gehari, confented; and the unhappy father and his fon defcended from the fide of the fhip into the boat, which Gehari had prepared for their reception, while the captain and his mariners poured after them the unavailing tears of friendfhip and compaffion.

The boat was about three leagues diftant from the fhore, when it parted from the fhip, and the wind blowing fair, Sadak fteered it brifkly for the ifland of the waters of oblivion.

The nearer they approached, the more tremendous looked the rocks which furrounded the ifland, againft which the fea beat and roared, as if it ftrove in vain for a place whereon it might reft.

Being arrived within half a league, the boat ftruck on a quickfand, and Sadak could neither move it, nor would the treacherous fand bear his weight, when he attempted to wade forward on its furface.

After many fruitlefs endeavours, he took feveral fmall boards, which formed the bottom floor of the boat, and tying them together, made two rafts, which he laid on the fand, and moving one forward, while he ftood on the other, he thus made fome fmall progrefs towards the ifland.

But this was an imperfect attempt, as the raft would bear but one at a time, and Ahud was left an helplefs fpectator in the boat.

To conquer this difficulty, Sadak returned again to the boat, and, by the help of the oars and rudder, he made a third raft; so that Ahud, by following his father's steps, and giving the raft which he stepped from to Sadak, who went before him, they, with difficulty, moved forward to the rocks that surrounded the waters of oblivion.

The tide had been several hours falling from the rocks, when Sadak arrived under their prominent horrors, and had left a narrow beach, on which he and Ahud rested, after their perilous journey.

Here Sadak and his wretched son recruited their wearied bodies, with such refreshment as they had brought in their garments from the boat, which, though scarce sufficient for the next day's support, was the only means of living they could see before them; unless they should be able to scale the over-hanging precipices, whose heads seemed wrapped in the dark clouds that were gathered around their rugged summits.

Sadak and Ahud having refreshed their limbs, arose and went about under the rocks in search of some opening, which might afford them an entrance into the island; but ere they could discover any passage, they came in sight of the burning torrent, and were obliged to retire from its destructive influence.

To add to this distress, the tide retired with violence around them, and the swelling ocean arose on the beach, so that Sadak and his son were half covered by the sea.

Thus

Thus wretched, they waded backward and forward on the beach, till Ahud difcovered a fmall cavern in the rock, whofe bottom the tide had not reached, when Sadak and his fon afcended into it.

In this gloomy cavern, which dripped with the falt tears of the ocean, they obtained a few moments relief; but the afcending fwell followed them ere long into the cavern, and dafhing its rude waves againft them, drove them on the ragged face of the rock.

The tide, however, rofe not above them; but, after a long perfecution, retired, and left them nearly exhaufted by its rude buffetings; and the wretched father, and his duteous fon, overcome with unnatural toils, flumbered on the fea-weed, which the water had left them for their miferable bed.

Yet, fhort were the flumbers of thefe afflicted Muffulmen; the rocks, and the mountains around them were heaved in the night with dreadful earthquakes, and the ifland trembled with the adventurous Sadak and his fon, as the wounded elephant fhakes the tottering turret in the armies of the vanquifhed.

The fea, agitated by contending winds, rofe in wild fragments to the clouds; and meteors gleaming through the troubled air, caft horrid light upon the watry profound, where monfters rifing on the fcattered waves, ftirred up a new commotion, and waged bloody war among themfelves, increafing ftill the terror of the night with their difcordant roarings, which the concave echoing rocks again repeated, and over all the thunders from above, joined in the general discord.

Ahud, said Sadak, starting from his sleep, (as he beheld the horrid scene before him), such would all nature be, were evil spirits masters of our fate; but fear not, Ahud, these gloomy rocks hide not this disordered prospect from our Prophet's sight: He, through the tumult, looks on us, and watches lest our faithless spirits sink from their just dependence upon Alla's power.

True, answered the duteous Ahud, O noble parent! and the man, whose righteous heart obeys the dictates of his God, may calmly view these desolated scenes.

In us, replied Sadak, whose slight frames were formed to tremble at every shock, these visions must awaken fear and horror; but the tumults of the whole ocean, and the crush of the wide earth itself, would be less disgustful to the blessed Alla, than the rebellious workings of a wicked heart, though hidden beneath the gay trappings of a voluptuous infidel. A wicked soul, O Ahud, is more dark and tumultuous than these horrors that surround us; yet often doth the coward run with terror from the lightning's flash, or even from an insect's presence, when he dare cherish in his bosom the most dreadful of monsters, a disobedient and rebellious spirit.

But in the midst of his religious expressions, the afflicted Sadak could not prevent some fears that arose in his mind, when he reflected on the exposed situation of his beloved Kalasrade, who, since her Lord's departure from the seraglio,

glio, had suffered far greater terrors from oppression and lust, than Sadak had experienced from contending elements.

For several days she was permitted, without molestation, to moan the fate of her Sadak, who she feared would be secretly destroyed by the malice of Amurath.

But the wild Amurath could ill brook his absence from Kalasrade; every day he sent for Doubor, to enquire how she bore the loss of Sadak; and but for the prudent interposition of the chief of the eunuchs, he would have teazed the fair one every hour with his offensive solicitations.

Doubor, who knew that persecution would rather inflame than assuage the sorrows of the virtuous Kalasrade, framed daily some new excuse to prevent the applications of Amurath; and at last, when the monarch would be no longer with-held, he went before, and assured Kalasrade that Sadak was safe, and on his search after the waters of oblivion.

The presence of Amurath renewed the sorrows of Kalasrade; she looked upon him as the murderer of her beloved, and all his softness and eloquence met with reproof and severity from the eyes and the heart of the much injured Kalasrade.

The proud Amurath, vexed at his ill success, cursed the faithful Sadak; and although his oath prevented him from executing the desires of his heart, yet he resolved to attack the fair one, through those who were dearer to her than her own existence.

Full

Full of these resolutions, he left the fair Kalasrade in wrathful haste, and flew from her presence, as the enraged tyger springs from the pursuit of the valorous huntsmen.

Immediate orders were given to the janissaries to seize on the children of Sadak, who were, with their grandsire Mepiki, on the opposite shores of Asia. But ere the janissaries could reach the village, the two elder were flown away with the aged Mepiki.

Amurath in wrath cursed the janissaries for their neglect, and ordered Doubor to dispose of the five that were taken in the prisons of the seraglio.

The next morning the malicious monarch appeared before Kalasrade, and commanded her to yield to his desires.

The affrighted Kalasrade, trusting to the monarch's oath, refused to comply; and Amurath enraged, found one female in his seraglio, who thought herself not honoured by his lascivious offers.

Pride and fury possessed his soul, and he commanded Doubor to bring the eldest of Kalasrade's children before him.

The little innocent was dragged out of the dungeon, and came with trembling limbs into the presence of Amurath.

Doubor, said the Sultan, unsheath thy cimeter, and sacrifice that accursed pledge of Sadak's love before my eyes.

The heart-wounded Kalasrade, who had long been torn from her children, rejoiced at the sight of Rachal, the elder of her daughters; and the little Rachal, when she perceived her

tender

tender mother, forgot the terrors of the dungeon and the frowns of Amurath, and ran from the chief of the eunuchs, and hid herself in the folds of Kalafrade's garments.

The bold affections of a mother at that instant animated the tender Kalafrade, and folding her daughter in her arms, she passionately embraced the beauteous Rachal, and bedewed her little cheeks with maternal tears.

The mighty Amurath could not behold the scene unmoved; but the thoughts that Sadak was the father of Rachal, soon changed his breast from pity to malice, and the enraged monarch again commanded Doubor to lead forth the little Rachal to instant execution.

At the voice of Amurath, the eyes of Kalafrade glistened with rage, and she viewed the Sultan as the lioness darts forth indignant flashes from her eyes, when disturbed in the lonely caverns of the rocks by the adventurous hind.

Tyrant, said she, death only shall divide my best loved Rachal from these widowed arms; though Sadak might have civil duties to struggle with against his love, a mother knows no superior tie to with-hold her from succouring those who were the offspring of her womb, and the children of her breast.

Doubor, said the wavering Amurath, what means this foolish heart of mine, that dares not encounter with a woman's will? But, slave, thou well mayest read thy master's mind; yet four are left in thy possession; those sacrifice to my neglected love; and teach this stubborn beauty, what she owes to Amurath and her prince.

Ah! what saidst thou, tyrant, interrupted the distracted Kalasrade; shall Camir, the lovely image of his father's strength? shall Elphan, ever submissive to his mother's will? or the fair Ophu, pretty mimic of my playful actions? or the lovely Isadi, sweetly smiling when Kalasrade smiles? shall these dear precious innocents bleed beneath the murdering knife of a slave's hand? O righteous Alla, who gave these pledges of my Sadak's love, in painful labours to my arms, remember, what I suffered for their lives, and let not a vile wretch at once destroy, what thou, with many a groan, didst bring to light and life.

Art thou too turned to stone, by this wild woman's talk, said Amurath to Doubor, that, like a striken hart, thou pantest for thy breath? Slave, instantly retire, and bring the heads of these early rebels to my sight, who ape so soon the treacherous features of their father's crimes.

Doubor, with slow reluctance, obeying his Sultan, left the apartment, and went with downcast looks, to seek the children of Kalasrade in the dungeon of the seraglio.

As soon as the little Camir and Elphan saw the venerable eunuch approach, they ran with sparkling eyes, and seizing on his trembling hands, they lifted up their smiling countenances, and told him they were glad to see him, for the black ill-natured men who had
watched

watched them, had given them no provision for the day.

Doubor, who had before secretly cherished the little offspring of Kalasrade, wondered not at the innocent freedom of Camir or Elphan; but the good eunuch's eyes ran down with floods of tears, when he beheld the smiling countenances of those, whose blood he was so soon condemned to spill.

Conquered by their artless love and freedom, the tender Doubor took them to his arms, and kissed them with a father's fondness: Then partly drawing forth his shining cimeter, the little family of Kalasrade, affrighted at its glittering sight, fled swiftly to the extremity of the dungeon, and Doubor, overcome with friendly tenderness and zeal, thrust the cruel blade back again into its scabbard, and fell to the earth, unable to perform the cruel purposes of his master's will!

While Doubor was thus employed in the murky dungeon, Amurath was not less irresolute in the gilded apartments of Kalasrade; now fully bent to execute his rage on the sweet smiling Rachal, he drew his crooked faulchion, and made up to the wife of Sadak, when awed by her maternal tenderness, the weapon fell from his hand, and he dared not strike where every blow would prove a wound to his Kalasrade's peace.

At length mad with his ineffectual toil, the monarch with a frown boding severity and wrath, broke suddenly from the apartment of Kalasrade, and beckoning to some mutes which stood at the entrance,

Slaves,

Slaves, said he, take that little urchin from her frantic mother, and with your griping hands cast over her infant face the rigid countenance of death.

The mutes, obedient to their royal master's orders, hastened into the apartments of the much-trembling Kalasrade, and regardless of her entreaties, tore from her struggling arms her daughter Rachal.

The distracted Kalasrade in vain cast her snowy arms around her beauteous daughter, in vain called on Alla, on Sadak, nay even on Amurath, to relieve her: The unmoved wretches in silent steadiness pursued their cruel orders, and, with their barbarous gripe, left Rachal in the agonies of death, at the feet of her frantic mother.

Kalasrade being released from the mutes who held her fast, while the rest executed the horrid commands of Amurath, sprang toward the expiring infant, and kneeling on the ground, she took the struggling Rachal in her arms, and pressed her to her panting breast; then lifting up her languishing eyes, wearied with many a fruitless tear,

O Prophet, holy Prophet, said the distracted fair one, look down on all a mother's anxious love, and spare my Rachal! Spare her, Prophet of the just!

After which, wildly folding her in her arms, the miserable mother poured on her livid face the copious streams of sorrow, and with a sigh, that might have pierced even the heart of Amurath, she cried, Ah Rachal! Rachal! Heaven spare thee!

Buried in tears, and sobbing over her child, Doubor, with a pale face and bloody hands, entered before her; and while the faithful eunuch strove to utter his melancholy tale, he saw the afflicted mourner hanging over her expiring infant.

At such a woeful sight, pity touched his aged breast, and the venerable eunuch hasted to her assistance, with all a father's soft affection.

Wretched! miserable! and afflicted fair one! said the trembling eunuch, what fatal grief has seized thy heart? Ah, said he, looking on the distorted features of the innocent Rachal, what rude murdering fiend hath spoiled this lovely image of Kalasrade's beauties?

Kalasrade, whose eyes were dim with grief, saw not the eunuch, till he came up to her, and poured his lamentations over her wretched infant; but as the fair one eyed his bloody hands, about to take her Rachal from her arms,

Bloody and relentless villain, said she, avaunt! thou shalt not feast upon my Rachal's flesh! Then recollecting herself, God of the faithful, said she, 'tis the murderous eunuch, stained with my children's blood! Steel-hearted executioner, hast thou eaten the hearts of Camir, and his brethren? but thou shalt not bereave me of my Rachal's heart.

My much honoured Kalasrade, said the affrighted eunuch, I have no orders to bereave thee of thy beauteous Rachal; I came here, seeking Amurath, my Lord; but whatever
misfortune

misfortune has befallen thy child, Doubor will gladly remedy the evil.

What, officious eunuch, said the hasty Kalafrade, hast thou destroyed, and canst thou also mock my griefs? Full well thou knowest the bloody orders of thy master's heart; four of my babes thy murderous hands have stolen for ever from my sight; their bodies are now perhaps cast forth, the portion of some ravenous animal, not half so fell in heart as thou and Amurath. O my children, is the dear flesh I have so often printed with a fond mother's kiss, now torn between the fangs of a merciless beast, or trodden under the feet of black unfeeling slaves! O Prophet, save me from the pangs of such heart-riven thoughts!

The righteous Alla knoweth, answered the chief of the eunuchs, how Doubor's heart was racked at Amurath's command; but here, Kalafrade, I have no command to hurt or to distress; and unless my art deceive me much, I can with ease recall this tender infant into life again.

Just reeking from the bloody scene, art thou become an instrument of life, deceitful eunuch!—Ah! forgive me, Doubor! excellent Doubor! said she, recollecting herself, didst thou not say, thou wouldest recall my dearest Rachal into life again? I will forgive thee.—No, continued she, pausing, I never can forgive thy murderous arms. Alla, said she again, recollecting herself, distracted with ten thousand ills, I know not what I utter; but thou, O Alla, knowest all! and not to

I 5   this

this base eunuch, but to thee, I lift my expiring Rachal. Thou, Alla, canst call a blessing from his bloody hands, and raise my child to life, through him who has already scattered fourfold death among my Sadak's lovely offspring!

The patient Doubor heard with deep anguish of heart, the wild and awful ejaculations of the miserable Kalasrade; yet unwilling to lose a moment, he answered not, but pulling out a phial from the folds of his garments, he poured some of its contents into the mouth of the gasping Rachal.

The powerful medicine wrought a quick change in little Rachal's frame; the strong convulsion ceased, and the reviving female opened its blue eyes, which sparkled with returning life, like the morning star.

As the eyes of Rachal brightened, so flashed with new life and spirit, the watery eye-lids of the fond Kalasrade; and much her full heart meant to say, when a mute abruptly entered, and commanded Doubor instantly to attend his lord.

Doubor, leaving the apartments, found the seraglio in confusion. The rebel janissaries proclaimed aloud in the courts the tyranny of Amurath, and their leaders demanded the brave Sadak at the hands of their monarch.

Amurath, fearful of their rage, sent for his faithful Doubor to appease their clamour; and when he saw the eunuch enter before him with bloody hands, his conscience darkened every hope of safety, as the black orb of night,

when

when she spreads her envious mantle o'er the face of the sun.

Wash, Doubor, in the sea, said Amurath, those murderous hands, and rather stain the whole Propontis with thy crime, than but one drop of blood appear to rob thy master of his tottering throne. O Doubor! Doubor! what seas of wealth would I not pour forth, to gather up the innocent blood thou hast this day spilled. Go forth, good eunuch, and appease these clamorous spirits; but with thy guilty hand, hide thy far guiltier heart, and over all throw the thick specious covering of deceit; and, Doubor, if success attend thy friendly cause, Sadak shall be restored to all his honours and his children.—His children, Doubor, we'll forget. This day, O Prophet, save me from destruction, and all my future life be thine!

Doubor, in obedience to Amurath, endeavoured to go forth among the tumultuous janissaries; but in their rage they would suffer none to speak, unless the brave Sadak was delivered to them.

Doubor returned with pale looks to Amurath's apartments.

My lord, said the affrighted eunuch, 'tis vain to stem the torrent. Your enemies increase each moment; and unless Sadak is delivered to them, they vow revenge on thee and all thy slaves.

Then, Doubor, said Amurath falling, I am lost indeed; and life, dear precious life, like a departing friend, will take a short farewell of me.

I 6 Glory

Glory of the Othman race, answered Doubor, suffer not your fears to interrupt your safety, but send some slave among the janissaries, and promise, in a few hours to give them Sadak; in the mean time, I will remove thy best effects through the water-gates, and we may fly to some neighbouring city, where thy loyal subjects shall still defend their Sultan against these bold undaunted rebels.

Friendly Doubor, said Amurath, thy words recall my sinking spirits; and, Doubor, neglect not, among my mutes and slaves, to carry fair Kalafrade with thee.

The honest eunuch sighed at his master's words; but in such perilous circumstances, he thought obedience was a double virtue.

With the fair Kalafrade, wondering at her fate, Doubor conveyed the reviving Rachal to the shores of Asia, whom Amurath soon followed, disguised like a mute, among the slaves of the seraglio.

The faithful Doubor led the royal family to Iznimid, and there proclaimed the arrival of Amurath, and the rebellion of the janissaries.

Abdulraham, the governor of Iznimid, immediately assembled the troops of the province; and the royal standard being displayed, the army of Amurath increased daily.

During these preparations, Kalafrade was confined in the women's apartments of Abdulraham's palace, and the little Rachal was suffered to attend on her wretched mother.

The janissaries of Constantinople having chosen the brave Boluri for their general,

after

after they were apprized of the departure of Amurath, resolved to march to Iznimid, to attack the royal troops, before they were sufficiently strengthened by the neighbouring provinces.

The governor Abdulraham went out to meet the forces of Boluri; but the battle soon proved favourable to the rebels, and messengers arrived from the defeated Abdulraham, advising Amurath to leave Iznimid, and fly to some other city.

Boluri, elated by his success, the next day marched to Iznimid; but the royal tyrant was fled to a neighbouring castle, with a number of friends, who came too late to join the forces of Abdulraham.

Here, in a place defended by nature, the Sultan and his family remained several months; during which time, the rebels were unable to force the defenders of Amurath from their impregnable castle.

A long and fatiguing siege succeeding, many of the janissaries grew tired of a war, where there were no hopes of plunder; and Boluri, fearful that Amurath might recover all, if suffered to depart from the castle, would not listen to the advice of his soldiers, who wished him to rove over the provinces of Asia, and plunder those who would not acknowledge his authority.

This misunderstanding produced discontent in the rebel army; and many of the officers seeing there was little prospect of plunder under Bolusi, secretly offered to give him up, if Amurath would pardon his janissaries.

Amurath

Amurath with great joy accepted the unexpected terms; Boluri was privately strangled in his tent, and the janissaries laid down their arms at the feet of Amurath.

The royal monarch being thus re-instated, forgot his obligations to those who had betrayed Boluri; and he commanded the ringleaders of the rebel army to be destroyed.

Thus secure from a second insurrection, he marched back at the head of his army to Constantinople; and soon reducing the rebellion there, he in a short time found himself re-instated in the seraglio of his ancestors.

But now forgetful of his former dangers, his heart beat with new passion for Kalasrade; and, fixed again on his throne, he wondered that a weak oath should so long have withheld him from the rapturous possession.

Doubor, apprized of his master's thoughts, laboured in vain to prevent the breach of his oath; and Amurath found, that while his faithful slave stood beside him, he should ever meet with an opposition that he could not brook.

To remove this obstacle, the vicious Sultan ordered Doubor to repair on a trifling message to Iznimid, resolving to force Kalasrade to his will, during the absence of his officious eunuch.

While these dark clouds were gathering over the miserable Kalasrade, Sadak and his son were the victims of the storm; beneath the rocks of the Island of Oblivion, and on the same night that Doubor departed from Iznimid,

mid, Ahud and his father were buffetted by the tempest and the storm.

But the piety of Sadak, and the submission of Ahud, alleviated, in some measure, the dreadful hours of that night of horrors, till day arose, and chased from their eyes the gloomy visions of the night: But with the friendly day, returned again the unfriendly tide, buffetting their bruised limbs, and smothering them with its waves, as the insect which preys upon the plantain leaf is washed by solstitial showers.

After waiting with patience the reflux of the tide from their cavern, Sadak, unwilling to lose the benefits of the day, led Ahud out on the narrow breach, while as yet they were forced to wade through the sea; and directing their steps toward the left, they endeavoured to surround that part of the island, which was opposite to the burning torrent.

This toilsome journey, though executed with the utmost difficulty and hazard, was yet as hopeless as the former; the black rocks, which had been hollowed by the waves, hung in rude arch work over their head each step they took, and formed a continued barrier, without any interruption, except where the sea broke inward in deep eddies, and formed in the fissures of the rock, the giddy whirlpool.

Wearied with this fruitless search, the wretched Sadak led his duteous son back to the cavern, before the swelling ocean rose again to exercise his severity on them; and after having encountered its fury, they gladly

sunk

sunk into a repose, which lasted till the returning tide obliged them to rise.

But now their provision being exhausted, or spoiled by the water, still severer distresses encompassed them, and the miserable Sadak beheld his son wasted with fatigue, and overcome with hunger and thirst.

One drop of wine yet remained in a little vessel, which he had fastened to his sash; this the tender parent offered to pour on the parched tongue of his afflicted Ahud, and this the duteous son refused, and with uplifted hands pressed the vessel toward his parent's mouth: An affectionate struggle ensued, and the duties which arose from nature prevailed over nature; till Ahud, receiving strength from the dictates of duty, started up, and before his father was aware, suddenly forced the liquor into his mouth; then falling on his knees at his feet,

"Ever honoured parent, said the trembling youth, forgive the first disobedience I have practised against you; let these tottering limbs bear witness, what terrors possess my soul, in that I have dared to exert my strength against the author of my being. Pardon, said I, O Father, rather strike me to the earth for my presumption, and cast from thy sight these rebel arms, which have prevailed against thy revered image."

"O Ahud, my son! my son! said Sadak, stooping. Alla shall doubtless bless thy filial prowess; thou hast indeed prevailed, most noble youth, but thou hast prevailed in duty,

and

and art thy father's superior in the triumphs of affection; yet, how dear, O my son, shall thy victory prove, if, to add a few moments to thy father's age, thou hast suffered the fair blossoms of thy own life to wither and decay!"

The words of Sadak gave comfort to the duteous soul of Ahud, and the cravings of hunger were suspended, while he heard the sweet rewards of his duteous labours; but short were the pleasures of Ahud, excessive thirst parched up his lips, and his supplicating eyes looking upwards on heaven and Sadak, expressed the silent anguish of his heart.

To see thee thus, O my son, said the distracted Sadak, falling upon him, is worse than the death thou hast, for a moment, driven from me. Oh, cruel Ahud! I will recall my forgiveness, for thou hast robbed me of a life far dearer than my own.

As Sadak spake these words, the wretched Ahud, overcome by his hunger, fastened on his own flesh, and greedily sucked the issues of his life; which unnatural relief, for a short time, subdued his thirst, and he waited with patience, till the tide permitted them again to go in search of some escape from their distresses.

Passing along the narrow beach, Sadak observed the water pouring from a small fissure in the rocks.

Ahud, said the miserable Sadak, his eyes sparkling with the distant hope, let us watch till the tide turn, and observe whether the water returns through this fissure of the rocks.

Ahud rejoiced in his father's hopes, and the two descendants of Elar sat waiting in silence on the fragments of the rocks.

The

The conjectures of Sadak were right; at the return of the tide, the waters formed a whirlpool, and were drawn inwards through the fissure of the rocks.

Whatever be our fate, said Sadak, this passage only seems to promise us the means of life; for on this beach, ere two suns are passed, we must perish by famine; wherefore, Ahud, continued his father Sadak, let us plunge together through this dark eddy, and either meet an end to our toils, or a reward to our labours.

Father, said Ahud, faintly, let us not attempt together the dangers of this whirlpool; but as I have less means of life remaining in me than yourself, I will first explore the secrets of this watery cave.

Thus spake the duteous Ahud, not expecting any relief from the undertaking, but desiring to prolong the life of his honoured parent.

Sadak, hoping his son might succeed, yielded to his intreaties; and Ahud having promised, if possible, to return with the ebbing tide, plunged into the foaming whirlpool, and disappeared from the sight of his anxious father.

For a few moments, the heart of Sadak was buoyed up with pleasing expectations, and he doubted not but Ahud was already in the land of plenty; but, as the wretched parent looked on the foaming whirlpool, and saw its tumultuous eddies roll ungulphed beneath the rocky bed whereon he stood, his weakened spirits sunk within him, and he cried out, in the agonies of despair, " Oh Ahud, my son! my son!

son! Oh treacherous ocean! thou haſt robbed me of both my ſons."

The tide riſing, obliged him to return to his cavern, where the emaciated Sadak ſat wringing his hands, weeping for his children, and bemoaning the fate of his miſerable Kalaſrade.

The calls of hunger alſo increaſed with his diſtreſs, and he cut the ſandals from his feet, and gnawed from them a poor lifeleſs ſuſtenance, till the waters prevailing, obliged him to combat their reſiſtleſs fury.

The next tide, the worn-out Sadak returned to the fiſſure in the rocks, and although the waters paſſed out, yet Ahud appeared not on their ſurface.

Sadak now waited impatiently the return of the tide, and with the firſt wave that entered, in leaped the adventurous hero into the jaws of the whirlpool.

For ſeveral moments he was hurried through the rocks, and bruiſed and wounded on all ſides by their rugged points, till light appeared through the waters, and he found himſelf in a deep cave, ſurrounded with rocks, and open at the top.

The rocks growing wider and wider, formed an irregular aſcent, and with ſome difficulty, the wounded Sadak crawled upwards, till he had attained to the ſummit of the rocks.

Here he found an extended country irregularly planted with fruits and herbs, and plentifully watered with little rivulets, guſhing out of many parts of the earth.

As

As Sadak looked round on this delightful prospect, he fell with his face to the earth, and said,

"O Alla, thy creature poureth forth his praises towards thee, and the wretch whom thou hast blessed adoreth thee for thy bounty!"

As Sadak spake these words, the pleasant vision faded from his sight, and he found himself cast forth by the waters on the beach, from whence he had leaped in the morning.

The heart of the unfortunate warrior fell at the sight, and the spirits of Sadak were nearly overwhelmed at the unexpected change.

But hold, said the submissive Sadak, if this change cometh through my devotions to Alla, blessed be that change, for Sadak had rather acknowledge his God on the barren rocks, than forget him in the mansions of festivity.

As Sadak spake these words, he perceived the eddies of the whirlpool to rise with an unusual swell, and a female in vestments of gold came forth from its surface.

Righteous Sadak, said the genius Adiram, I rejoice in thy fortitude, and I am happy in being the messenger of thy comfort; but ere I unfold to thee the wonders thou hast seen, permit me to lead thee in security to that place, from whence so lately thou wast torn, as a sleeper from his dream.

So saying, the waters ceased from the fissure, and the Genius and Sadak descending into the cave shortly after, attained to the summit of
the

the rocks, where Sadak had before seen the plains of plenty.

As Sadak arrived on the plain, Now, said the Genius Adiram to him, arise and satisfy thy exhausted nature, and then I will instruct thee in the lessons of our race.

But first, answered Sadak, O Genius, since such is human weakness, that even seeming good may be real mischief intended, let me address myself to that God in whom no one shall be deceived; for, if I partake of these viands, he first whom I serve shall be blessed for his bounties.

As Sadak spake thus, he fell on the earth, and said,

"O Alla! thy creature poureth forth his praises toward thee, and the wretch whom thou hast blessed, adoreth thee for thy bounty."

This noble instance of thy gratitude and dependence on Alla, said the Genius Adiram, is even beyond my hopes of thee, O Sadak, thou highly beloved! To be brave and duteous when misfortune cometh, is the lot of many, but few have fortitude to withstand temptations of pleasure, and the delusions of security: As joy approacheth, the knowledge of Alla vanisheth from the minds of mortals; and when the prize is attained, the elated conqueror looketh not on him that bestoweth it. The delusions of self-sufficiency arise out of ease, and man looketh on the undeserved gift, and calleth it a reward, and the price of his merit: But happy is he who receiveth with thankfulness, and forgetteth not,

not, that to Alla belongeth the praise and the glory.

O bountiful Genius, answered Sadak, tho' much I am fortified by thy religious dictates, yet doth my heart pant after Ahud, whom I have lost, and after Kalasrade, whom I left in a tyrant's power.

As to Ahud, answered the Genius Adiram, his fate cannot yet be unrolled to thy sight; and Kalasrade still suffers for her contempt of that life, which Alla had commanded her to preserve. Ah, poor Kalasrade! the bird of Adiram can no longer comfort thee, and the oath of a lawless tyrant is as a flaxen band around the flaming pile! But haste and pursue the waters of oblivion, for many dangers yet surround thee; yet thou hast well learned, to be most aware when perils are unseen. Thy way is onward to the flaming mountain, in which the waters are hidden.

The Genius Adiram then departed from the sight of Sadak; and after the laborious warrior had finished his repast, he walked onward toward the burning mountain.

The plain whereon he walked, led him into a deep valley, overgrown with bushes and trees, through which he broke with the utmost difficulty; and when unsupported by the branches of the trees, he fell into watery bogs, where he had perished, but for the broken fragments and boughs which he had gathered, to prevent his sinking.

Having passed this morass, he arrived at a river which ran among the rocks, whose source sprung from a wild cataract, which came foaming

foaming with a terrible noise, in two divided torrents down the rocks.

Here the astonished Sadak stood looking on the frightful water-fall, in wild amaze, and, stunned with the rapid dashing of the torrent, for some time paused, unable to pursue his course, or retreat from the dizzy scene.

No way appeared to pursue his journey, unless he dared venture up the craggy precipice, which broke the two cataracts, and divided the roaring currents from each other by its bed of stone.

Toward this middle rock, the brave warrior crept, his nature trembling at the bold determinations of his heart; and although his eyes swam, and his imagination tottered, yet the steady Sadak seized on the rock, and arose by degrees on its prominent fragments.

The foam and the surf of the neighbouring torrents washed him as he arose, and the noise of the impetuous currents overpowered him, so that he heard not the fall of several rocky fragments, which came tumbling on every side.

After his fatigue, and scrambling upward, he reached a broad, flat, prominent rock, whereon he laid his wearied body, and looked downward on the waves below. Ten thousand colours played in his eyes, and the rock whereon he lay extended, seemed, in his fancy, to break, and falling with him, to tumble headlong through the foaming waves.

Fear seized his body, though fortitude possessed his soul, and nature, tired of the struggle, kindly stole him from himself, and consigned

signed him to oblivion; for a few minutes he lay entranced, and as he waked, forgetful of his situation, he rolled over to the brink of the rock, and was falling downward, when he clasped the rock, and secured himself with his hands. Having gained his former situation, by long struggle and labour, he ventured not to look down from the precipice he had escaped, but turning his eyes upward, he perceived he had yet a third part of the rock to climb, ere he could reach the top.

His perseverance in a short time prevailed, and Sadak stood on the utmost summit of the rock, from whence he looked over an extended lake to the burning mountain, whose smoke and eruptions darkened the air, and filled it with sulphureous stench.

To pass this lake, Sadak determined to plunge into it, and swim across; but he saw, that unless he could steer between the two currents, he should be hurled headlong down the perpendicular torrent.

Unabashed by the danger, Sadak boldly leaped into the flood, and striking forth his limbs with the utmost dexterity, in a short time gained the opposite shore of the lake.

Here the hot cinders blown from the mountain, fell in black showers upon him, and scorched his raiment and his flesh; till Sadak, gathering a large bundle of wet flags, which grew on the watry banks, he tied them with his sash, and placed them over his head for his security against the burning coals.

In this manner he marched onward, the hot soil scorching his feet, and the sulphureous stenches

stenches blasting his lungs, till he perceived an huge cave, through which ran a rivulet of black water.

Sadak doubting not but this was the water of oblivion, ran eagerly into the cave, and saw at the extremity of it a fair virgin, sitting in a musing posture.

At the sight of Sadak the virgin arose, and welcomed his arrival.

Noble stranger, said she, it is now two hundred Hegiras since any one has been able to reach this scene of horrors; but to you it is given to taste the waters of oblivion, and to enjoy the blessings of our immortal race.

As the virgin uttered these words with a pleasing aspect, she drew of the fountain in a goblet of gold, and presented the dark waters to Sadak, who, turning the goblet from him with an easy motion, thus replied to the solicitations of the blooming virgin.

Fair keeper of these inchanting fountains, excuse my refusal; it is not for myself that I seek the fountain of oblivion; bound by a fatal oath, I come a miserable exile from the Othman throne, to seek a death more cruel, by succeeding, than others have found, who failed of success.

Then drink of this refreshing stream, answered the virgin, and forget the curses which Amurath hath heaped upon thy head; here drown thy former anxious thoughts, and rise refreshed in the lethargic stream, to untried scenes of pleasure and amusement; thy sins, thy follies, and thy pains forgot, here

Vol. II.   K   take

take a blessed renewal of thy life; the past be blotted from thy care-worn breast, the future all in prospect, all untried; then shall the golden dream of hope spring forth afresh, and the gay vision of unbounded joy again dance on thy sprightly fancy; wealth, power, and beauty, rich in possessions, eminent in fame, in extacy dissolved, shall all by turns solicit thy divided mind, while not a thought of what thou once hast felt, shall ever again molest thy troubled brain.

Such pleasures, answered Sadak sternly, may captivate the wretch, whose conscience wishes all the past one universal blot, but Sadak has not lived to wish the thread of life unravelled and destroyed. No, virgin, tho' great are the ills I feel, yet this, in every ill, supports my mind, I have not sought, nor yet deserved, the evils that I suffer.

For the weak child of man to boast, replied the virgin, argues neither sense nor merit; conceited, vain, and ignorant, their path of life is stained with error, and perplexed with doubt; purblind they grope along, in the bright meridian day, and every action past, they wish undone.

It is not presuming on a well-spent life, that I refuse your boon, replied Sadak to the virgin of the cave; but conscious of no studied ill, I thank my Prophet for his mercies past, and value the great Alla's former gifts too largely, to desire oblivion may prevent my future thanks; whatever afflictions are endured, were meant as blessings, to increase my faith; these surely to forget, were base

ingra-

ingratitude. Whatever are the blessings that Sadak has received, these yet reflect new comforts on my soul, and these to lose, were little to deserve the future mercies of my God. No, virgin, one moment's recollection of Kalasrade's truth, is more delightful far to me, than years of pleasure with a second flame. Though dead, shall I forget thee, Codan! whose pious cares so lately honoured good Mepiki's grave. Though lost to me, yet never from my mind shall Ahud's righteous image pass. Ahud, duteous name! who doubtless now beyond life's tyranny, quaffs the pure milky streams of paradise above, richly repaid by his kind prophet, for those few drops of life, he nobly gave the fountain whence he sprung. Hail, righteous suffering family of Elar! And thou, great parent of my life, look down, and curse this ungrateful head, when Sadak wishes to forget thy truth! perhaps, partaking of this stream, I might turn christian, and sell my God for some base bargain; or, like the evil Genii, lift up my rebellious arm, and brandish my weak weapons against the Almighty power.

Noble Sadak, answered the virgin, thou alone art worthy to succeed, who hast learned rightly to value the gift thou hast obtained: Take then this goblet, and carry to thy Prince these waters of oblivion; and fear not the toils of returning, for as soon as thou art in possession of the goblet, thou shalt stand at the gates of the seraglio of Amurath.

But, gentle virgin, replied Sadak, ere I receive from thy hands this inestimable gift, inform me, I beseech the, where is the duteous Ahud, the glory of my years?

Ahud, answered the virgin, is hidden from my knowledge; but let this content thee, that thou alone haft prevailed, and been able to bear from hence the waters of oblivion.

Thus speaking, the virgin gave into Sadak's hand the golden goblet; and as he received it, the cave and fountain rolled off in a dark cloud from before him, and Sadak found himself at the gates of Amurath's palace.

The janissaries, who recollected the features of their long lost general, shouted for joy; and the populace in tumults proclaimed the arrival of Sadak.

The slaves of Amurath hasted to inform him of Sadak's arrival, and the eunuchs of the seraglio brought him without delay before the impatient sultan.

As Sadak entered the royal apartment with the goblet in his hand, he perceived Amurath sitting with a disturbed visage on the embroidered sofa.

Sadak thrice prostrated himself before him, and Amurath, with a frown, commanded his slaves and attendants to retire.

What, slave, said the royal tyrant, as Sadak arose, hast thou succeeded in thy employment? Or dost thou bring thy forfeit head a tribute to thy prince?

Lord of the Othman race, answered Sadak, the great Alla whom I serve, hath blessed the cause of thy slave, and Sadak is returned with honour and success to the Othman court.

Curse

Curse on thy honours, vain slave, replied Amurath hastily, and cursed be the pride of thy heart: Thinkest thou that thou shalt triumph over thy prince? or that Alla hath reserved for thee joys superior to those which Amurath possesses?

The blessings of Alla, answered Sadak, have refreshed my heart, and the bounteous smile of my all-gracious Maker, hath enlightened my soul in every horror I have passed.

Blasphemous slave, said Amurath, rising in haste, thou liest; Alla meant not to bless thee beyond thy lord, but has buoyed up thy heart with treacherous hope, to make thy disappointment greater. Yes, slave, thy master has resumed himself, destroyed thy children, and blessed Kalasrade with these outstretched arms, that thou mightest curse thy God and die.

Hast thou prevailed, thou tyrant? said Sadak trembling; then welcome the black contents of this infernal bowl, for now oblivion's all I ask.

Slaves, said Amurath, clapping his hands, seize from the frantic slave that precious bowl; it were luxury too great for him to taste and to forget.

As Amurath uttered these words, the slaves of the seraglio entered, and wrested the goblet from the struggling Sadak.

Give me or this, or death, said Sadak to the slaves around him.

No, pious wretch, answered Amurath, 'tis I alone have blessings for thy heart. Chained to a damp dungeon's side, each day I will visit, and provoke thy memory with all the joys I lately tasted in thy Kalasrade's arms. When with amorous struggles, the half reluctant female gave denial to my fondness, and increased my flame; when heaving on love's tumultuous ocean, her breath my gale, her tears my sea, I seemed like the proud Venetian on his holy festival.

Thy faith, thy oath, thy honour lost, call not, base Amurath, said Sadak, on Alla more; even yet, since death and oblivion are denied me, I'll triumph over thee; for in all the curses that afflict poor Sadak's heart, none can overwhelm his conscience with such shame as thine.

Slave, replied Amurath, thy speech is free, I love to hear thy pious resignation; but death overtakes thee, if again thy words reflect dishonour on thy prince; for, think not, wretch, so meanly of me, that I approve of broken vows; none are so hardened, but must tremble, though they can't relent: Yes, slave, the joys I felt with my fond mistress, leave an irksome sting behind them, and while I triumph o'er thee, I curse myself; but these dull thoughts shall be driven from my anxious breast. The waters of oblivion are designed for mine, and for Kalasrade's peace; wherefore, bring me, slaves, the refreshing goblet, for my gloomy soul pants for oblivion, and I long to sin, and think it virtue. Slaves, give me the goblet: Now welcome peace! and conscience, thou base intruder; a long farewell to all thy wretched admonitions; but, slaves, remember, ere I drink this, Sadak dies.

As

As Amurath spake thus, he received the golden goblet from the hands of the slaves, who had rescued it from Sadak, and looking with a ferocious smile on the wretched husband of Kalasrade, "See, Sadak, said he, how greatly Amurath doth honour to his slave: I drink this bowl to be like thee, and fair Kalasrade having tasted its sweet contents, shall look on Amurath and think him Sadak."

The greedy monarch then raised the goblet to his lips, and drank of the dark liquor it contained; which quickly spread its fatal influence through his veins, and the disappointed Amurath too late perceived, that with oblivion death goes hand in hand.

Sadak surprised, started at the unexpected effects of the deadly goblet, and the slaves of Amurath, who ran to his assistance as he fell, finding their endeavours to recover him ineffectual, now fell trembling at the feet of Sadak, whom they imagined the janissaries would doubtless place on the Othman throne.

Lord of our lives, said the minions of the seraglio, Alla hath justly punished the wretched Amurath, for his broken vows, and thy slaves wait thy commands, to cast his wretched carcase forth a prey to the fowls of the air.

Wretches, said Sadak sternly to them, I seek not the power you are so ready to bestow; let the faithful Doubor be called, that the subjects of the Othman throne may be acquainted with their loss.

Heir to the Othman glory, answered the slaves, Doubor, by Amurath's command, is gone to Iznimid on the affairs of state.

Then, said Sadak, carry forth the body of our departed Sultan, and shew his pale limbs to the brave soldiers of the court, to whom (since no successor by inheritance or will is left) the choice of a new monarch falls. As to myself, tell them, I seek no honour, cursed in all I hold most dear. To me, honour were a grievous burden. Kalasrade, the virtuous Kalasrade is defiled, and Sadak shall retire for ever from the world!

The report of Sadak's arrival, and the death of Amurath, was now spread through every part of the seraglio; and while part of the officers hasted to acknowledge Sadak for their Sultan, others found out the melancholy Kalasrade, and declared every circumstance of the joyful news to the mourning fair one.

Is he returned, said the transported Kalasrade? Is Sadak, my lord, unnumbered with the dead? Then are my past sorrows like the vision of the night; and I again shall rise to a joyful day of constancy and love: But lead me instantly, continued she, to his beloved presence, that I may bless his conquered arms with love, and clasp him once again within these fond encircling arms!

So saying, she hasted with the slaves to the apartment where Sadak stood, with his surrounding guards, and flying in transports, she fell at his feet, and bathed his sandals with her overflowing tears.

Sadak

Sadak saw her approach with a mixed countenance of love and terror, and his soul divided by affection and resentment, knew not how to supply his tongue with a proper utterance; but perceiving her at his feet, the tender wretched husband stooped to the earth, and bowed himself before her.

What! noble partner of my thoughts, said Kalasrade, in amaze! art thou dumb with joy? Oh foolish wretch, continued she, why came I so suddenly into the presence of my beloved? My loved, my honoured Sadak, behold thy tender wife, and bless me with one look of love. Alas! guards, said she, turning to the eunuchs, as she perceived Sadak still immoveable, with his face to the earth, surely the death of Amurath hath not seized on Sadak; my beloved hath not drank of the pernicious goblet!.

Oh that I had drank thereof, said Sadak, groaning, when I stood before the virgin of the fountain of oblivion!

Speakest thou, my beloved, said the affrighted Kalasrade! speakest thou, my beloved! and not to me? Oh! oh! am I changed, my beloved? or—art thou not Sadak?

The tender Kalasrade shrieked at these words, and fell into the arms of her attendants.

At the shriek of Kalasrade, Sadak rose in wild haste, and clasped her in his arms.

Partner of my soul! said he, wildly, look on thy much injured lord; look up, Kalasrade, it is Sadak calls thee!

Dost

Doſt thou call? ſaid Kalaſrade, faintly: doſt thou, O Sadak, on whom my ſoul hangeth, call thy Kalaſrade back to life? Oh, Alla! ſpare me yet, for I am Sadak's!

Oh that thou waſt! ſaid Sadak, relapſing at the dreadful thought; Oh that thou waſt thy Sadak's only, that I could again preſs thee to my heart, and call thee only mine!

I am, my Sadak, I am only thine, replied the faint Kalaſrade; thine only could I be. Not Amurath, and all his lawleſs power, could ever tempt a thought from Sadak's love.

Wretched Kalaſrade, ſaid Sadak, ſternly; Alla knows my heart bleeds at thy diſtreſs, yet ſeek not meanly to diſguiſe the dark ſins of tyranny and luſt: Thou canſt not ſurely be ſo baſe, to wiſh thy Sadak in polluted arms.

O Alla, replied Kalaſrade, what means my lord? By all our righteous conſtancy and truth, I ſwear thou never haſt been injured in Kalaſrade's love.

Vain woman, replied Sadak haſtily, ſtrive not to deceive me; the lawleſs tyrant boaſted of his crime, and curſed my ears with the deſcription of his injurious luſt.

At theſe words, Kalaſrade looked in wild amaze at her offended lord; and her eyes, unwilling to expreſs reſentment, melted into tenderneſs and love.

The conſtant Sadak ſaw the ſufferings of his beloved, and his conſcience checked him for increaſing the diſtreſſes of his injured wife.

Forgive, ſaid he, running to her, forgive, O virtuous Kalaſrade, the cruelties of thy Sadak; thou cameſt ſeeking eaſe and conſolation

tion from thy lord, and I have doubled the curses of Amurath upon thy much suffering heart.

One word, though but one echo, of my Sadak's love, answered the afflicted fair, blots all resentment from Kalasrade's heart.

Whatever is past, though grating to my soul, thine were the keenest pangs, said Sadak, in return.—but to hold converse on a public stage, where love, or where misfortune is the theme, but ill befits the tender sufferers; wherefore, retire, my best Kalasrade, and when the royal janissaries have heard my tale, I'll come and weep with thee in mutual wretchedness.

The fair Kalasrade bowed at her lord's commands, and left Sadak with his surrounding nobles.

Sadak, having given audience to the officers of the army, the visiars and the bashaws of the Othman court, declined their proffered honours; but the voice of the multitude prevailed, and he was constrained to bear the weight of empire on his brow.

The shouts of the faithful rent the air with notes of triumph, when Sadak yielded to his people's supplication.

In the midst of their clamour, a messenger arrived, in the seraglio, and declared the approach of Doubor from Iznimid.

A gleam of comfort shot through Sadak's soul, as he heard the name of Doubor pronounced, and he sent his visiars to welcome his arrival, and bring him into the presence of his friend.

The faithful Doubor soon arrived, and having learned from his friends the wonderous change, fell prostrate at the feet of Sadak.

"Since he whom Doubor long revered is dead, said the faithful eunuch, Doubor rejoices at the public choice of Sadak's virtue to succeed him; yet, forgive me, royal master, if Doubor play the courtier but aukwardly before thee; born for his service, I lived in the smiles of Amurath, my lord; and, let these tears bear witness for me, I cannot ever forget so great a master."

Doubor, said Sadak sternly, thou art not the only afflicted soul that Amurath hath left behind him; deep are his curses stricken on Kalasrade's heart, and woes unutterable are Sadak's portion.

Surely, my lord, returned Doubor, the chief of the eunuchs, the mighty Amurath did never presume to break his oath?

Yes, he broke it, slave; nay more, and triumphed in his sin, said Sadak fiercely; and thou, I fear, hast borne a part in all his vengeful malice: All other evil I with patience bore, but this extremest cruelty loads my distracted thought past human sufferance.

My lord, answered Doubor, permit me to lead thee to fair Kalasrade's apartment; I yet must hope, some mystery unravelled hurts your peace.

To sooth with words ambiguous, when misfortunes past can never be redeemed, is a slave's province, said Sadak, but Sadak has a soul not to be lulled by women's tales; for know, tame wretch, I have already seen

Kalasrade,

Kalafrade, and viewed the graceful ruins of my once loved wife. O Prophet! Prophet! where was thy all seeing eye, when to unhallowed lust thou gavest up the purest of her sex?

Noble and royal Sadak, answered Doubor, prostrate on the earth, I beseech you to consider what mighty ills you heap on fair Kalafrade, if, unheard, you cast her from your presence, and accuse our Prophet, whose boundless mercy, like the mountain's shade, preserves and comforts every faithful mind.

Doubor, replied Sadak, thou ever wast to God and man an acceptable slave, and duly temperest submission to thy Prince, with faithfulness to Alla. I yield, good Doubor: Lead the way to dear Kalafrade's apartments, and Alla grant success attend our search!

The chief of the eunuchs preceding the trembling Sadak, led him to those apartments of the seraglio, where he had formerly been seized by the guards of Amurath; and commanding the doors to be flung open, Sadak discovered Kalafrade, sitting on the sofa, with her surrounding attendants.

At sight of Sadak, the beauteous Sultana arose, with wild distracted looks, and turning to her slaves:

"Who is this, said she, who basely apes the majesty of Othman's Prince? Whoe'er thou art, bold slave, continued she, depart, or by my beauties, the godlike Amurath shall sacrifice thee to our mutual loves."

O Pro-

O Prophet of the juſt, ſaid Sadak, haſting to her, what means this wonderous change? 'Tis Sadak, my beloved: Sadak, who comes to be convinced thou never haſt ſubmitted to baſe Amurath's love.

Submitted, wretch, ſaid Kalaſrade, with an haughty frown! doſt thou then call the royal preſence of the love-bringing Amurath an evil? On my ſoul, to me no joy was ever equal to his fierce embrace, when with reluctant ſtruggles I increaſed his love; but thou, rude ſlave, forbear, nor with unhallowed touch defile that form, which ere has ſerved to bleſs thy royal maſter's heart.

Juſt, righteous God, ſaid Sadak, falling back, what are theſe ſounds that rack my jealous ears? Have I then lived to hear Kalaſrade prize a tyrant, and deſpiſe her lord? — No, it cannot be. I ſee wild paſſion rolls her eye, and madneſs has poſſeſſed her brain; borne down by former evils, and depreſſed by anxious cares, the unexpected change ſeized too quickly on her ſoul, and the tranſported fair one ran to meet me, ere that her mind was calmed by reaſon or religion. In ſuch a ſtate thou cameſt, ſweet Kalaſrade, to thy Sadak's arms; and when thy fluttering heart with haſty pulſe demanded comfort, I gave thee baſe ſuſpicion, and with rude hand repelled thy tender love; as not contented with thy ſufferings paſt, I, in my firſt royal act, I played the tyrant on my wife, and curſed thee more than Amurath had done. But, righteous Prophet, thou haſt well repaid my baſe

ingra-

ingratitude! Blind as the dark mole, I dared accuse thy wonderous sight, and in the puny balance which my ignorant will held out, presumptuous weighed the mercies of my God!

The pious words of Sadak were attended with unusual omens; from the left the vivid lightning flashed, the palace shook, and a thick cloud filled the apartment where Sadak stood, out of the midst of which came forward the stately Adiram, and thus addressed the consort of Kalasrade:

"Noble Sadak, the trials of your fortitude are now finished, and Adiram is the joyous messenger of your future peace. The beauteous female who stands before you, is not the real Kalasrade, as you will perceive, when she shall restore to Doubor the enchanted ring.

"After your departure from the seraglio, in search of the waters of oblivion, I perceived that the obligations of an oath could not bind the man, that was influenced by revenge, and unmoved by the tender calls of humanity: I therefore sent by my little winged messenger an enchanted ring to Doubor, declaring its virtues, and bidding him use it when Kalasrade's distress should most require its assistance. The friendly Doubor had in vain employed both artifice and persuasion, to prevent his master from yielding to his passions; every contrivance proved abortive, and Amurath was determined to force Kalasrade to his will.

"In

"In this distress, I sent the enchanted ring to Doubor, commanding him to put it on the finger of one of the ladies of the seraglio, who should thereby be enabled to personate Kalasrade, and deceive the Sultan. Doubor, overjoyed, carried it to the fair and haughty Zurac, who had long pined unnoticed in the walls of the seraglio. Zurac tenderly loved Amurath, but her lord had never returned her affections."

Zurac, said Doubor to the fair Princess, you are well acquainted with Amurath's passion; every beauty of the seraglio is neglected, and Kalasrade alone possesses the heart of Amurath.

Say then, fair one, should Doubor give to Zurac the powers of pleasing the mighty Amurath, if Doubor should make him neglect Kalasrade, and seek only thee, what reward should the chief of the eunuchs meet at thy hands?

He should be, answered Zurac, as the clear fountain to the desert, or as pardon to the wretch condemned.

Take, therefore, answered Doubor, this ring, and while you wear it, your speech and person shall be as the speech and the person of the favourite Kalasrade; but beware lest your tongue betray the deception, and be cautious, and seemingly reluctant, that the change of behaviour awaken not in Amurath any suspicions concerning you.

Zurac readily yielded to the proposals of Doubor, and the eunuch secretly removed Kalasrade lafrade from these apartments, and brought Zurac in her stead; but the monarch, fearful that Doubor would seek to prevent his desires, sent the faithful eunuch to Iznimid, and the next day commanded the false Kalafrade to yield to his desires.

Zurac, happy that Amurath should so soon seek after her, made a faint resistance, and the passionate monarch took possession of her charms, the day before you arrived from the fountains of oblivion.

Though born to indulge his passions, without control from any human power, yet was Amurath shocked at the wild effects of his lust, and he repented of his folly when you arrived; but the submissive resignation of Sadak, and his superior virtue, stung the soul of the faithless monarch, and yielding to revenge, he poured his malice on your heart, for which the vengeance of Alla was levelled at his head, and he was suffered to drink down the deadly potions of oblivion.

As soon as Amurath was dead, I appeared to Doubor, who was travelling toward Constantinople, and I commanded him not to take the ring from Zurac, or to reveal the secret to any one, till he should see me again.

And now, Doubor, continued the Genius, be you the messenger of these happy tidings to Kalafrade, and prepare her heart to receive her lord; and acquaint her also with the safety of her children, whom Amurath commanded thee to destroy, but whom thou secretly hast preserved, having stained thy innocent hands with the blood of a kid. And that no consideration

may

may damp your joys, know, that Ahud is living, whose failure on the burning island, was the consequence of his filial piety. Having passed the whirlpool, and ascended the rocks, he came to the fruitful plain, and overjoyed at the sight of the fruits that grew thereon, the duteous youth plucked several, and folding them in his garments, he descended down the rocks, resolving not to taste them, till he had carried them to Sadak, his father: But, as through his haste to relieve the fainting Sadak, he neglected to thank Alla for the gift, the evil Genii claimed a power over him, and the cause was debated between our race and the impious Genii, before the footstool of Mahomet. Long were the contests of each, and every argument was used, which either mercy or malice could suggest; till at length Mahomet determined, that the youth should neither succeed, nor be condemned, but that he should be conveyed to the ship of Gehari, which was sailing toward the Othman empire. He therefore shall, if Alla permit, return within the space of a year to his parents arms, and in compassion to the race of the faithful, he shall not ascend to the enjoyments of his brother Codan, till, after thy death, he hath swayed with fame and glory the Othman sceptre.

Thus spake the Genius Adiram, and retiring into the dark cloud, she left the brave Sadak in the royal seraglio; who, after he had assured the fair Zurac, that she should enjoy the honours of Amurath's Sultana, hasted to meet his beloved.

Doubor,

Doubor, who, in obedience to Adiram, had imparted the glad message to Kalafrade, was presenting her five children to the happy fair one, when Sadak entered the apartment. The sight of his long lost children filled the happy father with the liveliest transports, and the honour of his Kalafrade so happily restored to him, gave new graces to his beauteous consort. They met with tears of joy, running like fountains from their pious eyes; and while in silent rapture they hung entwined in each others arms, their beauteous children kneeled around, and bathed their robes with streams of tears.

Conscious that passion had formerly transported them beyond the bounds of reason, they both in secret prayed for Alla's grace to moderate their joy; and, having borne the trials of adversity, they now strove to obey the sober dictates of calmness and humility.

And first, kneeling in the midst of their duteous family, with hearts and eyes uplifted to the throne of heaven, they poured forth their pious praises for their Maker's mercies; then in modest tenderness, indulged in mutual converse, by turns embracing all their children, and blessing their long lost offspring; and with their tears of joy, fell some few piteous drops for righteous Codan's loss, and duteous Ahud's absence.

These happy duties finished, the royal Sadak arose, and went toward Doubor, the faithful eunuch.

Friend

Friend of my bosom, and great instrument of all my joy, said Sadak, embracing him, not all the monarch of the Othman throne can do for thee, can ere repay thy generous services: Happy am I, to think that Alla will reward thee, with the heart-felt pleasures of an approving conscience, that, Doubor, shall be thy chief reward;—for worldly pleasures, command thy Sadak's fortune, the wealth of all my empire is at thy disposal.

The beauteous Kalasrade and her children followed the example of Sadak, and all with joy acknowledged Doubor's generous kindness.

The good old man, overcome by the affecting scene, in silence lifted up his watery eyes to heaven, then fell at Sadak's feet, and would have kissed his sandals; but the grateful Sadak raised him up, and seated him beside his amiable Kalasrade.

Serenity and mildness succeeded in the affectionate interview, where all were happy in each other, and where all acknowledged the source of their happiness in the bounties of Alla.

The Genius Adiram thus finished her tale, and Iracagem and the surrounding Genii bowed from their thrones; the children of earth were filled with firm resolutions of fortitude, and the noble image of Sadak fired their youthful imaginations.

While

While the sons of the faithful, said Iracagem, have received the impressions of fortitude from the lips of our sister Adiram, the daughters of our Prophet have been well instructed in constancy and truth, by the glorious example of the firm Kalasrade; and doubt not, ye beauteous offspring, but virtue and fidelity shall be as greatly distinguished, and as fully rewarded in the female sex, as ye see it honoured and approved among the sons of men. Born for each other, and alike endued with an ever-living soul, the great Alla impartially regards the sufferings and the virtues of all his children; and where weakness most prevails, there most his gracious strength supports, and comforts in the unequal conflict.

Nor weakly think, ye daughters of affliction, your sex is loaded with superior ills; though man in strength surpass you, yet seldom, against the virtuous and self-resolved breast, prevails his brutal force: Guardians of your sex, our watchful race attendant view your toils, and turn, unseen, the base designs of man back on himself, or make your sufferings, when sustained with truth, appear far brighter ornaments, than the gem, which vainly strives to cast a lustre on your charms.

Fair daughters, persevere, and let no foul intruder sully the beauteous image of a female soul: From your approving smiles, the sons of Adam take their first impressions; and were every woman virtuous, man soon would blush at vice and copy you.

Thus

Thus said the smiling Genius to his tender charge; nor added more: Then turning toward the illustrious Nadan,

"Nadan, said the sage Iracagem, we next expect to hear the mild doctrines of thy persuasive tongue."

"Chief of our immortal race, answered the venerable Nadan, I obey."

MIRGLIP,

THE

PERSIAN;

OR,

PHESOJ ECNEPS,

THE

DERVISE of the GROVES.

TALE the TENTH.

IN the first ages of the Mahomedan faith, the kingdom of Persia was governed by Adhim, the Magnificent, who removed the royal palace from Ispahan to Raglai, and enlarged the glories of his habitation beyond the example of all his predecessors.

The palace itself was built on the mountain Orez, standing on an extensive plain, which was surrounded by four walls, two hundred feet in height, and covered with a platform of marble, whereon nine chariots might drive a-breast. The northern wall, which looked toward the Caspian sea, was three leagues in length, and supported by six and thirty towers, whose

whose turrets reached one hundred and eighty-two feet above the platform of the wall.

The wall to the south, which looked toward Ormus, the great city, was also three leagues in length, and was supported by six and thirty towers, of equal height with the former.

The western wall looked toward Assyria, and its towers were in number thirty and six, and its length from the first tower southward, to that which looked toward the north, was three leagues.

The eastern wall, which completed the fortification, looked toward the kingdoms of India; and its towers, and its platform, and its extent, were equal to the rest of the walls, which Adhim had caused to be built around the plain of Orez, the place of his habitation.

Within these walls, Adhim caused the plain to be divided into gardens; and because there was no river near, he employed three hundred thousand men to bring the great river Abutour from beyond Cascmabat to the eastern side of the plain, where it entered through the wall under an arch, whose center reached even to the platform, which Adhim had caused to be laid on the surface of the wall which he had built.

In these gardens Adhim built a thousand palaces for his nobles and warriors; and in the midst, on a rocky mountain, whose summit was eight hundred feet from the river Abutour, which was made to run round the mountain, stood the palace of the king.

And

And because the soil of the plain Orez was rocky and barren, Adhim employed fifteen thousand carriages, to bring the fat soil of the vallies within the walls of his habitation; and he removed the forest of cedars, which grew on the mountains of Esdral, and planted them in the plain of Orez, which he had fortified with walls, and with an hundred and forty turrets.

And now Adhim looked from his palace on the mountain Orez, and his heart leaped within him to behold the works which he had made; and he said to his counsellors, "Who is equal to Adhim, whose buildings are as wide extended as the Caspian sea, and whose works no man can count because of their number?"

And his counsellors answered Adhim, and said, "None is equal to Adhim, the viceroy of Alla."

And Lemack, his Viziar, replied, "None is equal to Adhim, our Lord, whose buildings are like the cities of the eastern princes, and whose palace is as a desirable kingdom."

Adhim, pleased with the flattery of his princes, retired to rest, and the next morning summoned them again to behold the glories of his reign.

The courtiers seemed to admire the magnificence of Adhim, and they said, "None is equal to Adhim, the Viceroy of Alla."

And Lemack, his Viziar, replied, "None is equal to Adhim, our Lord, whose buildings are like the cities of the eastern princes, and whose palace is as a desirable kingdom."

The enraged Adhim, difgufted by a repetition of the fame flattery, which had pleafed him fo much the day before, commanded his courtiers and his Viziar to retire, and he went up alone to the higheft battlements of the palace, to furvey at once the mighty works which he had lived to complete.

For a few minutes the extended idea filled his foul: He endeavoured to reckon the flocks and the herds which had been driven into the paftures, bordering on the river Abutour; but they might not be told for number, and he was pleafed to find, that it was in vain to attempt to count the inhabitants of the palaces on the plain of Orez.

But what, faid the difcontented monarch, fhall thefe glories avail me, if the minds of my courtiers are not dilated with their mafter's magnificence? Here are objects fufficient to diverfify the ideas of my viziars for a thoufand years, and yet the words which they uttered yefterday, are to-day in the mouths of my flattering court.

Difpleafed at viewing unnoticed the glories of his palace, Adhim defcended toward the women's apartment, and conducted feveral of his Sultanas to the terrace, which overlooked the buildings he had erected.

Yafdi, faid the Sultan to the female who ftood at his right hand, obferve the glories which furround Adhim, thy Lord: Canft thou reckon, O Yafdi, the glittering palaces which I have built? Or canft thou number the multitudes whom thy Sultan hath bleffed?

Glory

The Sultan Axiam looking on his Palaces from ye Towers of Orez.

Glory of the earth, answered the Princess Yasdi, great are the perfections of Adhim, my Lord; but O, if Yasdi, thy slave, might speak, if she might answer her Lord, who is but as the handmaid of his pleasures, Yasdi would kneel before thee in behalf of her relations, and thou shouldest give to the children of my father, an habitation in thy palace of the plain.

Yasdi, answered Adhim, thy request shall be granted: But what saith Tema to the palaces which I have built?

O, said Tema, let my Lord not be displeased, and I will speak. Tema, whose soul is love, and whose spirit is fondness for thee, my Lord, wishes to enjoy the smiles of Adhim in the grove, and to see none other than the face of her beloved.

Gentle Tema, replied the Sultan sighing, I thank thy love, but I perceive the cottager has charms sufficient to provoke the affections of Tema.

And what thinks Ahiaza? said the fond Adhim, smiling on his favourite Sultana.

O my Lord, answered Ahiaza, you have brought me to an hideous height, and my head swims, and my fancy totters at the dismal prospect.

Adhim could no longer conceal his resentment; he turned hastily from the Princesses, and descended from the terrace into the apartments of his palace.

Let Lemack, my viziar, said the monarch, be brought before me.

Lemack hurried into the presence of Adhim, and fell at the feet of his Sultan.

Since those who have chiefly experienced the bounties of their Lord, said Adhim, are most ignorant of his glories, I mean, Lemack, to go disguised, and hear my praises among my less favoured subjects: Wherefore, prepare the mean clothing of two artizans, and we will together issue forth out of the palace, and join the conversation of my subjects, whose buildings are without the walls which surround the plain of Orez.

The viziar Lemack endeavoured to sooth the pride of his prince with a profusion of compliments; but Adhim stopped his career with a frown, and bid him not by a stale artifice, increase the guilt of his former indifference.

Lemack obeyed, and ere the bat had spread its leathern wing amidst the sable clouds of night, the Sultan and his viziar issued forth in disguise into the suburbs which surrounded the palace of Orez.

After wandering some time through the streets, they were met by two merchants, who had just been paying the Sultan's tax at the receipt of custom.

Ah, said the first merchant, these are the cursed artizans who are employed by the Sultan, to work up that wealth, which is squeezed out of our honest employment.

True, replied the second merchant; but would Adhim be as easily satisfied, as one we are well acquainted with, how happy should the merchants of Raglai live!

My

My Lord, said Lemack to Adhim, let us return; your subjects, I fear, are but little disposed to commend the glories of your palace.

Nevertheless, answered Adhim, we will proceed: A Prince should be able to hear with indifference both the good and the bad: All my subjects, Lemack, are not merchants.

As they walked onward, they met several young Persians, intoxicated with the forbidden juice of the vines of Deran.

These, said Adhim, though rebels to government, will yet speak as they think; neither prejudice nor private interest hangs on the tongue of him who is drunken with wine.

Tell me not, said the first, of the river Abutour; was I Sultan of Persia, it should run wine, and the walls of my vineyard should surround a province.

'Tis indeed a petty place, answered the second; and I believe there are better wines drank without the wall than within it.

'Tis only fit, said the third, for the habitation of our sober friend the water-drinker.

Peace, replied the fourth, his fame can never be blown upon by the breath of drunkenness; and, with all my gaiety, I had rather be that sober water-drinker, than the brickmaker Adhim.

The Sultan hardly could conceal his rage at the opprobrious epithet which the last young man had bestowed upon him; but being determined to prosecute his search, he left the riotous

ous young men without endeavouring to confute them.

Lemack, the viziar, again attempted to divert the intentions of his Sultan; but, in the midſt of his entreaties, they were overtaken by an old man and his ſon.

Gentlemen, ſaid the old man, be judges between me and my ſon; the young rogue broke looſe from me this morning, and to-night he is returned hungry and cold; and though I ſet before him ſuch food, as his mother and myſelf have uſed from our infancy, yet he talks of nothing but the delicacies of thoſe who eat in the palaces of the plains of Orez.

And my father, anſwered the ſon pertly, would perſuade me, that our neighbour lives better than Adhim the Magnificent; and that he who eats little is happier than the Prince of his people.

Lemack, ſaid Adhim, let theſe, and the young men, and the merchants, be brought before me to-morrow, that we may know what they mean, by preferring their neighbour to their Prince.

Lemack promiſed to obey; and Adhim ſtill purſued his walk.

And now they met a little family, following the heels of a man and woman in mean attire, who filled the ſtreets with their piteous lamentations.

Pity, good Muſſulmen, ſaid the man, have pity on a poor family, who are oppreſſed by the hand of power, and who are ruined, that

their

their ruin may add a needless splendor to those who are capable of sporting with the miseries of mankind!

Of whom do you complain, said Adhim, kindly walking up to them?

Alas, answered the man, so wretched are we, that we dare not mention the name of our oppressor; and but for the bounty of one who this day relieved us, we had perished in the streets.

Lemack, said Adhim, whispering his viziar, relieve them to night; and to-morrow let them be brought with the merchants, and those we have already met.

Commander of the faithful, replied Lemack, thy slave will obey the voice of his Lord: But the unwholesome dew falleth from the heavens; and my Lord will be wet by the sickly steam.

Lemack, said Adhim, we will enquire what means that crowd before us, and then return to the royal palace.

Alas! alas! cried a frantic female, who preceded the crowd, Queshad, the faithful Queshad, who supported my tender infants with the sweat of his brow, is no more! Thy limbs, O Queshad, are broken, yet not by toil! Thy life is wasted, while as yet thou hadst strength to go forth to the labours of the day!

Unfortunate wife of Queshad, said one, who endeavoured to alleviate her afflictions, mitigate thy grief, and know, that Alla hath, for wise purposes, made this trial of thy faith: Queshad, O mourner, was indeed a tender
husband

husband to thee, but Queſhad was not thy God. There are yet left thoſe, who can pity thy misfortunes, and relieve thy diſtreſs; and doubtleſs, the righteous Adhim, when he hears thy huſband loſt his life, in finiſhing the mighty buildings he hath erected, will pour the bounties of a monarch into thy widowed arms.

O mighty Alla, ſaid Adhim, ſighing in ſecret to his viziar, are theſe the glories I propoſed, when I employed all my ſubjects in ſuch works of magnificence? O Lemack, Lemack, I fear I am wrong! However, bring this widow and her friend, who has ſo juſtly anſwered for his Sultan, before me to-morrow.

Lemack employed the greateſt part of the night in finding out thoſe, who were, the next morning, to appear before his Prince, while Adhim lay extended and reſtleſs on the downy ſofa.

In the morning, the Divan was crowded, and the people were in tumults to know, for what cauſe ſo many priſoners were brought before the throne of Adhim.

No ſooner was the Sultan ſeated, than Lemack preſented the two merchants before him.

Merchants, ſaid Adhim, what I heard not as a Prince, I ſhall not puniſh as a Prince; only be cautious for the future, not to load your governors with undeſerved calumnies; and tell me truly, whom you dared wiſh in the throne of Adhim your Sultan?

The merchants were confounded at the ſpeech of Adhim, but perceiving he had over-

heard

heard them the night before, they fell at his feet, and besought his pardon: And the second merchant said:

"Alla forbid thy slave should see any other than Adhim, my Lord, on the throne of his forefathers; notwithstanding, I confess, I meant to praise the temperate virtues of Mirglip the Persian."

Lemack, said Adhim, bring forward the young men, who despised the law of Mahomet; and, viziar, remember, that when all these are dismissed, seek out this Mirglip, and bring him before me.

The young men, ashamed of their debauch, fell with their faces before the throne; and Adhim, gently chiding them for their excess, enquired of them, whom they meant to praise for his temperate behaviour?

The young men returned their thanks to the Sultan for his clemency; and the third said:

"Next to our Sultan, Mirglip the Persian, is beloved in the streets of Raglai."

Lemack frowned at these words, and he cursed the speaker in his heart; but the viziar dissembled his rancour, and brought the old man and his son before the throne of Adhim.

From whence, O young man, said the Sultan, hast thou learned to despise thy parents, and to disregard the authority of those who are set over thee?

Prince of thy people, answered the young man, trembling, forgive the follies of an inexperienced youth, and I will ever hereafter frame

frame my conduct from the example of the temperate Mirglip.

What! said the King, astonished, is Mirglip the neighbour of all my subjects?

He was indeed, answered the old father, that bright pattern of temperance, which I last night proposed as an example to my son.

The old man and his son retiring, Lemack, the viziar, brought the poor man and his family before the Sultan.

Of whom didst thou complain last night, said the Sultan to him, when thy dark words did seem to cast a shadow on thy Prince?

Forgive me, Glory of Persia, answered the poor man, if an heart, overloaded with sorrows, poured forth a part of its distress in the ear of its Prince: Indeed, commander of the faithful, the miseries which my little ones have suffered, since my cottage in the valley was destroyed, to make room for the mighty engines which drew down thy cedars from the mountains, forced me to complain in the bitter anguish of my woes.

Slave, answered the Sultan, thou mayest well ask forgiveness for thy presumption; but I have resolved not to punish; and even thy slander shall not make void the purpose of my heart: But who was this stranger that relieved thee, of whom thou spakest in such terms of praise?

Master of my life, answered the poor man, to the good Mirglip do I owe my own and my children's existence.

These

These slaves, said Lemack, are confederates in their tale; and some enemy of thy peace, O royal Adhim, means to set up this hypocrite above his Lord.

Thy surmise, O Lemack, said the Sultan, is just: But let us hear these last whom we met yesternight, ere we proceed to pass on this upstart Mirglip, such judgment as his insolence deserves.

The poor man and his family being dismissed, he who had comforted the wife of Queshad came forward, with the sorrowful widow on his right hand, whose distresses he endeavoured to alleviate, by representing to her the amiable generosity of Adhim, before whom she was about to appear.

The disconsolate widow fell trembling at the feet of Adhim, and her words, which strove for utterance, were stopped by heaving sighs, and an heart swelled with affliction.

The stranger who attended the widow, viewed with compassionate eyes the sorrows of her soul, and with silent respect, seemed to wait the commands of Adhim, to speak in her behalf.

Stranger, said the Sultan Adhim to him, I applaud your compassion; and as you have been the support, be also the voice of your female friend.

Guardian of our faith, answered the stranger, this widow is indeed my friend, for she is a Persian, and also a follower of our holy Prophet; and although I never beheld her till yesterday, yet have her necessities knit us together in the bond of friendship.

Stranger, said the Sultan smiling, I understand you; you are charmed with the beauteous sorrows of this amiable widow, and you are ready to renew the vows, which Queshad doth now remember no more.

Prince of thy people, replied the stranger, thy slave would never wish to countenance ingratitude to those whom we have lost. Grief is the natural tribute of a fond heart, to the memory of the beloved. And though I have besought the widow of Queshad to moderate her affliction, yet should I grieve to see her change her pious tears for wanton dimples. No, Prince, moved only by humanity, I met, and as my poor endeavours could, I succoured the distressed; and now, by royal Adhim's kind permission, I kneel before my Prince's throne, an humble suppliant for an helpless widow.

Lemack, said the Sultan, turning hastily toward his viziar, thinkest thou the new favourite, Mirglip, has half the virtues of this man before me? Haste, viziar, and bring him here, and I will engage, our stranger shall, in every grace, exceed this upstart Mirglip.

As the Sultan Adhim spake thus, the stranger fell with his face before the throne, and he said:

" If Mirglip hath offended his Prince, let thy guards, O Sultan, here strike, and sacrifice him to thy just resentment."

What, said Adhim, starting, art thou too Mirglip? officious slave! Was it not sufficient to send this flattering crew before me, but
must

must thou also act thy base hypocrisy in person here?

Merciful Adhim, said the viziar Lemack, let this trusty cimeter lay bare the traitor's bosom, and relieve my Prince from such daring rebellion.

Hold, Lemack, said the Sultan sternly, and defile not my reign with so mean a sacrifice: No, let him live; and if indeed he be the man fame speaks him, he were well worthy of a monarch's favour.

The subjects of Adhim hearing the noble sentence of their Prince, made the vaulted Divan echo with their praise, and every eye but Lemack's sparkled with a joyous tear.

However, the cautious viziar perceiving the purpose of his master Adhim, and the satisfaction of the populace, veiled his malice with a courtier's smile; and descending from his seat, he gave his hand to Mirglip, and raised the prostrate Persian from the earth.

O royal Adhim, said Mirglip, ere he rose, if with a view to worldly honour only I had done my duty, or to court the soft air of gentle breathing flattery, then might my Prince with indignation view the rebel Mirglip; but surely, Prince, to follow the holy precepts of our law, in honour of my Prophet, is not a deed deserving royal Adhim's hatred?

Mirglip, said Adhim, rise; thy Prince applauds thy holy zeal, and thou shalt live within my spacious walls, that daily I may hear thy virtuous converse.

Bountiful Sultan, answered Mirglip, in humble meanness bred a native of the forest, the

the honours of my Lord would wear unhandsomely upon thy slave, and I should act the courtier with an aukward grace: Rather, if it please my Prince, let Mirglip still among the meanest wander, sufficiently rewarded for his labours, that Adhim once hath deigned to bless his life with an approving smile.

What, said the Sultan astonished, canst thou resist the offers of thy Prince? Are not the tribes of Xemi, the mightiest of my subjects? Are not the captains of the host of Feriz in the long toils of war renowned? Are not these all anxiously soliciting to be admitted into the palaces of the plain of Orez? and shall Mirglip, a base peasant, dare refuse the bounties of his Lord? Yes, peasant as thou art, continued the Sultan, thy folly be thy punishment! go live inglorious, in the cotages of the forest, and every hour lament the lost affections of thy prince.

Thus said the Sultan, nor suffered a reply, but hastily withdrew with Lemack from the divan; while the populace with tears departed, all wondering at the abstinence of their favourite Mirglip.

The pride of Adhim was severely rebuked by the indifference of Mirglip, and he looked on his palaces with contempt, since they were unable to raise his fame among his subjects, or to tempt the admiration of a rude peasant.

Lemack with pleasure saw the emotion of his master; the peace of Adhim was indifferent to the viziar, so long as no upstart favourite was likely to destroy his interest with his Prince.

The

The well-instructed and the ingenuous mind alone, said the viziar to Adhim, can admire the extensive works of Adhim, my Lord; to Mirglip, and his tribe of peasants, these beauteous piles look like the steep mountains, which the labouring hind toils over, without reflecting on its mighty Founder: As the bird, with out-stretched wing, poised on the buoyant air, obliquely skims upon a palace or a cottage; and in its native ignorance, knows not the Sultan of Persia from the peasant of the mountain.

Thy words, replied Adhim, though meant to sooth my gloom, do truly add a poignant sting thereto; I have seen, O Lemack, the busy thrush, with impotent anxiety framing its little nest; and I have smiled to view the insignificant beams of its dwelling-place: Yet, Lemack, that thrush, perhaps, is now, regardless of my palaces, with a few airy circlets circumscribing thy Adhim's magnificence; and, should I venture forth, might chirup out a careless note above, and mute upon thy Prince, whom all the armies of the Persian empire might vainly follow to revenge his pastime.

My Prince, answered Lemack, is merry with his slave.

Thy Prince, answered Adhim, is dissatisfied with his own magnificence, when he sees, that a peasant may be more esteemed for his private virtues, than the Sultan of Persia for his stately palaces: Nay, Lemack, I myself esteem this Mirglip, and thou shalt haste, and pay

pay that widow, whom he so charitably supported, an hundred sequins.

Alas, Glory of the East, answered the viziar, shall Adhim then, the Sultan of Persia, stoop beneath a peasant? Shouldest thou heap half the wealth of thy kingdom on this woman, not thine, but Mirglip's would be the praise, and the hypocritical peasant should seem to make thee but the treasurer of his coffers.

Sooner let the widow waste like the live ember, said the Sultan, than such reflections glance on Adhim.

But why, O Prince, said Lemack, should a peasant's follies haunt thy fancy? Hath not my Lord ten thousand slaves that wait upon his pleasure? For thee the undaunted huntsman rouses with his well poised spear the tawny monarch of the forest; or with dexterous eye marks where the panther hides its callous offspring; or drawing with keen aim the feathered arrow, buries its bearded point within the spotted tyger's back; for thee the clarion sounds, and the brisk trumpet blows its lively note to mark thy footsteps; for thee, returning from his watery bed, the sun lights up the grey morn, and kindles for thy pleasure the genial face of day; for thee the blooming virgins of the East dissolve in amorous sighs, while every eye, attendant on thy will, beams not, unless thy favour light it up, and give it life.

And where is the joy, said Adhim, that, tyrant of the wood, I spread destruction?
that,

that, curfed by me, the lordly lion dies, or that the tender progeny, which heaven gives the panther, I deftroy? What praife fhall Adhim challenge, Lemack, that the tyger writhes his bloody back, and groans out beaftly fighs to give me pleafure? That my fame hangs upon the filthy blaft of fome fwoln trumpeter? Or fhall I think the fun awaits my call, who, long before my realms receive a diftant ray, is liftening to the whiftle of fome eaftern hufbandman? Yet worfe than all thefe, thou fetteft my honour on a woman's fmile, and wouldeft perfuade thy Adhim, that greedy eye gliftens at me, which gliftens at my gold. No, Lemack, without a felf-approving confcience, and a virtuous mind, bafe are the pleafures of an human foul; and Mirglip, by one righteous deed, fhall gain more folid comfort, than royal Adhim on the Perfian throne.

Lemack, continued the Sultan, this Mirglip fhall be our friend, and thou ere morning dawns, fhalt court him to thy Prince.

The will of Adhim, replied Lemack, be his viziar's law.

Thus faid the jealous viziar, and retired from the palace of Adhim, unwilling to execute the commands of his mafter, and yet fearful of difobeying his orders.

This villanous flave, faid Lemack, as he went from the prefence of Adhim, has, by his ftale virtues, corrupted the magnificent heart of Adhim, my Lord. While Adhim led his rivers through the rocks, I led Adhim through the blind vallies of deceit; and when ambition

tion stirred, I set my royal builder to rise from stone to stone, and scale the clouds: Long with such fruitless toil, he pleased his infant mind; and, big with mighty plans of moving barren mountains, he left the lower offices of government to me: Then luxurious plunder filled my chests, and as I passed, the children cried, the widows shrieked, and the astonished populace hid their heads, and cried, Hush, prostrate fall, the viziar Lemack comes! Then every step I took, great Lemack trode upon some abject neck; and the deluded Persian thought, death by my hand was a safe passport into paradise: If with hot eye I caught a female glance, the husband trembling came, and offered me his wife, proud, that from Lemack's loins should rise his future progeny; or if the cold senseless matron sighed out a denial, her house erased, her children slaughtered, and her husband pierced with the bloody stake, were the first tokens of my least displeasure.

Such Lemack was, while Adhim was a builder; but now his plan complete, his tower erected, and his plain enclosed, his busy mind unsatisfied, seeks new diversion; and for want of vice, virtue has made a faint attempt upon his heart. But I will stir the infernal race, and raise up phantoms to elude his search; and chiefly, that no starch example lead him forward, this Mirglip shall find a ready way to that heaven which he longs for, that every pious fool may know, how dangerous it is to ape a saint, where Lemack reigns.

Such

Such were the thoughts of Lemack, the viziar of Adhim, as he paſſed from the preſence of his Sultan, to his own palace on the plains of Orez; and in the rancorous malice of his heart, he reſolved to ſend forth a midnight executioner to deſtroy the virtuous peaſant Mirglip, whoſe actions had made ſuch an impreſſion on the mind of Adhim.

But the crafty viziar ſoon conſidered, that the blaſt of oppoſition would increaſe the reviving flame of Adhim's virtue, and that to deſtroy one vigorous plant, would be to raiſe a thouſand ſhoots around the expiring ſtock; he therefore reſolved to work in ſecret craftineſs, and that very night to go in ſearch of the ſorcerer Falri, under whoſe tuition he had been bred in the dark caves of Goruou.

For this purpoſe, the viziar Lemack exchanged his gorgeous robes of ſtate, for the religious weeds of a poor devotee; but that his ſanctified appearance might not have too much of the reality of religion, he hid under his outward rags a meal of royal delicacies, and a flaggon of the delicious produce of the vintage of Tihi.

Thus equipped, he walked forth toward the caves of Goruou, which were in a ſecret part of the foreſt, about three leagues from the royal buildings; and, fearful of a diſcovery, he avoided every Perſian in his walk, leſt they ſhould know the diſguiſed viziar, and revenge themſelves on the public author of all their wrongs.

The cave of Falri was ſurrounded with unhallowed ſwine, who grunted on the dark and filthy

filthy leaves of corn, which the forcerer had prepared for their fuftenance and their bed; an ill-favoured fteam arofe from their hides, and the neighbouring woods were filled with the loud fnarling of the guards of Falri.

As Lemack, preffing the beaftly muck, with his wet fandals, paffed the hot fmelling fwine; they all, with erected briftles, endeavoured to oppofe his paffage, till fcenting the delicacies which were hidden beneath his rags, they run upon him; and unlefs he had fuddenly entered into the prefence of Falri, they had deftroyed the viziar.

The cave of Falri fmelt not more delicately than the fwine before it; on every fide appeared the difgorged marks of drunkennefs and gluttony; and the four fteam which iffued from the covered pavement, affured Lemack, that he came too late to partake of the debauch of Falri.

At the upper end of the cave, the forcerer lay extended, preffing his aching forehead with an hand befmeared with greafe, and with the lees of wine; his little red ferret eyes were half fqueezed by anguifh from their bleared fockets, and his cheeks fcalded with the fiery rheum, and bloated by excefs, fhone difcoloured with a thoufand hues. Blotches, carbuncles, and warts, adorned his glowing nofe, and in his filthy beard, the different fauces of a week's extravagance were clofely matted: His lips, chapped and divided by the burning fteam of his overloaded ftomach, difcovered his foul teeth, clogged by corrupted food, and black with rottennefs; and on his furred and
fever-

fever-parched tongue hung not a drop of moisture. Over his unwieldy paunch, and lifeless limbs, were thrown a few difordered garments, but in contrary fashion to their real use; the turban, unfolded, covered his feet, and the vest was wrapped round his head, while his unseemly parts were left exposed, and emblems of his beaftlihood. Beside him stood his tube, burning with the fœtid herb tobacco, filling the cave with its poisonous odour; and on his right hand was placed a calabash of the spirituous juice of rice.

As the viziar Lemack entered, the sorcerer Falri filled the cave with curses and imprecations; but when he perceived it was his pupil in difguife, the wretch arose with many a ftagger on his tottering legs, and ran with out-stretched arms to hold him in his nauseous gripe.

What bringeth Lemack, said the ferret-eyed sorcerer, from the feafts of Raglai, to the caves of Falri! Are all the oxen of the plains of Orez devoured? or are the royal flaggons of Adhim exhaufted?

Thy fon, answered Lemack, fighing, was once the pride of Orez, and the voice of his mouth was a law in Perfia; Adhim was magnificent, and Lemack was absolute; my days were crowned with feftivals, and my nights with debauch; but foon thefe joyous caroufals shall be no more; Adhim awakes to virtue; and an abftemious peafant will fhortly be his guide, unless the power of Falri shake from his fecurity the abftemious Mirglip.

What,

What, Lemack! answered Falri, art thou a vizier in Persia, and comest thou to me to destroy a peasant for thee? Let thy guards this night dismember the abstemious Mirglip, and to-morrow rise, and fear not to meet thine enemy in thy paths.

The nature of Adhim, my Sultan, replied Lemack, will not be deceived; when Mirglip shall be missing, his whole pursuit shall be after the murderer, and Lemack at length be sacrificed.

Then, answered Falri, leave him to thy friend; return in peace to thy palace, and to-morrow, when thou goest into the presence of thy Prince, boldly declare that Mirglip could not appear before him, because he was drunken with wine.

Alas, replied Lemack, the Sultan, jealous of my tale, will haste to summon Mirglip before him; and I, detected in my falsehood, shall fall for ever from before my Prince.

If such suspicions, answered Falri, rise, do you engage, by the succeeding night, to shew your Sultan, Mirglip drinks the forbidden wine, and leave the rest to me.

To Falri's artifice, replied the vizier, I will leave it all; and haste again to Raglai, and the plains of Orez.

Thus said Lemack, and departed, not forgetful of the viands which he kept concealed in his garments; but willing to feast alone, in the wood, after he had left the sorcerer: For his purpose gained, the vizier, who was exhausted by his journey, wished for no partaker in his gluttony.

In the morning, when Lemack appeared before Adhim, the Sultan enquired after Mirglip the Persian.

Glory of the earth, said the viziar, bowing, who is he that is like Adhim in the greatness of his mind? over whom custom hath cast no chain, and who knows not the sceptred power of appetite and passion? Mirglip, O Sultan! hath won the hearts of all the people; he riseth and scattereth abroad the gifts of benevolence; he healeth the breaches of neighbours; he comforteth the afflicted: But, fatigued with the severe duties of the day, his wasted strength requireth recruit; and at night, after all his toils, he is renewed with the precious tears which fall from the luscious grape.

Hah! Lemack, said Adhim starting, is Mirglip, the wise, the temperate Mirglip, the slave of wine! No, Lemack, it cannot be.

O thou, answered the viziar, before whom hypocrisy flieth dismayed, and in whose presence falsehood dare not stand! forgive the tongue of thy slave, which wisheth not to utter the failings of its brother: To me, O Adhim, Mirglip is allied by the ties of virtue and religion! and not without my own distress, do I discover the little spot which sullies the glory of Persia: But my Prince requireth truth from his slave. Know then, O Sultan! that in obedience to thy command, I entered this morning the cottage of Mirglip; where I saw, O piteous sight! his out-stretched corpse unwashed on the ground, and the empty flaggon, which stood beside him. Struck dumb
with

with the fight, I hasted away before Mirglip awoke, to relate to my Prince the disagreeable tale; and having heard from his neighbour, that this is the only failing of Mirglip, which he repeats every night, my Prince may himself to-night discover the truth of my assertion.

That, answered Adhim, I mean to do, in the same disguise which we lately assumed. Wherefore, Lemack, leave me now, and prepare to convince me this night of what you have said.

Lemack obeyed, and night being come, Adhim and his viziar departed silently from Orez, to the cottage of Mirglip.

In the mean time, Falri, disguised in the habit of a merchant, entered the city of Raglai, and knocked, in the dusk of the evening, at the cottage of Mirglip, who invited him into his house; and understanding he came from a far country, set before him such plain provisions as he used himself.

The pretended merchant having eaten his fill, sighed, and telling Mirglip that he was greatly fatigued with his journey, he desired him to bestow one cup of wine upon him.

Mirglip started at the request of the merchant. What! said he, have I received under my roof one who despiseth the precepts of Mahomet, and the command of Alla?

Alas! answered the pretended merchant, Mahomet knows what a force I put upon my conscience, when I besought thee to favour me with the cordial of the vintage; but surely, when my nerves quiver, and my strength

fails,

fails, Mahomet will approve of your righteous deed.

As the false sorcerer spake thus, he tumbled from the sofa whereon he was placed, and he sighed aloud, " O Prophet, save my exhausted frame!"

Mirglip perceiving the distress of the sham merchant, and supposing it real, ran to those who dealt in sherbet, and bought a pitcher of wine, which he carried home, and set on the ground before the sorcerer.

It happened, that as Mirglip was entering his cottage, Adhim and Lemack passed him in disguise; and the Sultan saw plainly, that Mirglip was carrying into his cottage a pitcher of wine.

The enraged Sultan at first resolved to sacrifice the hypocrite, as he supposed, to his just resentment, which Lemack the viziar advised. But a few moments reflection made the Sultan rather choose to condemn him publicly, than to gain the hatred of his people by a precipitate execution.

Adhim disgusted, returned to his palace, ordering Mirglip to be brought before him in the morning; and Lemack retired to a joyous banquet, of which he partook with a new relish; as he doubted not but the fate of Mirglip was determined.

Early in the morning, the guards of the Sultan surrounded the cottage of Mirglip; and the viziar Lemack commanded a few chosen guards to enter, and seize on the hypocritical peasant.

Mirglip, though surprised at the tumult, yet shewed no marks of fear; conscience spread no alarm within, and he was satisfied that the sword which might deprive him of his existence, could not destroy the inward peace of his soul.

The guards, who were accustomed to strike terror into their captives, supposed they had been mistaken; and that the man who kneeled not for mercy, nor trembled through fear, could not be Mirglip, whom they were commanded to seize.

Being assured from his own lips, that he was Mirglip the Persian, they brought him before Lemack; whose eyes were swoln with intemperance, and whose brow was laden with malice.

What calm hypocrite, said Lemack roughly, have we here, who has so soon forgot the revels of the night, and the fumes of wine? But Adhim, the royal Adhim, shall judge thee, thou vile sycophant. Guards, continued the viziar, were there no partakers with this Mirglip? was no one with him in the cottage, where ye found him extended on the floor with drunkenness?

Just judge of Persia, answered the false sorcerer, who then came forward, let my pardon be sealed by the lips of the righteous Lemack, and I will speak.

If thou declarest truly before our Sultan, what passed between thee and Mirglip last night, answered Lemack, thou shalt be forgiven; but till then, guards, seize on him,

him, and let us bring them both before our Sultan.

The croud gathered as Mirglip and the viziar paſſed; and when they entered before Adhim, the Divan was crouded with anxious ſpectators.

The Sultan ſat on his throne, when Lemack brought Mirglip in fetters before him.

This, O royal Adhim! ſaid Lemack bowing, is the man whom Perſia loveth more than her Prince; who in his midnight haunts pours out the ſpacious goblet; who cheats the deluded populace by ſanctified expreſſions in the day, and at the decline of the ſun curſeth Alla, and his Prophet, in the cups of his drunkenneſs.

The populace ſhuddered at the malicious expreſſions of Lemack; and they doubted not, but the viziar would prevail, and deſtroy their favourite.

Viziar, replied the Sultan, we ſit here to judge from real facts, and not from the warm expreſſions of zeal. Who is it that accuſeth Mirglip?

This merchant, anſwered Lemack, whom he entertained laſt night, ſhocked at Mirglip's hypocriſy, and penitent for his own accidental ſhare in it; he, without compulſion, offered to diſcloſe the truth, if Adhim would forgive the partaker in the crimes of Mirglip.

The viziar then brought the ſham merchant forward before the throne.

Son of Persia, and guide of the faithful, said the Sorcerer, prostrate before Adhim, let my Lord forgive, and I will speak.

Speak then, answered Adhim, the truth, and justice shall, for this offence, forget to strike.

As I entered this city last night, said the sham merchant, yon Persian accosted me, and willed me to partake with him of the plain food of his cottage; thankful for his offer, I followed him, and he set before me some roots, and some boiled rice. After which, Merchant, said he, can you be secret? you are fatigued with your journey, and a cup of wine will enliven you. It was in vain that, in answer, I urged the commandment of our Prophet, and the law of Adhim. Mirglip would be obeyed; and he gave me a small cup, but in his own hands he held one large enough to contain a measure of rice. By frequent pledges, we soon emptied our first pitcher of wine; and Mirglip, not content, went forth to those who sell sherbet, and purchased a second.

The more we drank, the more lively we grew, and Mirglip waxed communicative; Merchant, said he, I invite only strangers, and after the first night I see them no more: You will, perhaps, be surprised to think that I, but a mean cottager, can every night support such an expence; but your wonder will cease, when you shall hear, that I am bountifully supplied by the rich merchants and widows of Raglai, with money to distribute among the poor; half of their supplies I regularly distribute every day; and the populace have made a saint of me for my labour; the other half exactly supplies me with an entertainment and wine each night for myself and a stranger.

And how cometh it to pass, answered I, that none of these strangers discover you?

That, answered Mirglip, is a secret which you never must know.

This, O Sultan, made me suspect, that Mirglip at last gave some potion to his guests, to take from them all memory of his feast; and therefore I resolved to taste nothing more in his house.

What I suspected was true; when I was about to depart, he brought out a small stone bottle, This, said he, O stranger! is a wine of the most exquisite flavour, I can afford you but a little of it; to every guest I give a cup, and no more.

Mirglip then poured forth a cup full, and I pretended to drink thereof; but in truth I turned aside, and poured it secretly into my bosom; by which means I preserved my memory, and have been enabled to detect the hypocrisies of Mirglip.

As the sham merchant uttered these words, a deep groan was heard through every part of the divan, and the populace incensed, cried out, That Mirglip, the deceitful Mirglip, might be delivered to their fury.

The words of the merchant, said the Sultan, are too true; a part of his tale I myself did witness, when going through the city in disguise,

disguise, I met this Mirglip with a pitcher of wine in his hand.

No more proof seemed wanting, nor would the Sultan suffer Mirglip to answer for himself.

Thy tongue, said he, is used to deceit, and I will not hear the hypocrisies thou art prepared to utter.

Lemack, rejoicing, seized instantly on Mirglip, and commanded the guards to gag him, that he might not, in the malice of his heart, utter any blasphemy against Alla, or rebellion against his Prince.

The unfortunate Mirglip, overpowered by force and tumult, was led away, Lemack hoped to instant execution; but the Sultan, in the midst of his anger, felt his heart yearn toward him, and he commanded, that till his sentence was pronounced, he should be cast into a deep dungeon, at the foot of the rock, on which stood the palace of the king.

Mirglip peaceably submitted to his fate, and seeing no present hope of answering for himself, meekly followed the guards of Adhim to the dungeons of the mountain.

The viziar Lemack having thus blasted the reputation of Mirglip, resolved to divert the thoughts of Adhim by some sudden scheme, that he might the easier destroy the unhappy peasant in secret.

For this purpose, he commanded his emissaries to procure some of the most beauteous slaves, that, if possible, the king might be moved from his present thoughts on temperance and virtue, to the looser phantasies of dalliance and love.

The orders of Lemack were always executed with precipitation; the viziar, impatient in his purposes, would brook no delay, so that neither rank nor condition was considered, but every beauteous female within the Persian empire, was suddenly dragged to the royal seraglio.

Out of these the artful Lemack chose thirty, who surpassed the rest in proportion, beauty, elegance and grace, and led them, adorned with the sumptuous luxury of the East, to the painted Dome, where the royal Adhim constantly refreshed himself, as soon as he arose from his mid-day slumbers.

The Sultan, who, though he had banished Mirglip from his presence, could not banish him from his thoughts, was displeased at the officious zeal of his viziar, and ordered Lemack to retire with his females.

Lemack seeing the determined countenance of his Sultan, was obliged to obey, and he made the signal for the virgins of Persia to retire from the painted Dome.

The Sultan, though indifferent, could not help observing the joy which one of the females expressed at the signal of Lemack, the viziar. During the time of their standing in the painted Dome, her eyes were cast on the ground, and her arms were folded in despair; but when she heard the voice of Lemack commanding them to retire, she alone lift up her sparkling eyes in transports to heaven, while every other female was disgusted at their Sultan's neglect.

Viziar, said Adhim, who is she among the virgins of Persia, that rejoiceth to be driven from the presence of her Sultan?

The fair Nourenhi (for that was the name of the Virgin) started at the voice of Adhim; she perceived that the Sultan had noticed her transports, and the pale mantle of fear overspread her cheeks.

But the fear of Nourenhi could not deprive her beauteous frame of its delicate symmetry, nor her lovely black eyes of their radiant lustre.

O Alla! said Adhim, as he beheld her, who art thou, O virgin of Persia! whose limbs are like the polished pillars of the temple; whose breasts heave like the roe panting for the thicket; and the arch of whose forehead is glorious as the enlightened hemisphere?

Lord of thy slaves, and terror of the earth, answered Nourenhi, thou seest at thy feet the daughter of a poor countryman, whose age and infirmities are now without support, since ten days was my dear sister Kaphira stolen from his embrace, and now is thy handmaid dragged from his trembling arms.

The man who, but in thought, hath injured him who gave thee life, O daughter of heaven! said Adhim, stooping to raise her, shall meet the fierce resentment of this arm.

Lemack, continued Adhim hastily, from whence came this fragrant flower? has she been plucked by force, O viziar! from her parent

parent ſtock? or, by her beauties awed, led ye her hither as the queen of Perſia?

Author of mercy, anſwered the viziar, this flower by chance we found, and who her parents are, thy Lemack knows not.

To thee, then, muſt I kneel, ſaid the fond Adhim, thou maſter-piece of nature, to know, from what deep mine thy artleſs luſtres ſprang, that in the plains of Orez I may plant the whole family of my beloved, and heap ſuch honours on them, as Perſia's throne may give, and thy fair beauties merit.

To frugal virtue long inured, anſwered the fair weeping Nourenhi, my aged ſire would curſe his daughter, ſhould you tranſplant him here. Curſe, ſaid I? alas! I wrong my gentle ſire; no, Sultan, ſweet endearing ſmiles hang ever on his cheek; and what he thinks amiſs, in ſuch ſoft accent is pronounced, that even guilt is pleaſed to hear itſelf condemned.

By the great Founder of our faith, ſaid Adhim, deſcribed by ſuch fair lips, and ſuch ſoft words as thine, thy peaſant father ſeems a ſaint to me! O what power is in thoſe lips, to make whomever you pleaſe as amiable as you are! But name him, beauteous virgin, that Lemack with a ſumptuous embaſſy may court him to our preſence.

Forgive me, mighty Sultan, ſaid the fair Nourenhi, but I dare not; for when the panders of thy royal court came to the happy grove, which late in vain concealed thy ſlave, Nourenhi, ſaid my ſire, let no man know' this ſafe retreat, which long hath hid thy father from the eyes of power.

If such were his commands, thou shalt obey him, fair Nourenhi, said the Sultan; and hereafter, when the imperial diadem of Persia glitters on thy brow, thou shalt surprise him with thy presence, and tell his aged, unbelieving heart, that Adhim is his son-in-law.

Alla forbid, replied Nourenhi firmly, that e'er his daughter should so soon forget the temperate lessons of her tender sire: No, royal Adhim! Nourenhi long hath learned to value the chaste Mirglip's virtues, more than all the splendors of the Persian throne.

So! said Adhim pausing, viziar, this is well; unsatisfied with his drunken lusts, this hypocrite hath also gained the Persian females to his interest.

Bred from our infant years together, said Nourenhi, we long have loved with an holy love; and Alla and his Prophet oft have heard our plighted faith.

No more, said Adhim; slaves, remove this daring female from my sight; and, viziar, continued the Sultan, let the axe this moment fall, and free the realms of Persia from the hypocrisies of Mirglip.

The mutes and the viziar both hasted to obey the Sultan; Nourenhi, with folded hands and streaming eyes, in vain besought his pity; the mutes hurried her from the presence of Adhim, and the Sultan was left alone in the painted Dome.

Adhim, enraged, seated himself on his sofa, and impatiently desired the return of the viziar with the head of Mirglip; but, hearing a noise in the court beneath, he looked forth through the lattice work of the Dome, expecting that Lemack, to please him, had ordered the execution of Mirglip within sight of the Dome.

But the corpulent sides of the viziar had so far retarded the speed of his malice, that he hardly reached the middle of the court, when Adhim looked forth through the lattice work of the Dome, where he saw Lemack stopped in his course by two reverend imans, who kneeled before him.

Vicegerent of Persia, said the first to Lemack, we come to inform our Sultan of one, who has dared to abuse the sacred ears of justice with the tales of falsehood.

Vile doating priests, said the viziar Lemack, panting for breath, avaunt; our Sultan is too wise to listen to the dreams of priests; and mark me, reverend grey-beards, if again, with step officious, you enter the palace of our royal master, I'll send your heads aloft above the gates, to preach without your bodies.

Viziar, said Adhim, opening the lattice of the Dome, I will not have the servants of my God disgraced without a cause; if, contrary to their faith, they have offended against our laws, I bid thee, viziar, be severe; as they who teach, should practise first the duties they enforce; but if led alone by honest truth, they come to warn me of some secret falsehood, they, viziar, act as duteous servants to their Prince, and I will honour them. Venerable imans,

imans, continued the Sultan, you who have a free access to Alla, shall never want access to me: Yet take heed, and use these sacred freedoms as becomes the ministers of truth; a flattering priest, who bids us look to heaven, that he may ransack earth, shall meet with Alla's curse, and man's abhorrence.

The viziar Lemack, finding he was overlooked, endeavoured to retract from his severity.

Glory of the earth, said he to Adhim, I have indeed injured these children of our Prophet; warm with indignation, that Mirglip should so often offend my Prince, not even the messengers of heaven could stop my fury; and those, whom in my cooler hours I love to honour, the favourites of Mahomet, these holy imans of our faith, have I with hasty words abused.

It is enough, O Lemack, said Adhim, from the window, I know thy temper is jealous of thy Prince's honour; but bring these holy men before me, and till their audience be passed, let Mirglip live.

Lemack obeyed with a dissembled alacrity; and, taking each iman by the hand, he led them upwards toward the painted Dome, blessing Alla aloud, who had placed him in the midst of two such holy supporters.

The imans, entering the Dome, fell prostrate before Adhim, who commanded them to declare the cause of their coming.

O thou Prince, said the elder, to whom Alla hath committed the government of thy people, forgive the boldness of thy slaves, who

come

come to declare to thee the innocence of thy servant Mirglip.

Good old men, said the Sultan to them, look well that you do not utter falsehood before me; the villanies of Mirglip are too glaring to be covered over by a specious tale.

Lord of Persia, answered the first iman, it is now six days since the viziar and his guards came into our district to seize on Mirglip; and we knew not till yesterday, that he was accused of drunkenness, by a merchant, who lodged at his house, or we might long ere this have refuted the calumnies of the merchant.

Mirglip, O Prince! the night before his imprisonment, came to us, and with distressed looks informed us, that a stranger was taken ill under his roof, who was so overpowered with fatigue, that he besought him to give him a cup of wine, left he should die. Wherefore, good Iman, said the charitable Mirglip, let me beseech you to haste to his assistance, that ere the veil of death be drawn over him, his soul may be comforted by your religious prayers.

The words of Mirglip were so urgent, that we both hasted to gird ourselves, to follow him to the house, where we found a merchant on the ground, who assured us, that he had but a few moments to live.

Mirglip joined in our devotions, and we spent the greater part of the night in prayers to our Prophet; till the base merchant, pretending to be relieved by our prayers, arose from the ground, and begged leave to repose himself on the sofa.

Mirglip

Mirglip yielded to his intreaties, and we departed from our friend's house, but not till he had poured forth into the yard, the remainder of the wine which the merchant had left; left his slaves should taste of it, and break the law of their Prophet.

Viziar, said Adhim, as the first iman had finished his relation, let these good men be detained in the palace, till the criers of the city have given the merchant notice to appear before my throne; and in the mean time, defer the execution of Mirglip, till the truth of this tale be made manifest.

Lemack went forth to obey the Sultan with an heavy heart, for he supposed that his friend the sorcerer was returned to his cave; and he knew there was no opportunity of seeing him, till night had closed the eyes of the inhabitants of Raglai.

The criers having in vain summoned the fictitious merchant, returned to the palace, and assured the Sultan, that no one could discover to them the merchant who had accused Mirglip.

There is yet, said Adhim, one circumstance that may declare the truth. For as none have had access to Mirglip, whom in our hasty zeal we would not hear, he cannot know these imans tale, if out of kindness they have forged it to release their friend.

The Sultan Adhim then commanded the prisoner Mirglip to be brought before him;—but, said he to Lemack, " Viziar, attend him to our presence, that no officious look or speech betray the purport of our calling him. And, imans, said he, do ye retire into that apartment,

ment, where, unseen, you may be witness of your friend's defence.

As Lemack entered the dungeon of Mirglip, the unfortunate youth doubted not but that he was the messenger of his death, for Lemack seldom visited the royal prisons, except he came on some malicious errand.

But the viziar, who began to fear, lest he should have appeared too officious in condemning Mirglip, and doubting not but that the love of Nourenhi would soon work his destruction, resolved to put on the appearance of friendship, that, should every engine fail, the promotion of Mirglip might not be the means of his own discredit.

Wherefore Lemack endeavoured to divest himself of that surly frown, which usually hung upon his bloated face; and with aukward flattery he addressed the unfortunate prisoner:

"They that are all goodness, need not fear the malice of their enemies; for Mahomet will guard them from hurt, and make the worst of men their friends. As to my part, Mirglip, I am astonished at your goodness, and have severely chid all the officers of the state, that they did not tell me of your virtues, that while my royal master Adhim had been employed in the glories of creation, I might have had the satisfaction of preferring the most religious of mankind."

Whatever is my Sultan's pleasure, said Mirglip, bowing, I submit.

My Sultan, said Lemack, somewhat offended, hath, at my request, resolved to hear thy defence;

defence; therefore haste with me unto the royal presence, and as you well are able, tell some well-coined tale before him, till his soft heart relent, and pardon follow.

If truth deserves no pardon, said Mirglip firmly, falsehood ever must deserve it less.

The viziar replied not, but led Mirglip through the dungeon into the painted Dome; for he perceived the young Persian suspected his sincerity, and pride and resentment prevailed over his hypocrisy.

Adhim having examined Mirglip, found by his answers, that the imans had declared the truth, and that the strange merchant had belied the innocent Persian.

Lemack, who feared the truth would prevail, was confounded at the noble simplicity of Mirglip; yet was he the first, at the permission of Adhim, to release the two imans, and congratulate them on the success of their information.

Adhim was also confounded at the patience and submission of Mirglip, who neither betrayed any fear in his condemnation, nor seemed elated by the gracious acquittal of his Prince.

But in the midst of his admiration, the beauties of Nourenhi possessed his soul; and the sacrifice which he dared not make to his pride, the Sultan resolved to offer to his love.

Lemack, said the Sultan, dismiss these venerable imans with costly presents; that my subjects may know, that Adhim will honour those who will boldly endeavour to relieve the oppressed.

The

The imans being dismissed, Viziar, said the Sultan, bring the fair Nourenhi into my presence, that I may know by what arts this base man hath practised on her innocence.

At the mention of Nourenhi's name, the pale Mirglip sighed; and all his precaution could not prevent the visible marks of fear which possessed his countenance.

Ah! base peasant, said Adhim, thy guilty conscience has taken the alarm; well mayest thou sigh to think thy iniquitous purpose is revealed, and that thy Prince is witness of thy fraud.

If to love the fairest of her sex, said Mirglip; if to engage in vows of constancy, with those whom Alla gave as social blessings to mankind; if, in obedience to the laws of nature, to follow those affections, which religion sanctifies; if these be crimes, said Mirglip, then hath Mirglip greatly erred.

I did suppose, said Adhim, that a man possessed like Mirglip, with a temperate soul, had no occasion for the dreams of love: Though to the world you seem austere, yet to Nourenhi you can relent, young man; and while you preach of virtue, teach her dalliance.

Virtue, I have heard, O Sultan, said Mirglip, reaches not the rigid, nor the soft extremes: She ne'er dissolves in wanton luxury, nor plants her foot, without occasion, on the prickly thorn. With the fair Nourenhi, I first imbibed the lessons of our Prophet; and while we hung attentive on the honeyed lip of her dear father Phesoj Ecneps, we both resolved

resolved to aid each other through life's rugged trial.

The good old Dervise saw our rising love, and checked it not; but, children, said he, restrain its bounds, and let prudence and religion lead it onward to your mutual peace.

From that hour, O Sultan! we gave our plighted faith; and had not these unforeseen misfortunes hindered us, to-morrow's sun was destined to behold our marriage rites.

False slave, said Adhim, amuse me not with such a senseless tale: But here comes our faithful viziar, with his beauteous charge.

Lemack then entered the painted Dome, leading the fair Nourenhi, supported by a female slave.

The stately Nourenhi entered with downcast eyes, and beheld not her beloved Mirglip, till the Sultan commanded her to look up, and cast her eyes upon her prince.

Nourenhi shrieked at the sight of Mirglip, and Lemack rejoiced to see the agitation of his Sultan, when he perceived the lovesick eyes of the beauteous virgin.

Virgin, said Adhim, take thy Sultan to thy arms, or see my viziar make an instant sacrifice of Mirglip.

The eyes of Lemack sparkled at the speech of his Sultan, and he stretched forth his hand to seize on his cimeter.

If my perpetual absence from this loved image will please thee, Sultan, said Nourenhi, I consent, but never can my heart desert its vow.

Then,

Then, Mirglip, said the Sultan, yield her to me, and I will place thee next myself upon the throne of Persia.

At these words the heart of Lemack failed, for he doubted not but Mirglip would consent.

Prince of thy people, answered Mirglip, how shall I answer the proposals of my Sultan, who wishes Mirglip to falsify his oath?

It is enough, said Adhim, I perceive both are fixed; Lemack, invent some punishment that may reach their crimes.

For Mirglip, said the viziar, drawing forth his cimeter, this shining blade shall soon suffice; but Lemack leaves the beauteous female to her master's mercy, who yet may see, when this base peasant is destroyed, new beams of sprightliness awake within her.

Hold, viziar, said the Sultan, for Adhim likes not the meanness of thy poor revenge; no, Lemack, thy Sultan only can devise a punishment adequate to their crimes.

Mirglip, continued the Sultan, and you, proud haughty fair, draw near.

Mirglip and Nourenhi slowly obeyed the commands of Adhim, falling prostrate before him, and both seemed more to fear for each other, than for themselves.

Love, vassals, said Adhim, drawing forth his cimeter, was your crime; be love your punishment: Rise, and enjoy each other, and so far shall Adhim be from separating your constant hearts, that I now draw this shining cimeter against your enemies; and he who loves not Mirglip and Nourenhi, is a traitor to his Prince. Nor think it, constant pair, a small conquest I have made; for even yet, while

reason

reason and while justice persuade me to bless you, intemperance and passion urge to your destruction; therefore withdraw, lest some fond sigh from fair Nourenhi's breast, kindle anew the fever of my blood.

Lemack, who was thunderstruck at the unexpected change, had time, in some measure, to recover, while Adhim spoke, and, courtier-like, he employed it, in framing a compliment, which, though true, yet came but aukwardly from the mouth of the fat speaker.

Thou hast indeed, most noble Sultan, blessed this happy pair; now let not Mirglip's temperance be more remembered; for thou, O Adhim! by this single deed, hast shewn more mastery of thy passions, than this Persian has atchieved in all his life.

True, noble viziar, answered the thankful Mirglip, to obey the dictates of temperance and virtue, where obedience is our greatest pleasure, and our best reward, argues but little merit; to boast in such a cause, were to call natural appetite a virtue; but to give up desire, possession, and a hundred fancied charms, to follow rigid virtue, this indeed ennobles man, and makes the prince his people's parent, and his subject's joy.

Nor think, O virtuous Sultan! said the fair Nourenhi, falling at his feet, that thy slave's beauties are too great to gaze on, though glowing with a sense of royal Adhim's generous kindness; shall not these watery eyes, which thou hast blessed, O Sultan! reflect more pleasure on thy soul, than all the brutal joys which force could give thee? Yes, noble Adhim, continued she, clasping his knees, thou art our Father, and our Prince, and from thy bounties, as from the lofty mountains, flow the streams of goodness on thy lowly slaves.

The generous Adhim, overcome by the gratitude of his slaves, dropped his arms on them, as they kneeled at his feet, and wept over them, and said to his viziar, with a sigh, Lemack, I feel more joy in this one action, than all my labours past have ever given me; but I long to see the reverend father of this beauteous virgin, from whom such virtues are derived.

Joy of thy slaves, and sovereign of hearts, answered Mirglip, we are bound by every tie to do as thou commandest; and the good Phesoj Ecneps, when he hears how greatly Adhim has condescended to bless his slaves, will, doubtless, haste to fall prostrate before thy footstool.

There is no need of that, answered Adhim; your father, doubtless, wishes not again to enter the busy scene of life, and mix with anxious courtiers; and much instruction shall thy Sultan lose, if Phesoj Ecneps regards me as the Prince of Persia; for though the sovereign of a kingdom, I am not yet above the wise direction of a temperate sage, whose heart uncankered with the rust of gold, sends forth the purest streams of piety and truth: Yes, Mirglip, I am resolved in secret guise to tread those paths, where thou hast learned the first great wisdom to be good, that I may kindle at the glorious presence of your animating sage,

sage, and treasure up such knowledge as shall bless my people.

The astonished Lemack heard the resolutions of Adhim with surprise, and feared, lest his Sultan should require his presence, at the mortifying lectures of the good Dervise of the Groves; but his grim countenance shone with joy, when Adhim, taking him aside, declared his intentions of leaving the reins of government in his hands till his return.

The subtle viziar, hearing his resolutions, fell at his Sultan's feet, and besought him not to think of hazarding his life alone amongst strangers; and that if he was resolved to persist, at least he hoped, that he would take him to the Dervise, that he might enjoy both the company of his Prince, and the lessons of the sage.

The unsuspicious Sultan assured his viziar, that he should take all necessary precautions, but that Lemack must submit to hold the reins of government till his return; and in the mean time, he commanded his viziar to send for a cadi, and to make all preparations in the palace for the nuptials of Mirglip and Nourenhi.

The city of Raglai, and the inhabitants of the plain of Orez, were surprised at the sudden alteration in Mirglip's favour, which was soon published about the palaces and cities; and every wish was, that Adhim would resume the power of administering justice to his people, and not leave his slaves in the hands of the viziar Lemack.

Adhim

Adhim caused the nuptials of Mirglip and Nourenhi to be celebrated with all magnificence; and Mirglip, who had received so much from the hands of his Prince, easily submitted to the pageantry of the court.

Two moons after the marriage of Mirglip, Adhim sent for his favourite, and reminded him of his promise; and told him, that he intended to pass for the son of a nobleman, who was desirous of enjoying the instructions of his father-in-law.

Mirglip and Nourenhi were rejoiced to hear, that Adhim intended to put his former resolution in execution; for they were both anxious to see the good Dervise of the Groves, and to acquaint him with the unexpected liberality of their Prince; and the constraint of a court was disagreeable to both, as Nourenhi had too much virtue to give encouragement to every fop that endeavoured to entertain her, and Mirglip was too temperate to join in the pleasures or the scandal of the emirs around him.

The time of their departure shortly arrived, and the Sultan and his two companions, Mirglip and Nourenhi, passed through the eastern gate of the citadel in palanquins, as part of the family of the old emir Holam, whom the Sultan had intrusted with the secret of his departure.

For three days they travelled eastward, and on the fourth, they entered a plain, on the right of which stood a noble grove of cedars and palms.

It is now time, said Mirglip (who was their guide), for us to send away these slaves back

back to Raglai, that none may know the recefs which hides our father Phefoj Ecneps from the eye of power.

The flaves being difmiffed, Mirglip and his Sultan, and the beauteous Nourenhi, walked forward into the Grove, and the young Perfian, by fecret marks, led them about two miles into the centre of the Grove.

The walk under the cedars and palms, though irregular, was pleafant and eafy; and the furface of the earth was covered either with mofs or fand, which, as no fun could penetrate, was cool and refrefhing to the feet of the travellers.

Having reached the centre of the Grove, they beheld a fmall irregular lawn, through which ran a narrow clear ftream; over this they paffed, by the affiftance of a rough bridge, made of unhewn timber, which brought them toward a plantation of laurels, plantains, youthful cedars, and fmall flowering fhrubs.

Through this delightful recefs they trod in mazy paths, till they beheld a fecond lawn, fmaller than the former, at the end of which appeared a neat and plain cottage, yet light and airy.

Yonder, faid Mirglip, O Sultan! is the retreat of the happy Phefoj Ecneps; and now permit me for a time to forget the honour due unto my Prince, and to look upon Adhim, the magnificent, as the pupil of the poor Dervife of the Groves.

The pupil of virtue, O Mirglip! faid the enraptured Adhim, is more glorious than the monarch of vice; and the foul of Adhim

has

has more ardent longings in this little spot, than it has ever experienced on the towers of Orez.

To this the good Mirglip could make no reply, for he perceived the Dervise coming forth from his cottage, and he ran and embraced the knees of his friend and his father.

My good Mirglip, said Phesoj Ecneps, with a joyous smile, you have made the heart of a poor Dervise flutter within him; a pleasing distress hangs on me, and the bright beams of goodness on thine eyes, revive my sinking soul.

Thou art indeed all goodness, said Mirglip, washing his trembling hand with tears; and so full of virtue and wisdom, that you seem to behold your own perfections in the meanest of your friends; if Mirglip has a thought that rises toward heaven, thou with thy pious breath hast blown it thither; from thee flows all the comfort I enjoy, to thee be all my praise.

Mirglip, said the Dervise gently, you have a courtly phrase, and would sooth my ears with prayers instead of praises; indeed, my good friend, I am neither Alla, nor his Prophet, but a weak old man, who cannot, by his taste, distinguish sweet from sour, and therefore you do play upon my weakness, as though I had forgotten, that God were alone the giver of every blessing.

Mirglip blushed at the gentle reproof of the good-natured Dervise, and was ashamed of that part of his salute, which love, rather than reason, hath dictated.

It is enough, said Phesoj Ecneps; forgive me, Mirglip, you know I seldom chide, unless my God be slighted; in his cause, though weakness be our strength, yet must we ever arm, not to support his power, but to declare our own obedience; for all the host of Persia could not create a grain of sand to swell his seas, or in his fleeting clouds suspend one falling drop.

Lost in attention, I could ever hang upon the honey of those lips; but thy fair daughter, the beauteous Nourenhi, said Mirglip, is at hand, and waits, with a young Persian nobleman, who pants to hear thy sweet instructive tongue.

My daughter, saidst thou, kind Persian, my lost Nourenhi! Is she with thee, on the plain? O bring her to my arms, and thou shalt see me weaker still than ere thou yet hast known me.

Mirglip was strongly affected at the passionate expressions of the tender Dervise, and he feared he had been too precipitate in disclosing to him the return of his daughter; but the fears of Mirglip were unjust, for the tenderness of the father, when Mirglip led his daughter to the Dervise, did but increase his piety to Alla.

O righteous Alla, said the affectionate parent, as he embraced his daughter in his arms, blessed be thy name, for thy comforts have refreshed my soul! nevertheless, teach me, O Father of life, to love thee above all things!

Adhim was not an idle spectator in this tender interview; for the piety of the Dervise enlarged

larged his soul, and he looked upward toward the heavens, and contemplated his own meanness, and the glories of Alla.

"I see! I see! said the enraptured Sultan, that neither riches, nor honour, nor power, nor might, nor beauty, nor dominion, can ennoble the soul of man; which then only is most glorious when it is most humble in itself, and most grateful to Alla!

The Dervise, whose joy and pious sentiments at the recovery of his daughter, had for a few moments taken his thoughts from the stranger, was startled at his noble exclamation, and excusing himself to him, he said,

"Pardon me, noble stranger, in that I have neglected to thank you for the honour you do this poor cottage by your presence; but the calls of nature are strong, and she will strive to be obeyed: In our weakness is her strength; and happy are they who do not always blindly follow her undistinguishing impulse. Attempered by reason, and awed by religion, her lively sallies are the great springs of human actions; and had we no passion, we should need no instruction.

"Alas! continued the sage, I forget that your natures, my children (for so, O stranger, I esteem all who enter under this roof); are harassed and exhausted by the fatigues of your journey; rest, I pray you, on these mossy seats, and I will set a few roots, and a bowl of water, drawn fresh from the stream, before you; the poor Dervise of the Groves has nothing more to offer you; but even these, perhaps, said he, setting them before his guests,

guests, may become more grateful to you, when you reflect, that they all are the bounties and blessings of Alla; and that there is more wisdom discovered in the growth of a root, than is displayed in the most sumptuous entertainment of the Sultan of Persia."

Adhim was pleased at the easy conversation of the good Dervise, who, on every subject, found an agreeable method of mixing his instructions with his hospitality and good humour.

After their frugal repast was finished, Mirglip told the Dervise by what means he became possessed of his daughter; and that the Sultan of Persia ordered the nuptials to be celebrated in his palace at Orez; and the good Persian was happy in the opportunity of displaying his generous sentiments before Adhim, who was unable to suppress the relation.

Phesoj Ecneps was so much enraptured with the description of Adhim, that he told the disguised monarch, he was sure the Sultan must be like him; which so confounded Adhim, that he had discovered himself to one whose eyes had not been dimmed by study and age.

The fair Nourenhi then began her tale, from her separation from the good Dervise, her father, to her meeting with Mirglip, in the palace of Adhim.

You may remember, Sir, said she, we were walking at the extremity of the Grove of Palms and Cedars, and sighing at the loss of my dear sister Kaphira, when the minions of the vizier Lemack arrived at the entrance of the wood, and seeing a female, pursued me through the groves:

groves: It was in vain that you called upon me to stop; I feared that even the eloquence of my father would be disregarded by the mercileſs brutes, who were ſent by the proud viziar, to ranſack the provinces of Perſia, and therefore I fled; and with reluctance returned, when two of them had overtaken me in the wood: After we reached your preſence, the diſtreſs of my father hung more heavy on my imagination than the evils I was likely to ſuffer; and even Mirglip was forgotten, when I ſaw the trickling tears ſteal ſoftly down the cheeks and the ſilver beard of my honoured parent.

The officers of the viziar ſhewing their orders to ſeize on every female they thought capable of pleaſing their maſter, my father found it in vain to reſiſt; and therefore, only begged leave to ſpeak a few words in private to me, which Nourenhi never can forget.

My child, ſaid he, we are the creatures of Alla, and whatever the hand of power or oppreſſion worketh, is by his permiſſion; therefore bear with calmneſs and moderation the afflictions of life; and in whatever ſtation it ſhall pleaſe the Juſt One to place thee, let this retirement of thy father be never revealed.

This was all I was ſuffered to hear; the officers ſurrounded me, and carried me, ſhrieking and crying, acroſs the plain, toward the city of Raglal.

In a few days, we reached the viziar's palace, and I found ſeveral hundred other virgins in the ſame ſituation with myſelf; but they rejoiced at their fortune; and what threw me

into

into the greatest distress, was to them the highest enjoyment.

The viziar Lemack selected but a few of our number, among which, I, unhappily, as I then thought, was placed in a foremost rank: But the gracious Alla, whose ways are unsearchable, made me happy, by denying me what most I wished for; and by sending me into the palace of the Sultan, gave the virtuous Mirglip to my constant arms.

And I, said the good Phesoj Ecneps, embracing his daughter, and the virtuous Mirglip, who arose to kneel before him, I will constantly beseech the Father of all men, to sanctify and bless you; nor shall ye, my good children, despise the blessing of your father, which Alla hath ever honoured with peculiar efficacy.

The good old man then entered warmly into the praises of the generous Adhim; and the disguised Sultan was obliged to bear a disagreeable part in his own praises, till evening warned the happy family to retire to their respective couches.

Two slaves were all that Phesoj Ecneps employed in his houshold; one had formerly preserved his master's life beside a dangerous precipice; and he, the good Dervise would say, claimed a constant return of tenderness, while that life remained which he had preserved: The other, animated by the bright pattern of his master's virtues, preferred the enjoyment of the good Dervise's presence, to the liberty he had frequently offered him.

These

These attended the disguised Sultan and the happy Mirglip to their separate apartments, where nothing luxurious or inconvenient appeared.

Early in the dawn of morn, when the birds of the Grove began their natural hymns of praise for the returning bounties of the day, the Dervise arose; and, dressed in neat and artless simplicity, he entered a small mosque, which was built at one extremity of his cottage, and where Mirglip, knowing the custom of his father-in-law, had before brought Adhim and Nourenhi.

The Dervise first saluted his guests with a pleasing cheerfulness; and then, putting on the robes of religion, he began the morning devotions of the faithful; mixing a lively sense of the mercies of Alla, with an humble dependance on his will, and diffusing the heart-felt joy which possessed his soul, into the minds of his attentive family.

As he had finished his devotions, the much-affected Adhim went toward him, and embracing him in his arms,

O holy Dervise, said he, forgive my emotions! but I must thank thy good religious heart, for carrying me so near the heavens of my God: Could every Persian hear thee pray, the mosque would be the seat of pleasure, and Adhim our Sultan, would leave the palaces of Orez, to live with thee in the temples of Alla.

My good and noble pupil, said Phesoj Ecneps, gently squeezing his hand, I am pleased to find you animated by the holy truths of religion; but your transports incline me to believe, you have not heretofore thought so frequently on the subject; the voice of religion, my good friend, is still and calm, is gentle and serene; nor elevated by passion, nor depressed by despair, but constant and uniform; the result of reason, and the daughter of truth; born for the world, and living for each other: Religion aims not to hide us from mankind, but to teach us the amiable lessons of social harmony, as well as the humble expressions of religious hope. Each morn we rise, our duty first to God we owe, and next to man; and to enter not the mosque with prayer and thanksgiving, is an unpardonable neglect; but to hide ourselves always in it, from the useful duties of life, would be to bury those talents, which Alla hath given us to improve.

I see you smile, continued the Dervise, and I guess your thoughts; sequestered in this pleasant valley from mankind, you look on Phesoj Ecneps as a rebel to his own instructions; but different stations best become the different stages of our life: Once like yourselves, youth strung my nerves, and health gave vigour to my arm; my voice was heard among the people, and I read continually the law of our Prophet in the mosques of Ispahan; till some of our reverend fathers sent me forth with certain of the sons of the emirs of the Persian court, to travel over the kingdoms of the earth, and guide their opening minds to useful knowledge; that, like the industrious bee, gathering the honey of each various clime, they

they might return laden with the best riches of a nation, sound policy, and experienced wisdom; nor blush I to declare, O noble guest! that Adhim owes the wisest of his emirs to my fostering care; though little be the praise to Phesoj Ecneps due, who but in gentle whispers, guided those streams of virtue, which appeared in the minds of the young nobles committed to his charge. These offices discharged, a private duty led me to this blissful seat, the gift of one who fondly glories in the name of pupil. Here an aged parent, depressed by years, though cheerful and resigned, called for the fond duties of a tender son; and here my long-lost Marinak blessed my arms with two fair beauteous daughters, whose minds, like opening buds of fairest blossoms, I have watched; and as each beauteous tint displayed its charms, I with soft hand gave every leaf its place and order, till my dear-loved Kaphira strayed, I know not how, from her fond parent's hut, and since, no traces of her footsteps can we find.

Here the good Dervise paused; the dear remembrance of his happy family drew pious tears adown his reverend cheeks; but turning quickly toward his royal guest,

Stranger, said he, these are not tears of weakness, but of love, and these I glory in; the heart which cannot feel the tender ties of social harmony, is more or less than human; to be above the calls of nature I boast not; to be beneath them I scorn; as Heaven gave me appetites and passions, these shall I wish to wear, and guide aright, nor aim at that

vain

vain philosophy, which would give to feeble man the unfeeling attributes of stone.

But, reverend sage, said Mirglip, thou hast taught thy guest but half thy virtues; for know, O noble stranger, there's not a family within ten leagues of this plain cottage, but feels the good effect of Phesoj Ecneps' presence; the youth of either sex he places under proper tutors and directors, and makes the rising progeny of Persia both loyal to their Prince, and duteous to their God. These streams, indeed, in secret flow; and, as the moon by night, which, though she but reflects the vigorous rays of the overshadowed sun, seems not to borrow, but to give her light: so are the minds of all this sage's neighbours cultivated, while few can see the light which kindles up their virtues.

Fie, Mirglip, said the good Dervise, to destroy the little merit of thy friend, by blazing it abroad. What we give in secret, we give as Alla's stewards; and unknown ourselves, on Alla, where alone 'tis due, the honour is reflected: but when our charities go forth, confessed as our own meritorious service, we bid mankind give praise to us, for what is not our own.

Nay, but, said Mirglip, to speak before our friend, is not to give our voice to public fame, though Phesoj Ecneps' virtues well deserve its loudest blast; but shall not this generous stranger hear how much the Dervise of these groves exemplifies the virtues which he teaches, when, with a fond generous affection, he made the life of his dear honoured mother smile

smile in age, and happy in affliction; when the chief glories of his youthful soul were to please her that gave him birth; when, like the stork, he made the nest of comfort for his parent, and bore her into light and life on his industrious wings; then, pleased alone with all mankind, when they were pleased with her. Or view him in his friendship unreserved, and blessing all around him, the virtuous smile light up where'er he stepped, and peace and joy attending at his side. Or see him condescending to the meanest of mankind, diffusing comfort, and enlightening ignorance, pleased at each reflected ray of knowledge which he shed, and healing what the rage of poverty or vice had maimed. Or view him in a stronger and a pious light, his soul in transports rising to the throne of grace, his body humble, prostrate, and submissive; no thought of his own merit intervening, to damp religion with the cloak of sin.

O my friend, said Phesoj Ecneps, interrupting Mirglip, 'tis rude indeed to break upon thy speech; and I have suffered while my pupil praised me, because this noble stranger will believe, O Mirglip, that amidst the lessons of the Grove, the voice of flattery has not been shunned; adulation is intemperate love, or base hypocrisy; the last can ne'er be Mirglip's vice, the first is his misfortune; generous in his soul, he over-rates the little favours which his friend has shewn him, and seeking to make him great, he makes him mean.

Indeed, answered Mirglip, it grieves me, pious Dervise, in ought to differ from thy amiable

amiable sentiments; to nothing but his own perfections is Phesoj Ecneps blind, and rather had his modesty conceal the brightest pattern of humanity, than that the world in whispers should declare from whence they caught the virtues of their heart.

The world, said Phesoj Ecneps, gentle Mirglip, is unconfined by language or by seas; and Persia, to this earth, appears but as a spot; yet even in Persia, the Dervise of the Groves at present is unknown; how weak then for the idle pigmy to stretch his slender neck the distance of a grain of rice, and fancy all men must admire him!——But I stop, for much I fear, my words are but an exercise for further flattery: let us walk, my friends, around the little spot, which I, with nature, jointly cultivate.

The friendly company obeyed the voice of the Dervise, and the good Phesoj Ecneps crossing the lawn, led them in the rising plantation before his cottage.

Here, in the irregular walks, they beheld several seats, on which the Dervise looked with a pleasing complacency, and seemed at sight of each, to smother in his mind some private thought.

Royal Adhim, said Mirglip, whispering the Sultan, we shall lose a great part of our pleasure in this short excursion, if you do not notice the silent transports of our friend.

Adhim, obeying the impulse of Mirglip, went toward the Dervise, and said,

Forgive me, generous Dervise, if I a moment interrupt your pleasing meditations; but

...ture in his first exception. It was to notice the heavy traffic at our time. Achan, obeying the impulse to Aijah, went toward the Duvile and had...

MIRGLIP and ADHIM hearing the Instructions of FINCAL, the Dervise of the Groves.

I see your countenance glow with peculiar pleasure at each seat we visit; sure some fond remembrance strikes you, and if it were just in us to ask it, that which gives such joy to Phesoj Ecneps' virtuous soul, cannot but enliven the hearts of his obedient and attentive pupils.

These seats, said the good Dervise of the Groves, which first I raised to rest my wearied limbs, reflection dedicated to the memory of my virtuous friends, whose loved images alternately strike my fancy as I walk. Perhaps, to hear their different trials, and their constant victories o'er life's uncertain passions, may be no unpleasing entertainment; at least indulge my friendly zeal, which loves to shew deserved honours on religious actions.

Thus spake the Dervise, and seated his company beside him.

The first memorial of friendship, said he, we have already passed; and though dedicated to my chief affections, I shall not affront my second friend, whose idea here, by constant practice, fills my mind, to found another's praises in his little temple. This seat, O Ellor, was raised to thee: sweet Ellor! gentle companion of my former years! with thee, I trained my early mind to piety and virtue; and, polished by thy inviting converse, life lost her rough ungrateful sting, and every change brought comfort to my mind.

This next sequestered seat, said the good Dervise, walking onward, revives the memory of peaceful Yeliab, a name sacred to every social virtue; whose heart, untroubled by ambition,

bition, yields only to the tender calls of nature and humanity; nor, though secreted from the world, as is this bench from the sun's fiery heat, by the o'erspreading cedar, is Yeliab therefore lost to public duties; the orphan claims, without a fee, his just assistance, nor claims in vain; and the poor do bless him daily for benevolence unsought.

The Dervise then passed out of the rising plantation with his company, and led them beside the small stream, till they arrived opposite two little islands, which were planted with the overspreading larix; between which islands, a rock, covered with shells, lifted up its irregular head.

These islands once, said the good Dervise, were barren and uncovered, but with assiduous care, I raised these waving heads upon them, and gave their naked surface the honours of the forest.

Why, Dervise, interrupted Adhim, it would require the mightiest engines to move these trees.

Now, replied Phesoj Ecneps, it might, but thy servant was content to raise their infant shoots from the bursting seed, and every year hath blessed me with a new appearance; improving hourly on my admiring fancy, I force not nature, gentle pupil, but I court her, and see her wide extended arms return my love.

The Sultan stood some time admiring the magnificent appearance of each island of larix, and it damped his pride, to reflect that the plantations of the Dervise were gaining new vigour from every returning sun, while his exhausted

haunted cedars were drooping their majestic heads in the plains of Orez.

They had now reached a third seat, which looked on the rock and the islands.

Lively Symac, cried the Dervise, somewhat elevated, here do we recollect thy bright and humorous converse, where sprightliness took hand with virtue, and laughter only pointed its keen raillery at impudence and vice: nor laughter bred intemperance, but was employed to elevate the soul, and not misguide the passions; knowing that our wise all-seeing Master gave us smiles to sweeten life, thou dost make goodness cheerful, and restore to slighted virtue the joys which sin hath long in vain usurped; nor loaded with the grievous pains of sickness or affliction, sinks thy generous mind; but while torture wrecks thy face, thine eye still sparkles, and like the smothered flame, breaks forth, and conquers every weight above it.

When life's amusing scenes are past; when anguish cometh, and the dark long day is lengthened out by bitterness of woe; even then my Symac can enjoy in fancy what is past, and in patience wait the future mercies of the bounteous Alla.

And here, continued the good Dervise, beside him is the seat of Eloc, calm and affable; a constant worshipper of Alla and his Prophet; one, whose mild instructions sink deep, whose reason pleases, and whose speech informs: unsuspicious, easy, and resigned, he views the stormy world with steady eye, nor studies to avoid,

avoid, by flight ungenerous, the casual ills of life, nor fears to meet them.

The good Dervise then led his pupils forward toward the Grove, where, mixed with opening spots and sheltered walks, he brought them onward to another seat.

Friend of my bosom, here Serahi holds my heart; our mutual esteem from early confidence arose, and happy I beheld him favourite of fortune, till a sudden blast overset his prosperous bark, and every former hope was lost. Then most I loved him, rising from the furnace of affliction with a noble mind, and leaving every tie of nature and of friendship, to seek alone his means of living in a distant clime; where now, obedient to his Prophet's precepts, he teaches those around him not to trust the flattering dreams of present life.

Mirglip perceiving the sage had finished his encomiums on Serahi, proceeded to the seat of Norloc, which was artfully hidden beneath the surrounding branches which rose above it.

Concealed by studious labours from the world, said Phesoj Ecneps, yet never from my mind, shall Norloc's righteous image stray, whose opening mind surmounted all the obstructions penury could cast upon it, and with eager and industrious toil fathomed the depths of learning and of science. But what, alas, avail thy learned stores! Those whom thou hast taught, shall rise above thee; and thou find no reward on earth, that the just Alla may reward thy patience more hereafter!

THE CONTINUATION OF THE TALE OF
MIRGLIP, THE PERSIAN; OR PHESOJ
ECNEPS, THE DERVISE OF THE GROVES.

BUT if the seat of Norloc, said Mirglip, is concealed, yonder bench, however, is sufficiently exalted, which looks upon half the provinces of Persia, from the eminence of that steep and lofty rock.

We will ascend the mountain, said the good Dervise, and examine the prospects which lie before it; and when our minds are filled with the wide extended scenes in view, we will still increase our astonishment, by considering the extent of his learning, to whom the summit of that rock is justly dedicated.

A spiral path winding easily round the mountain, soon brought the Dervise and his company to the seat of Stebi; from whence appeared on the left hand the Caspian Sea, and before them, and on the right, lay extended the wide dominions of Adhim the Magnificent.

The view of this territory, said the disguised Sultan, would fill me with surprise, did I not recollect the promise of the Dervise, to lay open before me the wonderful acquisitions of his friends.

The realms you see before you, said Phesoj Ecneps, contain a people, among whom the Persian language alone is used; but Stebi, the friend of my bosom, is master of every various

speech

speech which Asia knows; nay more, doth understand the different languages both of ancient and of modern Europe. But to him, language is only the handmaid of knowledge; fraught with all the science of each various clime, with all the wonderous truth philosophy can teach, he climbs the heavens, and explores her sparkling stars; from orbs eccentric drawing useful learning, and reading in the wide expanse, the mighty work of him whose wisdom planned the harmonious system of unnumbered worlds.

He then, said Adhim, is worthy of a monarch's notice, and fit to take his station on the towers of Orez, where Adhim hath invited the learned sages of his empire, to improve that useful study of the heavenly bodies.

Alas, said the good Dervise, what is merit, when unassisted by a courtier's smile?

True, answered Adhim (who well understood the artifices of courts), the officers of state esteem each place their perquisite, and monarchy itself must yield to them, and give his courtiers friends those honours, which more justly, in his private mind, he would confer on modest merit.

Mirglip smiled at the observation of the disguised Sultan; but he, willing to wave the discourse, descended from the mountain, and looking forward, said to the good Dervise of the Groves:

To whom is that seat dedicated, which I perceive is formed of rugged roots, and seems to offer but little comfort to those who will venture to seat themselves upon it?

This

This place, said Phesoj Ecneps, walking up to it, myself did raise, in fond remembrance of Smadack's zealous friendship and unhappy fate, that I might not enjoy an ungenerous ease, while my anxious thoughts did wander o'er his cruel fortunes. But why do I call them cruel, since the abstemious youth has but increased his virtues by forbearance? The trials and the conflicts of life are no misfortunes, when victory succeeds; and Smadack's fame shall ever be remembered, who dared with filial piety encounter love.

And love so chaste and temperate, said Miglip, interrupting the good Dervise, that might do honour to the breast of purity itself; and which, nor vain my augury, our holy Prophet shall ere long reward.

It must then, answered the good Dervise, first meet with parental blessings, for heaven seldom smiles when parents frown: Sometimes, indeed, by fortune blinded, or by age misled, forgetful of their offspring's real happiness, the parent urges his authority beyond the laws of God or man, commanding breach of oaths, or forced unnatural union. Then Alla must be first obeyed, for parents who derive their power from him, can plead no power to break his holy laws; but oftner far, thoughtless affection springing from fancy or from chance, the present good unfelt, the world untried, and dreams of happiness which never shall be found, stir up the children to engage in miserable alliance; these to prevent with tender care by mildness and affection, doth well become a parent's thought, whose

riper

riper judgment hath already tried the various scenes of life; whose expectations checked by the cold hopeless whispers of experience, lead not to the air-built fancies of a love-sick brain.

Yet far from me be speech which aims dishonour on the nuptial vow, by soundest policy approved, by every wise man honoured, and by Alla sanctified; the lawless voice of wild disorder shall cast its scoffs in vain against connubial truth, where friendship holds its purest empire o'er the soul; where love triumphant reigns, and from whose fruitful progeny spring all the sweet endearing blessings of society, the harmonies of nature.

But let us quit, said the good Dervise, this melancholy scene, and rest a while in yonder comfortable bower, with easy smiling Rezaliph; who, were he here, would join his ready voice to deck our matrimonial triumphs.

He is then, said the disguised Adhim, the father of a family?

Yes, continued the good Dervise, two smiling boys hang on his knees, like clusters on the vine; and Rezaliph is ever studious to implant his virtues on their infant minds.

The man who trains his children in the paths of virtue, said Adhim, is the best subject that a monarch knows.

And feels, said Mirglip, the most exalted pleasures of the human heart; nor when outstretched upon the bed of death, can he be said to die, whose virtues multiplied through all

all his race, reflect his righteous image to succeeding worlds.

The happy family of Phefoj Ecneps paſſed onward from the feat of Rezaliph, through a narrow path, ſhaded with the nobleſt trees of the Grove, and advanced toward a ſmall but beautiful lawn, round which were planted ſeveral lofty trees; under each of which the diſguiſed Sultan beheld the feats of friendſhip, and at the extremity of the lawn, he perceived the cottage of the good Derviſe of the Groves.

The Sultan ſtood ſome time amazed, not confidering that his walk had been circular, and that he was again returned round to the lawn which he had left; but he was ſatisfied of the deception, when he obſerved on one ſide of the lawn, the bench which they had firſt paſſed, without being acquainted with the virtues of him to whom it was dedicated.

I ſee, ſaid the good Derviſe to him, that you are reſolved I ſhall not forget my friend, whom I have placed under yonder ſpreading cedar of Lebanon, firſt in my eſteem, though laſt in the order of our walk. But here is alſo one, under this dark and majeſtic corktree, whom even Adhim, our Sultan, would rejoice to know. Nael Ecaf, the friendly and the upright; in juſt integrity of heart and ſteady virtue ſecond to none.

Nor is Talpar the mild and affable to be forgotten: nor the tender bounteous heart of Gapſac, ever ſmiling on his friend: or the noble ſpirit of Eirruc, indefatigable in his generous attachments; theſe each doth Phefoj

ac-

acknowledge as his friends, and holds their kindness as Alla's choicest blessing; who gave us social virtue, that in some degree we might experience heaven's holiest attribute, unbounded love.

The next feat, said Mirglip, passing onward, is unworthy of our good Dervise's notice.

What, replied Phesoj Ecneps smiling, shall I forget my son-in-law, whom I have placed under this shady and elegant tulip-tree? No, kind stranger, this tree is dedicated to the memory of my dear Mirglip; and see how I have suited the temple to the inhabitant; how open and expanded are the leaves of this tree, like the generous actions of him they are designed to represent; how noble and erect, and yet how pleasing; the stem, like the resolute virtues of the affable Mirglip; and see, to mark him more, how exactly are the leaves of this tree indented.

Adhim smiled at the cheerful sallies of the good Dervise; and walking forward toward an acacia—To whom, said the disguised Sultan, is this airy tree dedicated, and whom are we to recollect under its shade?

One, said Phesoj, who is like that tree, both pleasing and agreeable, while the sun-shine of life is upon him; but when the clouds arise, and the winds prevail, the acacia is not more torn and broken with the blast, than Maroh is by the violence of passion; yet who is free from weakness, or released from error; who can, through every scene of life, with

action

action juſt, and manner blamelefs, fupport the perfect character of faultleſs man?

If ſuch there be, continued the good Dervife, going up to the wide ſpreading cedar, and bowing before the feat, here, O ſtranger, ſhall we find the picture: Yes, friend of my boſom, bright example whom I wiſh to copy; holy Dervife of Sumatra! thou art he whom Genius with her choiceſt ſtores hath not honoured more, than virtue hath adorned with every godlike quality of mind; to thee I look, as to the ſpring and fountain of all the knowledge I enjoy; but chiefly haſt thou taught my wondering foul the mighty depths of Alla's law; raiſed and inſtructed my darkened fight, and o'er my wandering thoughts caſt all the amiable light of heavenly love. But who can paint the various virtues of thy foul, or give thy full idea to the admiring world, as parent, huſband, friend; as citizen of earth; as worſhipper of Alla, or teacher of mankind? Though fraught with all the uſeful knowledge of the world, yet eafy, gracious, and mild, you ſeem to learn from thoſe, whom you with ſweet complacency inſtruct. Nor, though by every good man loved, admired, and reverenced, can pride overwhelm thy modeſty of thought!

What, faid Adhim ſtarting, who is this of whom you ſpeak in ſuch fond raptures? By Mirglip's fame I firſt was rouzed to love of virtue, and looked on him as the great pattern of fuperior excellence, but he ſtill onward led me, and defcribed the temperate leſſons of his father Phefoj Ecneps, as the feed from whence

his

virtues sprung. And now, that I attendant watch thy much instructive speech, thou again dost raise my fancy upward to the pious Dervise of Sumatra's rocks.

And he, said the good Dervise, Phesoj Ecneps, were he here, would raise thy admiring passions higher still, and fix them on that God, whose worship he best knows, and best can teach mankind.

Mirglip was alike struck with the astonishment of Adhim, and the friendship of the good Dervise, and he every moment expected, that in the midst of his emotions, the disguised Sultan would discover his quality to Phesoj Ecneps.

The sun now had nearly attained the summit of his course, when the Dervise led his company from the cedar to his homely cottage, where, after a frugal meal, they retired to their repose.

The evening was spent, like the morning, in viewing the delightful prospects around the cottage of the Dervise, and sometimes resting on the seats which he had placed in the different parts of the country for the reception of his guests.

But each seat supplied the good Dervise with an opportunity of inculcating some moral or religious truth, or holding to the view of his pupils some eminent example of virtue or friendship: sometimes firing their emulous souls with a description of public patriots, and then, at others, recommending the amiable patterns of private and domestic virtue; among the latter, none was more engaging than the character of the mild and blameless Stevar, to whose memory the good Dervise had erected a seat among his departed friends.

Stevar, said Phesoj Ecneps, though bred where virtue more is blasted by the rude attack of sin, than countenanced or cherished, yet, amidst the boisterous elements of wind and seas, preserved an heart untainted with his comrades vices; nor clime, nor custom, could pervert his honest soul; nor specious argument, nor certain prospect of unbounded wealth, could shake his firm unalterable virtue.

The remembrance of the tender Stevar drew tears of friendship from the Dervise and his son-in-law, while Adhim, who never in his court had experienced the amiable effects of that social passion, gave thanks to Alla, who had kindly introduced him to those who were thus capable of elevating his nature, and giving him an higher relish of life, than the pompous luxuries of the court of Persia could teach him.

Several weeks passed thus agreeably, and the Sultan was every day so much enamoured with the delightful recess of the good Dervise, that he had little desire to return to his palace at Orez: however, the more he admired the lessons of virtue, the more he saw the necessity of putting her maxims in practice, where providence had placed him as a light to others; and he was about to disclose himself to the good Dervise, and require his further counsel in the arduous affairs of public justice, when an hasty mes-

messenger arrived in the Grove, where the family of Phesoj Ecneps was retired.

This messenger was no other than Bereddan, the son of the emir Holam, who, in the garb of a poor peasant, had wandered from Raglai in search of his Master.

Ah! said the Sultan, starting, who art thou, O young man, why art thou clothed in these mean garments? and why doth thy face betray so much anxiety of heart?

Alas, answered Bereddan, once Lord of all thy slaves, but now a traitor deemed in his own realms; flight only can preserve my royal master from the fury of his usurper, Lemack, who hath bribed the tribes of Xeri, and the captains of thine host, to call him Sultan of Persia. The cities of Raglai groan under the tyrannies of thy viziar, while a chosen set of villains, the creatures of Lemack, were, four days past, commanded to seek thee in these Groves, and bring thy head a tribute to their proud usurper. One of their number, repenting of his intended crime, came hastily to me, and told me, ere an hour was passed, the troops to which he belonged were ordered to surround my father's dwelling; and, having made him their guide to you, my Lord, they were to strike off his head, with the head of my Sultan, and bring them both to Lemack's court at Orez.

Astonished at the vile command, I called a peasant into my father's palace; and, changing garments with him, while Holam escaped in a different disguise, I bid him make what use he pleafed of my more dangerous trappings; and, mounted on an Arabian courfer, I rode both day and night to fave my royal Mafter's life. The fleet and noble beaft bore me with what fpeed he could, till I arrived within two leagues of this habitation, where, fainting through lofs of ftrength, I was conftrained to leave him, and have happily explored this deep recefs, which, with all its fecrecy, can never long hide my Prince from Lemack's malice.

The aftonifhment of Adhim, the Sultan, was not greater at the recital of Bereddan's tale, than was the wonder of the good Dervife, when he perceived that he had been entertaining the Sultan of Perfia in his humble cottage; he fell immediately at the feet of Adhim, and befought his pardon for the boldnefs of his fpeech; but the generous Sultan, feeing him on the earth, ftooped to raife him up, and affured him he fhould ever hold him chief in his efteem.

A hollow noife, like the feet of horfes hafting through the wood, increafed the confternation of Adhim and his friends; and they all advifed him to ftrike through the moft unfrequented paths, and conceal himfelf in fome remote part of the foreft, till the rebel troops fhould be withdrawn from the Groves and country which furrounded the good Dervife Phefoj Ecneps.

The love of life, faid Adhim, is fmall inducement to my flight, which were I unprepared to lofe, when fate fhall take it, I were indeed unworthy of a crown, and moft unfit to ftand upon the tottering verge of power;

but to desert my station, or yield to evil when virtue bids me draw the avenging steel of justice, this were baser flight than to avoid prevailing multitudes, and hide me for a time from superior malice; wherefore, friends, adieu, and Heaven grant my present flight bring future victory and peace to Persia!

Thus spake the monarch, and hasted from the presence of his friends, while Bereddan and Mirglip were disputing which ought to follow their Lord, and which remain with the good Dervise of the Groves. At length, Bereddan prevailed on Mirglip to remain with Phesoj Ecneps and his wife Nourenhi, and the son of the Emir endeavoured to follow the footsteps of his wandering Lord.

Adhim flew swiftly through the walks of Phesoj Ecneps to the neighbouring woods, where, penetrating into the thickest part of the forest, he wandered onward, but not without frequent alarms from the wild beasts that surrounded him.

At the close of evening he entered a deep valley, sheltered on all sides with noble and majestic cedars; and on the foot of a mountain found a small opening, which led him under its side.

Dubious of his course, he knew not whether he might safely enter the cavern or not, as it was probable some beast of the forest did use it as its den.

In the midst of his doubt he heard a voice calling unto him,

" Adhim! thou Lord of Persia, fear not!"

The voice from the cavern did rather increase the dread of Adhim, than encourage him to enter, and he assayed to run from its mouth, when a small figure appeared at its entrance.

Adhim, said Nadan, fear not, I am Nadan, the guardian of this forest, and the friend of virtue.

Whate'er thou art, said Adhim, if thy heart is warmed by virtue's sacred flame, thou canst not deal inhospitably by a stranger, though by thy speech, the wretched Adhim is no stranger to thee.

Adhim, indeed, said Nadan, is wretched, and though deserving of compassion, yet not free from error: born for thy people's happiness, thy noble heart did much mistake its pleasures, when it sought renown and comfort in the deep dug quarry, or the mouldering turret; these can no more ennoble man, than may the barren towery rock boast more utility than the fertile vale: be useful, and be great! From hence alone can justice raise thy fame, and millions bless thy fostering care; from hence alone can spring the heart-felt pleasures of a noble mind; which never, unless in blessing others, can be blest itself. Survey the wide extended earth, its steep formed rocks, and mountains raised beyond the clouds; yet these, tremendous to a human eye, are to the globe, no more than insects on the rind of yon majestic cedar; what then are all the labours of thy puny race, unless some future good to man do sanctify the builder's toil? What, but the weak effect of blind erroneous pride, mistaking both the means and end of what it aims to compass? Pride, indeed, directed to its proper object, is noble; or rather, to form my speech in fitter terms, I should call it emulation, and the brave spirit of a godlike soul, which stirs your race to every exercise of virtue; which marks the life of him who wears it, with distinguished honour, and gives mankind that best of characters, a virtuous patriot. For, think not, Sultan, that in the sequestered vale alone, dwells virtue, and her sweet companion with extensive eye, mild, affable benevolence: no, the first great gift we can bestow on others, is a good example; and he, who in his private life doth combat every duty, and lives at variance with domestic virtue, shall vainly ape the generous figure of his country's patriot; for what are the blessings of society, but those, which in a lesser scale we meet at home, peace, honour, faith, and love? Will he then, Prince, who gives up these within his house, cherish and extend their influence abroad? Or can the man who rives a parent's heart, and curses those whom first he's bound to bless, be ever deemed a friend sincere by those he knows not? Sooner shall the stork, leaving its nest, regardless of the calls its little offspring vainly utter to demand its care, roam to some distant rock, and nurse officiously the eagle's brood: sooner shall man stab man to feed the hungry lion's mouth, and call his murder, charity.

Then learn, the first advance to real fame is private virtue; which, though rooted in domestic love, must yet extend its branches 'till it reach the farthest boundaries of nature.
Hence

Hence springs temperance in yourself, to others justice. Hence, the sweet calm of an approving conscience, more valuable than the loud applause of tumult or of multitudes.

Nor yet, O Prince, despise the voice of fame; which, though o'erbearing in its first career, grows calm as it extends, and mellows into truth; 'tis noble to deserve applause, and he who scorns the censure of mankind, is more the slave of sullen pride, than conscious of desert: the best may pity, when deluded men affront the virtue which deserves their praise; but fools alone deride the public clamours of misguided subjects, whom it were better far by mildness to convince, than by neglect enrage.

Noble stranger, answered Adhim, I admire thy gentle and deserved reproofs, and doubt not but some superior being animates thy frame.

I am, indeed, said Nadan, of that celestial race, which watches o'er the actions of mankind; who may advise, but cannot force the human will. But, Prince, a while forget the base pursuit of Lemack and his ruffians; to-night within this cavern rest your wearied limbs, secure from danger or surprize; for this retreat is impervious to all, but those who are the friends of virtue.

Thus saying, the Genius Nadan led the Sultan Adhim into his cavern, which, though narrow in its entrance, was within both beautiful and spacious.

Elegant spars and stones, polished by nature, formed the inside of the cavern, which was enlightened by a magnificent diamond that hung in the middle, and which reflected its bright lustre on the stones around it.

Nadan set before his guest the fruits of the forest, and entertained him with his conversation, so that the Sultan seemed still to be in the company of the good Dervise of the Groves.

My Sultan, said Nadan, has been misled by his courtiers. Alla, O Adhim, gave thee the command of his faithful people, the inhabitants of Persia, and thou hast given thine inheritance to another, to one who was unworthy of the seat beneath thee, yet hast thou exalted him above thyself: he who seeth only through a favourite's eye, shall soon have no other sight to guide his ignorant uninstructed will; the counsel of the wise and good is a Prince's best security; yet even the best counsellor shall not always advise what is right, but in the multitude of sages is the truth. 'Tis not the sun, though glorious in his course; 'tis not the air, though sweet and salubrious; 'tis not the earth, though the great womb of nature; 'tis not the water, though refreshing and cooling; 'tis neither of these alone which giveth life and health to the corn, but all, in their several degrees, combine to form the blade, and fill the bursting seed.

But, continued the Genius, those limbs unused to toil, require repose; and see, Adhim, at the extremity of my cavern are the sofas of rest.

The Sultan obeyed the Genius, although his mind was desirous of still further converse,

and

A. Walker del.   Isaac Taylor sculp.

Avillm and Kaphira in the Forest of Gorvou.

and extended his wearied limbs upon the sofas of Nadan.

The sun, which, at the first approach of day, cast its bright beams into the cavern of Nadan, awakened the Sultan, and he sprang upward, revived by the wholsome entertainment of the Genius, and searched for him in the cavern, that he might thank his benefactor.

But Adhim, having in vain sought for the friendly Genius, issued out of the cavern, and began his course toward the city of Raglai, directing his steps by the sun.

The Sultan travelled all day, and at night he ascended a broad spreading palm, and rested on his boughs.

Adhim continued his journey two days more, subsisting on wild fruits; and at noon he rested under the shade of the trees of the forest, and at night slept upon the wide extended branches.

On the fourth day as he finished his repast, and was about to compose himself on a bed of leaves, he heard a rustling among the trees, and starting up, he perceived a female walking in the solitary paths of the wood.

The sight of the female stirred up the passions of Adhim, but his heart beat with double violence, when he perceived the form of the beauteous fair one, was as the form of Nourenhi, the wife of Mirglip.

Ah! said the panting Sultan, dost thou wander, O elegant Nourenhi, among these secreted paths? Dost thou seek me in the forest? Dost thou force me to thy irresistless charms?

charms? Then, justice, sleep, and passion, lead the way; nature is frail, and thou with a new blaze of beauty dost call me forth to love.

Yet hold, O trembling Adhim, stop thy forward limbs, while virtue yet commands them, nor yield thy body up a prey to violence and base ingratitude: thy pleasure will be fleeting like the passing clouds, and mixed with passion, cruelty, and horror; then shame, with all her stings and dark remorse succeeds; thy friend distressed, thyself abandoned, and life's fair blossom nipped by cankered thoughts, and conscience keen remonstrance: but how to move from such a scene of beauty! These sluggard limbs rebel, and every passion urges to possession: Ah! Adhim, thou art but half converted by the Dervise good example, or Nadan's firmer speech; to thee the base usurper Lemack is a saint, and thou dost seek to turn thy Mirglip's only subject from her loyalty.

As passion and honour thus took alternate possession of the breast of Adhim, he observed the fair one marked his advance, but seemed not fearful of his approach.

This rekindled the fires of his heart, and he ran, and fell at the feet of the lovely female.

O Nourenhi, said the admiring Adhim, fly from the base Adhim, who, forgetful of himself, of Mirglip, and the good Dervise, doth wish his nobleness of heart had never given thee from his longing arms. Ah! did I call it nobleness, to yield to the slave Mirglip such

grace

grace and elegance of form, as nature made to bless a sovereign's love! No, by my soul, 'twas basely done, to sacrifice thy beauties to the cold dull dictates of that phantom justice, which, when rigidly exerted, doth rather turn to injury than blessing.

Ah, continued the Sultan, pausing, see Nadan! Phesoj Ecneps calls! See, Mirglip bares his bleeding breast, and warns me to desist! And, oh! methinks the gracious Alla too looks down upon me, and awed with terrors, and with vengeful thunder, writes his perfect law in vivid flashes on the clouds. I yield, I yield, O holy spirits of my friends, and thou far holier God, I yield! O frame not such tremendous vengeance for a worm, but spare, and I obey!

The beauteous female was astonished at the prostrate Sultan, who having caught the hem of her garment, held it while he spake.

Whate'er thou art, said she, O stranger, (whom, by thy speech and nobleness of soul, I judge no despicable parent claims) fly swiftly from this dangerous place, where dark invisible spells surround thee, and where Falri holds his uncontrolled reign. But if I judge aright, you called yourself the royal Adhim, or fancy did beguile my credulous ear. Alas, Sir, here too doth vicious Lemack oft resort, and such sad scenes of horrors have these eyes beheld, as make me tremble at your fate, should Falri or his friend discover where you wander.

Who then, said Adhim in amaze, art thou, O daughter of the earliest light! for as I gaze, new beauties break upon me, and you seem most fair to make your friend most miserable. Art thou not Nourenhi, the wife of Mirglip, the daughter of the Dervise of the Groves?

I am, replied the fair one, daughter of the Dervise of the Groves, the sister of Nourenhi, the friend of Mirglip, the wretched, lost, unfortunate Kaphira!

Then, answered Adhim, O holy Prophet, I do thank thee, my friend is satisfied, and I am blessed. Yes, fair Kaphira, continued he, I am Adhim, once Lord of Persia, but now thy humblest slave; and rather had I live with thee in this dark gloomy forest, than again ascend my throne, and leave thee to another.

Alas, Sir, answered the lovely Kaphira, my deep concern lest Falri should approach, does make me hear you with an aching heart.

Sure, lovely maid, answered the Sultan, if thou canst escape his rage, Adhim has but little to fear from this vile sorcerer.

Noble Sir, replied Kaphira, my tale might seem too tedious, to gain the attention of a monarch's ear; and at present we are unsafe, as much I fear some secret spies do watch your footsteps; for, on every tree hang some foul imps of Falri's, ready to execute his horrid purpose.

As the fair Kaphira spoke, Adhim looked around, and saw the bloated Falri approach, surrounded by satyrs and monsters of the forest,
the

the sight of whom created both horror and disgust.

If, said the resolute Sultan, drawing his sabre, I cannot conquer, yet to yield were base: wherefore, fear not, adorable Kaphira, for while this arm retains its wonted strength, nor Falri, nor his vile associates, shall approach to hurt thee.

I would to Heaven, O kind Sir, answered Kaphira, you were as well secured as I am: But see, the monsters stop, as if they saw you not, and seem to wind toward the left, and seek the cave of their beastly master.

By my honour, said the Sultan, their base neglect bears harder on my pride, than would their utmost malice, had they dared my fury: what can this mean? Is every feature then of royalty destroyed, that the fell ruffians knew not whom they sought? or feared the cowards to meet an angry and offended Prince?

Majestic Adhim, answered Kaphira sweetly, thy form, alas, would instantly betray its noble master, did not some secret power defend thee.

Perhaps, said the Sultan, recollecting himself, I derive my safety from this curious ring, which, on the morning, when I waked on the sofas of the Genius Nadan, I found upon my finger.

Kind Genius Nadan, answered Kaphira, hast thou too given thy just protection to this noble Prince? Yes, royal Sir, continued the fair one, shewing him a ring like that he wore, these both, I am assured, are Nadan's
pre-

presents, and we are safe alike from Falri and his charms.

If such security attend us, answered the Sultan Adhim, permit me to ask, by what strange misfortune were you brought into these confines of the cave of Falri?

Prince, answered the fair Kaphira, as I was walking in the Grove of my good father the Dervise Phesoj Ecneps, I observed a small golden ball before me in the path: pleased with the shining novelty, I endeavoured to take it up; but as I stooped, it rolled forward before me, and I, eager to obtain it, followed it beyond the limits of my father's Grove.

No sooner had I set my foot upon the plain, which is the boundary of the Grove, than I perceived the ball to swell; startled at the sight, I endeavoured to run back into the Grove, but either fear or magic deprived me of motion, and I was constrained to stand, and view the further wonders before me.

The ball continued to swell for several minutes, till it hid the distant hills from my sight; when, bursting with a violent noise, it flew into ten thousand pieces, and discovered a bloated, ferret-eyed wretch, mounted upon a bristly boar.

The wild intemperate love of novelty, said the wretch to me, has ever been the ruin of your sex: at first, allured by shining trifles, they pursue in wantonness, and inattentive follow beyond the prudent limits of paternal care. While Kaphira was contented

tented with her father's Grove, Falri in vain attempted to molest her; but now fate has resigned thee to my arms, and thou shalt bless my nuptial bed with many a monster like myself.

I shrieked aloud at the voice of Falri, but in vain; the monster descending from his beast, seized me round the waist, and putting me upon the bristly boar, he seated himself behind me, and we were borne away with such swiftness, that I knew not how we went.

In a few hours, we entered this forest, and through winding paths were brought in view of Falri's filthy cave.

New horrors seized me at the sight of such variety of filthiness, which were still increased, when Falri bid me welcome to his native palace, and told me, the marriage rites were needless, as he doubted not his love would last, at least as long as mine.

As we entered the cave of Falri, I was surprised to see a little personage standing at the upper end, and supposing it was some relation of the sorcerer's, I cast my eyes on the ground, and would not look upon him.

Fair slave, said Falri, as we entered, to me, for I allow no higher character to your sex, than that of ministering to our pleasures, here you are secure, as by my magic power, I do forbid your regress from this forest, unless Falri approve your flight.

Thunderstruck at the words of Falri, and at his countenance, which shone with beastly lust,

lust, I sighed, and returned no answer to his imperious commands.

Fair Kaphira, said the little personage, fear not, I am the Genius Nadan, and no relation of Falri's, as you suppose. I am here invisible to that beastly sorcerer, neither can he hear the words of my mouth. I cannot, indeed, release you, because your own intemperate curiosity has misled you; but since you erred in innocence, I can baffle the design of Falri.

Here, continued he, extending his hand, put on this ring, and you shall be invisible to Falri and his accursed friends, so long as you remain in this forest of the inchanter.

I instantly took the ring from the gentle Nadan, with thankful eyes, and fixing it on my finger, I perceived the countenance of Falri to change.

Ah, said he, art thou fled, proud child of Phesoj Ecneps? then are my enchantments vain, and the power which I worship is accursed.

No, answered the Genius Nadan, thou accursed slave, Kaphira is held in the forest of Falri by the sorceries of thy art; but she shall, if she please, be ever invisible to thee and thy friends, so long as thou dost detain her in this forest.

The sorcerer enraged, felt about the cavern, hoping to secure me; but I easily eluded his search, and walked out into the forest; where I have supported myself till this time on the wild fruits of the place, and have too

fre-

frequently been witness of the debaucheries and immorality of its profane and wicked inhabitants.

Beauteous Kaphira, said the Sultan Adhim, I pity your misfortunes, nor am I able at present to relieve them; you, doubtless, have heard my unhappy fate from Falri and his crew; who, as Nadan informed me, has ever been the friend of Lemack, my deceitful viziar; and if it suit you to rest under this ancient palm, you shall be acquainted with such particulars concerning Nourenhi, Mirglip, and Phesoj Ecneps, your honoured father, as will doubtless be pleasing to one so nearly interested in their fortunes.

The Sultan Adhim then informed his beauteous friend of Mirglip's fame, of Nourenhi's captivity, of the fortunate issue of her love, and of his secret expedition to the Groves of the good Dervise: and having finished his relation, and asked the fair Kaphira's permission to love her with undissembled affection, he set forward to the city of Raglai and the towers of Orez.

But the night advancing, he was obliged to rest again in the forest; which gave him an opportunity of recollecting that his ring might possibly be of no further service to protect him, when he was past the confines of the forest of Falri.

This reflection made him resolve to stain his face with some berries, to cut his beard like a Calendar, and to procure, in the suburbs of the city, a garment suitable to the profession which he had assumed.

As

As the disguised Sultan entered the city, he perceived a crowd, and mixing with the multitude, he saw at a distance the public cryer.

Friend, said he to the by-stander, what doth this cryer offer to the public?

Ten thousand sequins, answered the man, to him who will bring the head of the traitor Adhim, to our Lord the Sultan Lemack.

Alas! answered the Sultan, when I last visited your city, Adhim was Sultan, how then is he become a traitor?

It is well, replied the man, that a friend of Adhim hears you talk thus; half what you have said would have cost you your life, had any of the emissaries of Lemack heard you.

How then dare you confess, answered the Sultan, that you are the friend of Adhim?

I dare not, answered the man, hold farther conversation with you here; but if you will follow me, and submit to the terms which I shall require, you shall hear more than you imagine.

The disguised Sultan rejoiced at the fortunate event, which brought him acquainted with one who seemed so ready to serve him though unknown, and hasted after the stranger through several streets and lanes.

At length the stranger stopped at a baker's shop.

Here, whispered he, friend of Adhim, thou shalt have security and ease. Enter fearless, and partake of such poor entertainment as I have; while I unravel to you some mysteries, which will surprise and rejoice you.

The

The Sultan entered with pleasure the house of the baker, who set before him some cakes and sherbet, and begged of him to eat freely, for his company was sufficient recompence for what he should consume.

Adhim, supposing he should shortly be able to reward the baker very amply for his services, eat heartily of what was set before him.

Our good Sultan Adhim, said the baker, as they sat together, had won the hearts of all his subjects; and the whole city laments the tyrannies of Lemack.

Was Adhim, then, answered the disguised Sultan, so much beloved?

You know but little of Adhim the Magnificent, answered the other, to ask such a question.

Yes, replied the Sultan, I think I know him now; though I confess I knew him but lately.

And where then, replied the baker elated, where is our beloved Sultan concealed?

I perceive, continued he, I am deceived in you, Sir; I thought to have communicated somewhat to you, but you are better able to inform me. Now, by my faith, Sir, you must bring me to our royal master, that I may honour him as I ought; and doubtless, many will be found in the city, who will be happy in falling prostrate before him.

Perhaps, said the disguised Sultan, ere long we may be able to shew him to his injured subjects: but at present, I do long to know what numbers espouse his cause, and wish him again on the Persian throne?

It

It is enough, replied the baker, I will go and bring several with me, who are as much the friends of Adhim as myself. In the mean time, kind stranger, solace yourself here in my house; and believe me, I am truly happy in meeting with one of your way of thinking.

The baker then hasted out of his house, and left the Sultan, surprised at his free and voluntary offer, to support the cause of a Prince, whom perhaps he had never seen.

I was wrong, said the Sultan to himself, that I did not at once discover myself to this baker; he frankly and openly assured me he was my friend; why then is the spirited Adhim more close and mean than an illiterate and narrow bred peasant? But I will, however, let the good man enjoy the first discovery; I will take him apart from the friends he shall bring with him, and he shall have the honour of introducing his sovereign to his faithful subjects; and if ever I again ascend the Persian throne, not Mirglip, nor Phesoj Ecneps shall enjoy a seat above this honest baker.

It was almost night before the baker returned to his shop: the Sultan saw him coming with a crowd at his heels; and he blamed him in his heart, that he had thus imprudently subjected his friends to the suspicious eyes of the vassals of Lemack.

The baker entering his house, enquired for his friend, the stranger, whom he brought with him in the morning; and Adhim hasted to meet him at the threshold.

There

There, my friends, said the baker, this is the man who was born to make a holiday in Raglai; seize him, continued he, O ye guards of Lemack, and carry him before our Sultan, as one who dares prefer the slothful Adhim to Lemack the Lord of Persia.

Adhim was thunderstruck at the perfidy of the baker, and the guards instantly seized on him, and having fettered him with heavy irons, dragged him toward the towers of Orez.

The crowd gathered as he passed along. Whom have we here? said they: A friend, answered the guards, of rebels and traitors, whom to-morrow's sun will, at its first appearance, behold on the public scaffold of execution.

The guards having conducted Adhim to the palace, enquired for their Sultan; but Lemack, who was solacing himself in the seraglio, ordered the prisoner to be cast that night into the dungeon at the foot of the rock, and the next morning to be brought before him.

The captive Sultan entered the gloomy dungeon with firmness and intrepidity; and the guards having chained him to the wall, barred up the prison doors and retired.

Monarch of Asia! Light of mankind! Terror of the earth! Glory of the East! said Adhim to himself, awake! Put on thy frowns, and make the nations shake; open thy mouth, and be thy speech a law; nod, and let the inhabitants of Persia fall prostrate at thy feet. Yet, hush, thou Man of might, Sultan of Persia, beware, lest some base peasant

fant come, and with a feigned tale, delude thy ready ears, and snatch the glories of thy kingdom from thee! Oh, Prophet, said the enraged Sultan, starting! ought but this I could have borne; after having heard the wise dictates of Phesoj Ecneps; after enjoying the instruction of Nadan, the tutelary Genius of my kingdom; after the reception of a magic ring, which preserved me from the brutal force of the sorcerer Falri, and having escaped the guards of Lemack; after all this, to be cheated of every purpose, by the low cunning of a base-born peasant! O Prophet, either take from me the pride of nature, and humble my conceits, or let me perish by some glorious feat, worthy the station to which thou once hadst raised me.—Yes, said he, pausing, I will be cool; weak are these joints to work deliverance, and these limbs to gain my native freedom! Here immured, within these walls I once possessed; confined by dungeons which I raised myself; and straitened by a chain I made for others; I'll learn the weakness and the pride of man, and bear with equal temperance the evils and the smiles of life. For me the sun did rise, said Lemack; but forgot to say, for me the dungeon gaped: the fool of fortune once, like the green leaf growing on the topmost branch, I now am cast by stormy winds beneath the traveller's foot: once Lord of Persia, now an iron-fettered slave; yet even now possessed of greater liberty, than all the ancient Sultans of the East, whose mouldering dust would little more than fill the hollow turban. Peace then, thou lively spirit, which doſt guide the trifling atoms of this mortal being; the little that I am is Alla's gift; be he then Lord and chief diſpoſer of my paths.

With ſuch thoughts did Adhim calm his hot, impetuous temper, waiting with coolneſs the return of the morning, which was to bring life to others, but death to him.

But ere the moon, which glimmered through the bars on the damp walls of the mould-fretted dungeon, was fallen from its midnight watch, the Sultan heard the doors of the dungeon grate, and preſently he beheld the reflection of a light on the winding paſſage, and could diſ-tinguiſh the fall of feet treading ſoftly on the pavement. Fear for a moment poſſeſſed his breaſt, as he expected death was haſting to him before its appointed time; and his firm mind was ſcarcely recovered from the boding ſhock, when he ſaw a female enter the place where he lay, with a lamp burning in her hand.

The gloomy cavern, and the cold midnight air, had chilled the blood, and terrified the mind of the affrighted damſel, and ſhe ſtood ſhivering before the Sultan, unable to utter the motives of her viſit.

The Sultan, not leſs alarmed, though leſs fearful than before, aſked her on what er-rand ſhe came through the horrors of the night?

Firſt, ſaid the damſel kneeling, let me, O ſtranger, looſe you from theſe ignominious chains.

Upon

Upon which she took from her bosom the keys which unlocked the fetters, and released the Sultan from his confinement.

Gentle damsel, said Adhim, what means this unexpected kindness?

I am, answered she, the only daughter of Colac, the keeper of these dungeons; and I am called Kufan, because of the blackness of my eyes: but were my eyes like jet, and more brilliant than the diamond, yet never can they be fixed on a more lovely object, than on him who now stands before me.

What, said Adhim, O wretched Kufan, has none of thy father's friends demanded thee, that thou comest at midnight among these damp walls to find thy paramour, and one, or I much mistake, whom thou hast never yet seen?

O foolish young man, said she, 'tis enough for you to know, that Kufan loves, and you are happy; happy indeed! when love's the price of liberty.

Disgrace to your soft sex, said Adhim, starting from her, avaunt! for rather had I bear my chains, than meet a monster who belies her nature.

Yet, hear me, fool, said she, ere day break in upon us, and cut off all future hope.—I have the keys of every barred door which shuts you from mankind, and freedom waits without, to lead you into safety, if my love be first preferred.

I would not wish to live, said Adhim, on such mean terms: no, Kufan, base minds
alone

alone can love for profit; but thou haſt caſt thy ſex's decent virtues far away, as I have heard in Europe's colder clime, where ſome bold females walk abroad, uſurping manly vice, and caſt their nauſeous wild embrace on every paſſer by.

Then, ſaid Kufan, her eyes flaſhing with indignant malice, die, cold ſenſeleſs wretch, and cheap thy ſacrifice of life, which is already more than half extinct.

As Kufan uttered theſe words, the arched paſſages of the dungeon echoed with an uncommon noiſe.

The Sultan Adhim, conſcious of his ſituation, was vexed in his heart that he had ſuffered Kufan to unlock his fetters; and he doubted not but thoſe who were entering, would ſuppoſe that he had conſented to the damſel, who was thus manifeſtly aiding his eſcape.

In the midſt of his anxiety and diſcontent, the vile Lemack entered the dungeon, ſupported by Colac the keeper, holding a bloody cimeter in his hand.

Slave, ſaid he to Colac, where is this rebel, whom juſtice wakes to puniſh at this ſilent hour of night? Other Sultans leave the execution of their orders to the meaneſt of mankind; but they who hope to have them well performed, ſhould act the executioner themſelves. Yet, ah! continued Lemack ſtarting, whom have we here? Damned Colac, doſt thou ſolace thus thy priſon gueſts, and makeſt a ſeraglio of my dungeon!

VOL. II. P Colac,

Colac, no less surprised at seeing his daughter with his prisoner than Lemack, was about to answer him, when the tyrant struck his cimeter into his heart, and fell with the murdered Colac on the ground.

Kufan screamed at the sight, for Kufan loved her dear parent with a noble fondness; and though vicious in her mind, was yet tender and grateful to the father of her life.

Lemac struggled on the pavement to recover his feet, but the fumes of wine overpowered him, and in broken accents he stammered forth execrations on the author of his misfortune.

Adhim, perceiving no one came to the assistance of Lemack, seized the cimeter which the tyrant had plunged into the breathless body of Colac, and was about to strike it into the heart of Lemack; but seeing him breathless and extended, the Sultan forbore: No, said he, thou art not fit to die, nor would it well become a noble spirit to finish that little of thee which vice hath spared. Then seizing on Kufan, as she knelt before her expiring parent,

Damsel, sa'd he, I admire your filial piety and tenderness, but the time is big with strange events, and will not yield her precedence even to nature; wherefore rise, and help me to drag this unwieldy corpse to yonder chains; and hear me, damsel, be obedient, and I will pardon and reward thee; for know, O Kufan, it is Adhim that directs your arm.

Kufan, astonished at the words of Adhim, fell at his feet, and was about to reply; but he obliged her to arife, and by degrees they pulled along the ftupified body of Lemack, and fecured him with fetters and chains; then taking off his royal veftments, Adhim put them on himfelf; and commanding the virgin to continue in the dungeon, without making any alarm, he paffed through the arched paffages, locking and barring the doors, and afcended into the court of the palace, with the bloody cimeter in his hand.

What Adhim expected, came to pafs; none dared meet him, as they fuppofed it was the drunken, blood-thirfty tyrant; and he arrived at the feraglio unmolefted, where he beheld feveral females weltering in their blood.

Thefe, faid he to himfelf, are the victims of Lemack's rage; but I muft yet diffemble.

The Sultan then afcended the royal couch, and having covered himfelf, he ftamped on the ground, to call the eunuchs before him.

It was fome time before any durft venture into the chamber, fuch dread had they of Lemack's drunken madnefs; but after a time, fuppofing him fallen afleep, the chief of the eunuchs entered the chamber.

Abelidah, faid Adhim to him, counterfeiting the voice of Lemack, call Holam, Pherizar, Humlack, Eupordi, and Melan before me.

Abelidah, the chief of the eunuchs, was aftonifhed at the commands of the fham Lemack, efpecially as three of thofe emirs whom he had mentioned, had fled as foon as Lemack was proclaimed Sultan.

However,

However, the prudent eunuch supposed remonstrances would be in vain, wherefore he sent for Pherizar and Eupordi, and acquainted them with the Sultan's order.

Pherizar and Eupordi were thunderstruck at the command; and they doubted not, but the prisoner who was betrayed by the baker, had discovered their secret attachment to their lawful Prince.

Wherefore the good old emirs came trembling into the chamber, and fell prostrate before the royal couch.

Abelidah, said Adhim, still counterfeiting the voice of Lemack, withdraw with thy fawning mutes and eunuchs.

Abelidah obeyed, and left Pherizar and Eupordi alone with the Sultan.

Adhim then rose from his couch, and discovered to his wondering friends their long lost Sultan.

For some moments the emirs gazed in silent transports, and knew not how to give credit to their eyes; but recovering from their astonishment, they did obeisance to their royal Sultan.

Pherizar, said the Sultan Adhim, it is not now a time to unfold to you the miracle which brought me here: we must be instant in seizing the captains of the army, who first supported Lemack, and the viziars of the court, who have basely deserted me, to fawn upon a vile usurper. Give me then, faithful emir, the names of these rebels, that we may, still counterfeiting Lemack, send for them into the palace, and secure them with those chains they meant to fix on us.

Pherizar,

Pherizar, in obedience to his Sultan, gave in a list of the ringleaders of the rebellion, and Abelidah was called in, and sent to bring them singly before the counterfeit Lemack.

The viziars and captains each expecting some further preferment, obeyed with great alacrity the royal summons; and as they entered, the emirs seized on them, and led each of them through a back way, into a separate place of security.

The first movers of the sedition being confined, Adhim discovered himself to Abelidah and his eunuchs, and commanded the trumpets to sound, and the criers to go forth, and proclaim the arrival of Adnim, the lawful Sultan of Persia.

This was done so suddenly, that the soldiers who had lost their captains, knew not which way to move; but throwing down their arms, many ran out of the city, while others repaired with great submission to the outer gates of the palace.

Pherizar and Eupordi went out to meet the penitents; and putting themselves at their head, they seized on all the strong places of the city, and sent around to the friends of Adhim, to repair under their standards.

The citizens, in general, rejoiced at the happy exchange; and those who were as wickedly inclined as the tyrant Lemack, were obliged to join the general voice, and cry, "Long live Adhim the Magnificent, our lawful Sultan!"

The imans, who had been driven out of their mosques by the tyrannies of Lemack, entered them again with joy, and gave praise to Alla, for the return of their Sultan.

Pherizar was now sent to the good Dervise of the Groves, requesting his attendance, with the excellent Mirglip.

When the faithful emir reached the Grove, he found the mild Phesoj Ecneps weak and infirm, and with difficulty brought him forward in a palanquin towards the towers of Orez, so that the emir feared, they should not reach Raglai by the tenth day, which was appointed for the trial of Lemack.

As soon as Pherizar was gone forth, couriers were dispatched also, with all haste, to the different provinces, to order their respective governors to repair to court, and men well affected to Adhim were sent in their stead; and this was done so quickly, that the Sultan had placed proper men all round his empire, before the news of his return was known.

These things being well executed, Adhim committed the keys of the dungeon to Eupordi, and informed him of Lemack's situation, and the assistance he had received from Kufan; commanding him to leave Lemack fettered, and to bring Kufan before him.

The damsel, who had received no nourishment during her confinement, which lasted till the evening of the day following her midnight adventure, was weak, and faint with hunger and terror, and the presence of Eupordi added to her fright, so that she fell motionless at his feet.

Eupordi seeing Kufan fall, ordered his attendant guards to raise and support her; then
going

going forward toward the usurper Lemack, who lay snoring on the ground, he caused double chains to be fastened on him.

Lemack awaked not till the chains were hung around him; when, shaking his huge corpse, and grunting forth a groan, he essayed to rise, but found himself pinioned to the earth.

"In what cursed region am I wandering, said he, rubbing his eyes? and who are these imps before me, who seem to personate the spirits of the damned? Surely death is passed, and hell awake! Ah! I shall eat no more! nor taste again the luscious grape! I must exchange the soft carpet, for this damp, slippery cave! and for the lively female, these cold, adamantine chains! O Alla, never did I pray before, but give me life and luxury again, and I will worship thee!

Gods! continued he, looking on the emir, is not that Eupordi? whom I meant, had life, dear precious life, been given me but a day, to have sacrificed for his cursed rebellion. Art thou too here, said he, cold canting emir, loyal slave! and could not Adhim and his virtues save thee! Then virtue was a farce as e'er I thought it, and he the wisest that made his paradise on earth. Come, friend of priests, religious, good Eupordi; come, learn to curse of me, and laugh at holy cheats, who have deprived thee of life's blessing, and now do leave thee here, a prey to this dark grave.

Blasphemous slave, answered Eupordi, thou art yet alive, if that be called life which thou possessest, which is indeed but life's slavery, a

fearful

fearful vassalage to disordered appetite, and craving passions; to live like thee, the drudge of luxury, were a curse, and not a blessing, a grievous burden, and no gift to be desired: but haply life with thee is short; for now our royal Master reigns again, and thou art Adhim's prisoner.

Prisoner! said Lemack confounded, his countenance falling, and his limbs convulsed with fear; righteous Eupordi! is then my royal master living, and returned to his long expecting subjects? O let me haste to kiss that garment which enrobes him, and to lick the dust which bears the pride of Persia on its surface; happy for me, my Lord again vouchsafes to rule his wide domain. Poor weak old man! the cares of state depressed my unpenetrating mind; and every day convinced me, none but our royal Master could sway with just impartial balance the royal sceptre of the Persian throne.

I now retort that canting phrase thou gavest me, said Eupordi, and from thy example judge, the vicious tyrant, when deposed, becomes a slave most abject.

Good Eupordi, replied Lemack in tears, hast thou no compassion on a fallen brother? Did I then suffer thee to live for this? O fly, kind emir, and at Adhim's feet beg mercy for thy friend.

Whatever our royal Master shall command, Eupordi must obey, said the emir; but think not that he means in secret silence to deprive thee of thy life; no, Lemack, just and noble in his soul, he has called the solemn divan,
and

and means to judge thee for thy crimes. Ten days are yet appointed to assemble the viziars and emirs to the Divan.

Then am I lost indeed, poor wretched man! said Lemack, to meet the frowns of our offended nobles, who will rejoice to spurn the man they saw with envy, favourite of our Sultan.

Speak not thus hastily, Lemack, said the emirs, of our Persian nobles: above the low conceits of envy or of malice, they will judge thee as their brother; and where doubt hesitates, there mercy shall prevail.

Thus said Eupordi, and retired, commanding the guards, who had in vain endeavoured to recover Kufan, to lay her body beside her father Colac.

Adbim, having heard the dismal tale of Kufan, ordered all funeral honours to be paid her and Colac, and continued to their family the post which the father enjoyed; commanding his treasurer, moreover, to pay the widow a thousand sequins.

In the mean time, Falri, surrounded by sorceries, had rendered the forest of Goruou impervious to the troops of Adhim, who, in the midst of his cares, had not forgotten the beauteous Kaphira; baffled by his inchantments, the Monarch wished himself to seek her in the forest; but he considered that his life was his people's, and that public utility must be preferred to private happiness.

Falri, knowing by his art the overthrow of Lemack, cursed the foolish drunkard in his mind; and he had left him to himself, to perish by the hand of Adhim, had not the success of the Sultan been a canker to his own breast.

Wherefore he resolved, by some secret contrivance, to ruin the happiness of Adhim; and as Nadan protected the Sultan from enchantment, Falri hoped to make his new fangled virtues, as he called them, the sources of his misery.

The following night he stood before Lemack in the dungeon, but the dispirited wretch could scarcely speak to his adviser Falri; and when he found the enchanter was not able to release him, he wept like an infant.

Wretched Lemack, said Falri, craft shall prevail, where force may not; did I not sacrifice Mirglip to calumny? then fear not but Adhim shall be snared by the deceits of Falri.

Thus said the sorcerer, and disclosed to Lemack the foul purpose of his heart; but Lemack, to whom revenge was of little value, when his life was forfeit, answered the sorcerer only with his groans.

On the tenth day arrived the faithful emir Pherizar, with Phesoj Ecneps the Dervise of the Groves, and the temperate Mirglip; but the good Dervise, fatigued with his journey, was unable to attend his royal Master; and when Mirglip came into the presence of Adhim, the Sultan having welcomed him to Orez, ordered him to watch his father's health, and excused every kind of attendance on himself.

The Sultan then entered the divan, and being seated on his throne, with his surrounding viziars and emirs, he commanded the
rebel

rebel Lemack to be led forth from the dungeon.

The unwieldy Lemack moved flowly through the ranks of guards, who were placed on each fide to fecure him, and his chains rattled on his limbs, as he heaved his diftempered fides with heavy fighs.

An horrid gloom o'ercaft his brow, and fear and difmay trembled on his eye-lids; foul tears ran trickling down his furrowed cheeks, and his jaw, falling from its worn-out focket, refted on his protuberant paunch.

As he came into the prefence of Adhim, he fell at the foot of the throne, and groaned for mercy, vowing everlafting fidelity to his Lord, and penitence for the crimes he had committed againft Adhim and his fubjects.

The royal Adhim, though enraged at his hypocrifies, was neverthelefs moved at his abject viziar; and in the noblenefs of his heart, he would have forgiven his crimes, had he not called the folemn Divan to judgment.

The rebellion of Lemack was too glaring to admit of any palliation; and Adhim found that none of the viziars chofe to fpeak in his behalf.

My fubjects and my fafeguard, faid the royal Adhim, fear not to fpeak in behalf of this poor prifoner; for I fwear on my fceptre, the man who pleads beft for Lemack, fhall have thanks from me.

The divan ftill continuing filent,

Then, faid Adhim, I will fpeak, and afk ye, nobles, whether this Lemack be guilty of death, who ufurped not our authority, fince it was delegated to him? and if he abused it, mine was the fault, not his.

Just and generous sovereign, answered Pherizar, more lovely to the guilty than to those who have never offended, you have called me here to speak the just sentiments of my heart; and therefore, I conceive Lemack had been acquitted by your voice, had he not publicly offered a reward for the life of his Prince.

The divan rang with applause at the words of Pherizar, for Lemack was so abhorred by the people, who knew more of his wretchedness than the generous Adhim, that the mildest of them thought his death was absolutely necessary to the general peace.

Adhim, overcome by the reasonings of his counsellors, yielded up Lemack to their will; and the wretched viziar sunk to the ground, while he heard on every side the sentence of his death pronounced.

The royal Adhim having determined the fate of Lemack, commanded him to be detained in the divan, during the trial of several innocent persons, who, in the usurpation of the viziar, had met with no redress.

The nobles in the divan were amazed to see, with what candour and perspicuity the Sultan decided; divesting himself of every prejudice, and not permitting royalty on the one hand, nor popularity on the other, to bias his judgment, or influence his decrees.

Lemack beheld these transactions with a different eye. The justice of Adhim struck the sharpest stings in his conscience; he saw with contempt,

contempt, virtue triumph, and vice abased; he saw private advantage yielding to public justice, and the law triumphant over partiality and affection.

And now the different parties were retreating, every one satisfied with the equity of their Sultan; and the public crier gave notice, that the causes were all determined, when a young man, from the extremity of the divan, called out, and desired to be heard.

The assembly were so much charmed with the address of their Sultan, who seldom before had attended the divan, but left the management of justice to Lemack (except where humour or caprice led him to be particular), that they were pleased to find there was yet another cause to be tried; wherefore, making room for the young man, they let him pass toward the foot of the throne.

The young man led in his hand a veiled virgin, and falling prostrate at the footstool of Adhim:

Pattern of every human excellence, just Lawgiver of Persia, said the young man, I beseech thy patience to hear me a few words.

I am, O Sultan of Persia, the son of a noble emir of thy court, and being smitten with the beauties of this fair damsel, I asked her consent to marry me, provided I could prevail with her father to receive me for a son-in-law. The damsel consented to the terms I proposed; and I went in search of her father, who yielded to my entreaties: and now, O Sultan, that I have done all that was required of me, the damsel refuses to go
before

before the cadi, and take me for her husband.

Damsel, said the Sultan to the virgin, who stood veiled before him, has this young man spoke the truth, or has he deceived thee into a promise?

The damsel held down her head, her hands fixed in each other, and answered nothing.

If, continued the Sultan, you make no answer, virgin, I must conceive you guilty, and enforce the promise which you seem now so unwilling to fulfil.

The damsel still continued silent, yet her breast heaved with sighs, and her knees shook with fear.

The modest distress of the virgin, said Adhim, will not suffer her to speak, and her fear arises from female delicacy. Lead her forth, young man, continued the Sultan, and let the cadi ratify your vows.

As the Sultan spake these words, the beauteous virgin fainted in the arms of the young man, and the attendants of Adhim hastening to unveil her, and give her air, discovered to the astonished Sultan the features of the long-lost Kaphira.

Adhim hasted from his throne, and was about to assist in recovering her, when, checking himself, and stopping:

Hold, said he, aloud, to himself, Sultan of Persia, forbear, for by Phesoj Ecneps' consent, by Kaphira's silence, and by thy own decree, she is the wife of another.

The Sultan Adhim spake this, with a firmness and resolution which astonished every hearer,

hearer, though they were ignorant of the cause; and as he left off speaking, he ascended the throne, commanding the eunuchs to spare no pains in succouring the beauteous Kaphira.

In the mean time, he dispatched Abelidah, the chief of the eunuchs, to request the presence of Mirglip in the divan, and as the good young man entered, Mirglip, said he, behold thy sister Kaphira!

Mirglip, elated at the words of the Sultan, ran towards his sister, who was then reviving from her faintness; and taking her from the arms of the young man, he embraced his sister Kaphira.

Kaphira looked on him with a look of tenderness, and with a deep sigh said, From whence comest thou, O Mirglip, my brother!

After a tender interview between Mirglip and Kaphira, the Sultan asked Mirglip, Whether he knew the young man who attended his sister?

Author of all my joys, answered Mirglip, I remember well the face of this noble youth, and am surprised that my Sultan recollects not the features of Bereddan the son of Holam, who came to inform you, at the Dervise's, of the rebellion of Lemack.

Just Alla, said Adhim, starting, I am indeed blind, not to acknowledge the friendly offices of Bereddan, to whose faithful services I owe my crown and life.

Bereddan, continued the Sultan, lead away the beauteous Kaphira; I ask no more; doubtless

less you have the permission of Phesoj Ecneps, and to suspect your faith were cruelty and injustice.

Indeed, replied Mirglip, he has; ten days since, the young nobleman returned to us in the Groves of my father, and told us, he had in vain followed the steps of Adhim his Sultan; but that journeying through the forest of Goruou, he had espied the fair Kaphira a prisoner to enchantment; and engaged, if my father would reward his love, to release her from the tyrannies of Falri.

The good old Dervise willingly consented, and Bereddan flew from the Groves in search of Kaphira; his success we knew not, but seeing him here with Kaphira, we doubt not but he hath well deserved the love of our sister.

The fair Kaphira looked in amaze on Mirglip as he spoke; and clasping her hands, and lifting them to heaven, O Alla, said she, defend me!

The Sultan, who would not trust his eyes toward her, fearing their well known influence, was, however, somewhat confounded at the preference which Kaphira had paid to Bereddan, after the sweet converse he had enjoyed with her in the forest; but he concluded, that gratitude, and her father's promise, had bound her to Bereddan, and he resolved to sustain the mighty shock with firmness and intrepidity.

But the resolutions of Adhim were vain; love, mighty love, possessed his frame; and

though

though his mind resolved to suffer, yet his body sunk a prey to his contending passions.

The emirs seeing their Sultan fall, crowded eagerly to release him; and Kaphira shrieked aloud at his fate, and had Bereddan suffered her, she would have ran the first to support her Lord.

By degrees the Sultan recovered, and turning toward Bereddan, Cruel emir, said he, forbear; far hence lead thy rich prize; and thou, O Prophet, learn me to forget myself and her.

The sorcerer Falri, who had personated Bereddan, to deceive the good Dervise and destroy the peace of Adhim, exulted in his success, and led away the unwilling fair one through the divan, blessing Adhim aloud for his disinterested justice.

The crowd saw with rage, the sham young emir hasting away; and had not the noble virtue of Adhim awed their minds, they had sacrificed the false Bereddan to their resentment.

As Bereddan passed along, the abject Lemack rose from the earth, whither he had cast himself after his condemnation, and turning to Adhim,

Disposer of my being, and just judge of Persia, said he, swear to forgive thy slave his iniquities, and I will unravel to thee such a scene of sorcery, as shall release Kaphira from him who now bears her away.

Speak then, viziar, said Adhim hastily, and relieve my doubts, and I swear to reward thee with thy life.

Seize

Seize on the sham Bereddan instantly, replied Lemack.

The words of Lemack were needless, for the crowd in the divan had seized him the moment Lemack began to speak.

The sorcerer Falri, perceiving that his false friend Lemack was about to betray him, began to mutter his inchantments; but he found a superior power withheld him, and the spirits who had served him, remained deaf to his secret incantations.

Instantly the Genius Nadan appeared in the divan, and turning to Adhim,

Prince, said she, fear not, for Lemack having given up Falri, his forceries will no longer protect him.

Speak then, O Lemack, said the Sultan to him, and discover to thy Prince, by what artifice has Falri prevailed on the beauteous Kaphira to listen to him!

First, answered Lemack, let these bonds be taken from me, which ill become the friend of Adhim, and the man who alone could restore Kaphira to his arms.

The spectators were enraged at the insolent change, and saw again with fear the deadly spark of malice issue from his eye, and his brows knit with surly importance.

Release him, guards, continued Adhim, but watch well his malicious cunning, lest some of my subjects curse the hour of his freedom. But hear me, wretched Lemack, said the Sultan, take heed that truth, a long neglected guest, come from thy lips.

On

On truth, said Lemack, hangs my juſt reward; then hear me, Sultan: by thy arts o'erthrown, and bound in yonder dungeon, this Falri, by his inchantment, contrived to ſee me, and told me by what artifice he meant to ruin Adhim's peace.

Firſt like thyſelf, arrayed with Adhim's viſage and with Adhim's form, he wandered round his own domains, ſeeking Kaphira, whom, by her ring concealed, he ſought in vain, till the artleſs virgin, ſuppoſing he was Adhim, diſcovered herſelf to him. By eaſy, ſmooth, and flattering diſcourſe, he ſoon prevailed upon her to yield herſelf to him, and brought her in diſguiſe beyond the power of Nadan. Then perſonating Bereddan, whom he had caught wandering in ſearch of his royal Maſter, and confined in his beaſtly cave, he went to Pheſoj Ecneps' happy Groves, and with a well-told tale, allured the unſuſpecting Derviſe to promiſe him his daughter.

His plan thus happily ſucceeding, he entered the cottage, where before he had left Kaphira, and now, no longer Adhim, but the ſham Bereddan, he claims her vow of marriage; ſhe, affrighted, declares her innocence; and Falri, under a pretence of juſtice, brings her to the ſolemn divan, hoping to blaſt the pleaſures of my Sultan, and to make his juſt reſolves the occaſion of his future torment; a feat indeed well worthy of his malice, but of little comfort to poor Lemack's heart, who, bound by ignominious chains, was left to periſh like a caſt-off garment.

ment. Indeed he promised fair, bid me not doubt, and preached up faith to one who never yet would credit Heaven; told me I should again enjoy the Persian empire, and fed me with an empty tale, thinking I would not help myself, when fit occasion served.

Yes, false deceiver, continued Lemack, shaking his hand at Falri, with all thy cunning hast thou yet to learn, a wise and cautious man will never suffer to oblige his friend. Born for myself alone, I move not at another's beck, unless I see my own advantage move where I do.

Base, wretched Lemack, said Adhim sternly, blast not the face of justice with thy odious speech, nor triumph in the life which ingratitude has obtained thee. From self alone, and not from public virtue, rises the informer's tale; a curse to those who trust him, and the scorn even of those his meanness benefits: go, then, vile wretch, detested by thy friends, despised by all mankind, with lasting infamy be branded, till, sick of life, and weary of your vileness, you curse the ungenerous means which lengthened out your shame.

As Adhim spake, Lemack looked pale with rage, and struck with just confusion, answered not, but limping forth, he left the divan, knowing not where to turn, or hide his head from the just fury of the multitude, who followed at his heels with hisses and imprecations.

In

In the mean time, the Sultan proceeded to pass judgment on the sorcerer Falri; but here the Genius Nadan interposed.

Falri, O Sultan, said Nadan, though now confined by my charms, is nevertheless not subject to a mortal's power; for he must ever live, while foul excess and bloated luxury controul mankind: however, Prince, thus far thy sentence shall extend, to drive him from thy kingdom and the Persian empire.

If such my doom, said Falri, release me, Genius, and I will fly far hence away, to some European clime, where art and science shall but live for me, and commerce raise her swelling sails, to bring varieties to feast my dainty palate.

Thus spake the sorcerer, and changed into his natural form; he spread his foul black pinions to the air, then waving them aloft,

Persia, said he, farewel; high pampered by fair Albion's luxuries, I'll soon forget thy simple, uninviting diet!

And now, said the Genius Nadan, leading Kaphira toward Adhim, receive, O Prince, the just reward of all thy toils, and haste to bless the lingering sight of the good Dervise with his daughter; and remember, that every joy you feel with fair Kaphira, was honest Mirglip's gift.

Nadan having finished his tale, bowed before the throne of the sage Iracagem, and that faithful instructor arose, and returned his salute.

Bounteous

Bounteous Nadan, said the sage Iracagem, we are indebted to you for much instruction, who have blended the doctrines of temperance with the exercise of justice; and taught our listening pupils, the love of virtuous friendship, and the sweet rewards which rise from generous and from noble actions. Nor have we more to teach, nor they more to hear. Hark, friendly Genii, the charm is broken! Our mansion totters on its mouldering base! The fleeting scene rolls far away, and all the visionary dream dissolves!

Kind reader! The Genii are no more, and Horam, but the phantom of my mind, speaks not again; fiction himself, and fiction all he seemed to write; nor useless shall his life be deemed by those, who blush at worse than Pagan vices in enlightened climes.

In friendly guise these sheets were written, to lead thee unto virtue; and the proud, gaudy trappings of the East, with all its wild romantic monsters, have risen far above their usual sphere, to serve the cause of moral truth. But then, perchance, you'll ask, What shall that truth avail, now all the beauteous wildness is no more, which was the spring and mover of this Pagan virtue? The Genii all are fled, who watched attendant the virtuous mind, and crown'd it with success; and the reward ceasing, the incentive to noble actions ceases with it.

If, then, you will yet spare me a few moments, and listen to me, I trust you shall not long

long lament the loss of Horam, and his friendly Genii; for were the foundations of morality laid only in phantom and imagination, persuasion would be so fruitless, that every moral writer, dissatisfied with his ill success, might justly cast his works into the flames.

Prepare then for a scene more worthy of your sight than human fancy could conceive, a scene tremendous! wonderful! and great! full of mercy and of truth! where Heaven itself inclines to earth! and God becomes an offering for mankind!

Behold the moral veil rent in twain, and from thick clouds of darkness, the Sun of Righteousness arise! Behold death nailed on the cross, and mercy springing from the grave! Redemption brought to man by an heavenly being, far superior to angels or ministering spirits; and the voice of God declared to us by his son, whom he hath appointed Heir of all things; by whom also he made the worlds; who being the brightness of his glory, and the express image of his person, and upholding all things by the word of his power, when he had by himself purged our sins on the cross, sat down on the right hand of the Majesty on high; being made so much better than the angels, as he hath by inheritance, obtained a more excellent name than they.

We then may make an happy exchange from Pagan blindness to Christian verities, and look upon ourselves as creatures dignified with Heaven's peculiar grace. For us cometh the wonderful Counsellor, the mighty God, the Prince of Peace; travelling from Edom in the greatness of his strength, mighty to save, the Lord our Father, our Redeemer; whose name is from everlasting, whose arm brought salvation unto his people, and his righteousness it sustained him; who put on righteousness as a breast-plate, and an helmet of salvation upon his head; the garments of vengeance for clothing, and was clad with zeal as a cloak; who preached good tidings unto the meek, who came to bind up the broken-hearted, to proclaim liberty to the captive, and the opening of the prison to them that are bound; our sun shall no more go down, neither shall our moon withdraw itself, for the Lord is our everlasting light, and God our glory.

Fear not then, worm of Jacob, and ye men of Israel; fear not ye who are come to the brightness of his rising; fear not ye who are the ends of the world, for your hearts shall be enlarged, and ye shall see the salvation of the Lord; for ye have an Advocate with the Father, who is above all, and over all, even Jesus Christ, the righteous Son of God.

To have God for our friend, is more noble and satisfactory than the mediation of departed souls or ministering spirits. To have Heaven for our Comforter, and the Holy Spirit for our Guide and Director, is far superior to the assistance of Genii or any intermediate being.

The meanest Christian is far above the most exalted Heathen; though clothed in poverty, he who sanctifieth, upholds him, and he who justifieth, hath been sacrificed for him. He is greater than kings, and mightier than the princes of the earth, for he is the temple of God, and the Spirit of the Lord dwelleth in him.

How greatly then are we beloved of God, and the children of mercy, through the light of that bounteous religion, which is the gift of an all-powerful Father, of an all-merciful Mediator, and of an all-sanctifying Spirit. What new worlds of bliss do these sacred truths open to our dim, faded sight? What scenes of endless glory do they unfold before the faithful eyes of those who seek the Christian law of truth? Thrones, not tottering, but triumphant and everlasting! Powers, principalities, and dominions, not gained by conquest and the sword, but the sweet reward of duteous faith and love! Myriads of angels singing their heart-felt hosannas of praise and thanksgiving, and conquering armies of martyrs, who have subdued the world by patience, long-suffering, and faith unshaken! All these, and glories unspeakable and inconceivable, blessings unbounded and everlasting, shall be the portion of the pious and faithful Christian, when even the earth itself shall pass away as a scroll before the wind, and moulder into atoms like a moth fretted garment!

In that awful moment, how glorious shall the faithful appear, when the omnipotent Saviour, clothed with a vesture, dipped in his own meritorious blood, and having on his high a Name written, KING OF KINGS, AND LORD OF LORDS! shall say unto them, Come ye blessed of my Father, inherit the kingdom prepared for you from the foundation of the world; enter into the eternal joy of your Lord, and become the sons and daughters of the Lord Almighty!

FINIS.

www.ingramcontent.com/pod-product-compliance
Lightning Source LLC
Chambersburg PA
CBHW030310240426
43673CB00040B/1118